January 1, 1938.

Dear Dave:

We've done a lot of work together, and have had some rich times in each other's company. I think you know the high regard I have for you as teacher, critic, fellow-writer, and, above all, friend. It will suffice for me to say that there is no one closer to me, among all my colleagues; and I want you to know how proud I am, Dave, of your friendship.

Mac.

LUCIFER AT LARGE

LUCIFER AT LARGE

BY

C. JOHN McCOLE

C. John McCole.

"Formerly the imagination created saints for
its legends, today it makes devils for its novels."
— St. Marc Girardin

LONGMANS, GREEN AND CO.

LONDON · NEW YORK · TORONTO

1937

LONGMANS, GREEN AND CO.
114 FIFTH AVENUE, NEW YORK
221 EAST 20TH STREET, CHICAGO
88 TREMONT STREET, BOSTON

LONGMANS, GREEN AND CO. LTD.
39, PATERNOSTER ROW, LONDON, E. C. 4
CHITTARANJAN AVENUE, CALCUTTA
53 NICOL ROAD, BOMBAY
36A MOUNT ROAD, MADRAS

LONGMANS, GREEN AND CO.
215 VICTORIA STREET, TORONTO

MCCOLE
LUCIFER AT LARGE

FIRST EDITION

PRINTED IN THE UNITED STATES OF AMERICA

To
RAMONA

CONTENTS

vii

CHAPTER I

ON FALLING OFF THE FLOOR

". . . the mere fact that a writer to achieve truly meritorious
work must express himself, in no way involves the deduction
that because he is expressing himself his work must have value.
Yet so some of our present-day critics would seem to wish us to
believe. In their eyes self-revelation's the thing, and the dis-
closure of no matter what paltry philosophies, illicit desires, and
undisciplined passions, is worthy of a respectful hearing merely
because it is a record of self. We submit that any such conten-
tion as this is the veriest bunk — that there are purlieus of the
mind and soul that no manner of literary skill in presenting them
can ever render other than waste lands ; that self-expression that
translates into words experience either so commonplace or so
intimate as to deserve the tribute of reticence is merely egotism
run riot, and that criticism that fails to grade its interest by the
caliber of the soul that is expressing itself is criticism not worth
its salt. . ."— Amy Loveman, in the New York *Evening Post,*
August 18, 1923.[1]

CHAPTER I

ON FALLING OFF THE FLOOR

1

A CRITIC is an ass gnawing at vines. So Shenstone thought. A critic is a butcher. Thus spoke Samuel Butler — illustrating his own contempt for the craft by assuring us that he himself wrote only that he might have something to read in his old age.

To Burns, critics were bandits and cut-throats; to Dryden, they were hangmen. Ben Jonson thought them tinkers who caused more damage than they could repair. Swift considered them rats, dogs, and drones. To Sir Henry Wotton, they were servile fools who brushed the clothes of noblemen. And to Washington Irving, they were freebooters pillaging in the republic of literature.

With some few highly interesting exceptions, we are to-day inclined to be somewhat less rabid in assailing our critics. And yet, to a certain extent, I firmly believe we have a just quarrel with some of them. We might wish that certain critics would not try quite so hard to out-do one another in amassing superlatives. (In one recent twelve-month period our attention was called to over one hundred and thirty novels; and we were told that *each* was *the best* novel of that year!) And we might wish that some few of them would not straddle so many literary fences: that they would be less compromising, and less inclined to relinquish certain standards.

On the whole, however, I am inclined to think that the profession of criticism in America has made genuine advances in the last few years. It seems to me that our critics are doing work at present that is characterized by an independence of judgment, an intellectual courage and honesty, that was almost rare seven or eight years ago.   I ask readers who may disagree with me to follow, *systematically* for a time, the reviews in our principal papers, literary supplements, and magazine book departments.   I am convinced that such readers will find themselves a bit surprised.   They will discover critics — a not negligible number of them — who do *not* always straddle fences.   They will come upon reviewers who are sometimes doing as many as four or five books a week, and who are nevertheless turning out rather surprisingly pointed and competent work.

By and large, however, the soundest criticism of our day has been that done by our Humanists.   They, at least, never sit on a fence, trying agreeably to dangle one leg on each side. They do not compromise with Naturalism, monoptic realism, defeatism, morbid cruelty, or any of the other tendencies which I deal with in my inquiries.   They write, moreover, without leaving too much of their sentence structure to God. And mere literary mediocrity they do not immediately hail as literary genius.   Young authors like Miss Kennedy's Fanny Baines, who write, not because they know how to write, but because they feel that a husband and a lover and a trip to Paris should not be wasted — such young authors do not get past many literary bases with Humanists upon them.

But Humanism — when spelled with a capital H — is sometimes a cold creed.   As Mr. Yvor Winters says,[2] one's objection is not to the Humanists' humanism, but to their lack of it — to their "spiritual bankruptcy."   Their credo finds itself too divorced from real spiritual sanctions to be either as effective or as warmly satisfying as it might be.

Mr. Paul Elmer More, for example, quarreled with those of our young moderns who conclude that there are absolutely no standards, merely because they have discovered no absolute standards.   But Mr. More himself failed to assure us that it is absolutely impossible to have any absolute standards unless one has that of *the* Absolute. Humanism does not permit us to forget that man is human. It ought also to remind us that he is, whether we like the word or not, at least somewhat divine.

Let me be more specific. Some twenty years ago Stuart Sherman distinguished between the animal, or naturalistic, impulses in man, and his human impulses, by telling us that, while it is the nature of the animal to look only to the preservation of its own life and the reproduction of its kind, it is the nature of the human animal to sacrifice his life, if need be, for his great-grandfather, and to control his instincts toward an indiscriminate reproduction out of a consideration for his grandson. In other words, the human animal has, among other distinguishing characteristics, an "impulse to refrain." [3]

This impulse, say what you will, does not work if it is made entirely dependent upon human relationships. And the proof of this lies in common experience. We should all of us begin at once a whole series of indiscriminate reproductions—if we had nothing more to deter us than the fear of dulling somewhat the memories of our great-grandfathers! Our recollections, indeed, must go further back than this, to account for the "impulse to refrain." Our recollections must go back to the Absolute.

2

My study, let it be said at the outset, does not purport to offer a complete survey of contemporary literature. Instead, it aims at tracing a few of the literary currents that began, let us say, just before the *fin de siècle*, gathered momentum in the early years of our century, and finally entered into the work of such writers as those I discuss in my book. Our critics have not, I feel, placed enough emphasis upon these tendencies or upon the vitiating influences which they have often had upon our contemporary literature. But let me suggest a few of the currents that I have in mind.

Moving Day for the Absolute. The first of them resulted, in part, from the "new science" of the nineteenth century — not from the genuine science, of course, but from what Carlyle called the "Rush-lights and Sulphur-matches" that some mistake for the more genuine "Torch." Spencer may have had a little to do with it, and so might have Huxley, and the gentle Darwin with whose experiments his wife found fault because they put "God further off." And Tyndall may have helped a bit with his insistence that all the older religious cosmogonies must absolutely "submit to the control of science" and scientists not forget that in Matter lies the real "promise and potency" of life.

But it was Ernst Haeckel who did the biggest part of the job of foreclosing the mortgage on the universe. God, "only a gaseous vertebrate" at best, had to move out. *The Riddle of the Universe* (translated into English in 1900) "proved" that He had no place whatsoever as a "deliberate architect" in the scheme of things.

E. L. Youmans, John Fiske, Josiah Royce, William James, William Cowper Brann, Robert Ingersoll, John Dewey, Bertrand Russell — the disciples in philosophy of the new evolution and pragmatism were quick to take up the idea. And many of our American novelists soon followed. In *Butterfield 8* — to give but one later example — Mr. O'Hara has Gloria Wandrous reflect: "What about God . . . ? She hadn't thought about God for a long time. . ."[4]

Nature Moves In. With God out of the universe, Haeckel and his disciples had to find a new tenant. Nature seemed a promisingly dependable one: at least she bore letters of recommendation that dated as far back as Rousseau. Haeckel asked her to move in — and put the place in order a bit with what he called her "eternal, iron laws."

Nature moved in. She took full possession of everything — including man, who was supposed, anyway, to be her handiwork. Man was told that he had to submit to her dictates, that he must surrender to her unchangeable rules and seek his felicity only in her mandates. In other words, she told him to trust the instincts which she had given him. "Sit down before fact as a little child," said Huxley. ". . . follow humbly and to whatever abysses Nature leads, or you shall learn nothing."

It was all rather hard at first, for man had been a bit used to following — not Nature and his own instincts — but ideas, principles, laws given him by the Absolute. But gradually he began to learn to accept Nature instead. Gradually, he learned, also, that when he wrote about life, it was a good thing to write, as the Goncourts put it, "with documents narrated or copied from nature."

The "common comfort of a caudal appendage." But writing "with documents narrated or copied from nature" was also somewhat disconcerting at first. It was a little difficult, especially, to be made to stop writing about Man :

> How poor, how rich, how abject, how august,
> How complicate, how wonderful, is man.[5]

It was difficult, that is, until Nature showed him what a pitiful thing he really was. For when she got through with him, he no longer seemed rich or august, complicate or wonderful. He seemed only abject. Haeckel's monophyletic evolution traced him, together with the other animals, "from a single common mammalian parent form." It called him a "placental mammal"— and this, after a while, did manage to seem more pleasingly scientific than Sir Thomas Browne's "noble animal," or Milton's "Two of far nobler shape erect and tall."

Mark Twain, among other writers, embraced the new

theory with alacrity, telling us that man is only a "museum of diseases" who begins his life in dirt and departs it with a stench.   Ultimately it became the fashion to compare man even unfavorably with the rest of the animal kingdom ; and, by now, our novelists go so far as to deride us because we are merely apes "reft of our tails."   In the words of Mr. Cabell, we lack even the "common comfort of a caudal appendage." [6]   And, as Mr. Wescott says of one of his characters, the only difference between ourselves and the other animals is that we "remember more and worry more."

By and large, the same point of view is encouraged by our critics.   Let me mention just a few representative opinions. Dogs, says Mr. Hazlitt, not only have a keener sense of smell than man, but show their gratitude more intensely.   And he adds that what we call the "impulse to refrain" is most certainly not common to man alone.   His proof of this ?   The "phenomenon of house-training."   Mr. Chamberlain wonders "What earthly difference does it make . . . whether man differs in kind or degree from the animals — even the lower animals ?"   Mr. Grattan insists that the Humanistic distinction of free will in man is but a "figment of the imagination." [7]   And Mr. Krutch suggests the new attitude toward man by saying that he is

> of all living creatures the one to whom the earth is the least satisfactory.   He has arrived at a point where he can no longer delude himself as to the extent of his predicament, and should he either become modified or disappear the earth would continue to spin and the grass to grow as it has always done.   Of the thousands of living species the vast majority would be as unaware of his passing as they are now unaware of his presence, and he would go as a shadow goes. [8]

"Big fish eat little fish."   When Nature moved in as the new tenant of the universe, she did much to place man in a deterministic world.   She made his destiny seem blind, pur-

poseless, futile. And she told him that his chief chance for surviving lay in his abandoning himself to the predatory instincts she herself had given him. To borrow an illustration from a contemporary novel, he was to survive like the lobster, by feeding upon human squids.

"Every drop of water is a battlefield," said Spengler in his *Man and Technics,* "and we, who have the land-battle so constantly before our eyes that it is taken for granted or even forgotten, shudder to see how the fantastic forms of the deep sea carry on the life of killing and being killed." [9] But all this should not keep us from remembering that the tactics of man's living are, in a similar manner, "those of a splendid beast of prey, brave, crafty, cruel. He lives by attacking and destroying." [10]

"The bird exploits the worm, the tiger the gazelle, the human being the tiger — endlessly," [11] says Mr. Fisher's Vridar Hunter. Living is "a game of big fish eat little fish, and little fish must still learn to swallow littler fishes ever to grow large himself," [12] observes one of the men in Paul Green's powerfully written *This Body the Earth.*

Slave Morality. In such a kind of lobster world, morality tends to have a rather small-change value. The squids are eaten up much too quickly to get any large amount of comfort from it; and the lobsters do not need it anyway.

This is Nietzscheism with a vengeance. For it will be recalled that the German philosopher divided all ethics into two classes: what he called Slave Morality and Master Morality. The former — what most of us understand by morality — exists for squids alone — for the weak. The latter — Master Morality — consists, we might say, in doing away with morality. The big fish is a law unto himself: he need, to be moral, only to continue to be a big fish.

Let the weak die, said Nietzsche. ". . . we will even help them to perish." "The Blond Beast has no altruistic considerations, and we can hardly conceive of an orderly universe in which the owl should give himself up to the service of the mouse." [13]

From such a point of view, morality becomes, at best, only a utilitarian concern, an arbitrary matter, something that can never be measured by any objective standard.

"Bottles of fluid dynamite." With objective ethical values thus nicely put away in the closet, Nature set up her new housekeeping with a handbook of biochemistry. Man came to be thought of largely as a creature of chemical compulsions.

An example might make this new point of view toward man somewhat more clear. According to the chemical compulsion theory, if Mr. X, on his way to work in the morning, happens to see Mrs. Y watering her flower garden, becomes enamoured of her physical charms, and arranges, then and there, an ardent courtship which is consummated in an elopement before nightfall, he does so only because a certain mixture of chemicals in Mrs. Y have brought themselves dangerously close to a certain mixture of chemicals in himself. If Mr. Dreiser's Aileen wishes to become Cowperwood's mistress and leave Mrs. Cowperwood at home to hang pictures on the wall all by herself — that is the fault of "temperament," and the fault of temperament alone.

The Positivist will tell you, of course, that Mr. X should have had a more due concern for Mrs. Y's husband. The Pragmatist might say that perhaps Mrs. Y should have been less impetuous, because later she might herself regret the step she has taken. The Nietzschean would probably insist that if Mrs. Y's husband was such a squid, he *deserved* to lose to the lobsterish Mr. X. And the Humanist, I suppose, would assure you that Mr. X did not have the proper regard for his great-grandson — or that he had not read his Plato very attentively that morning.

All of which leaves us just about where we were in the beginning, knowing only that Mr. X's mind was certainly not bent upon catching the eight-ten train.

The "clinic of love." The contemporary novelist who thinks of man's impulses as predominantly biochemical, tends to derive his technique from the laboratory. In the preface to *Germinie Lacerteux,* the Goncourts said that the "study which follows is the clinic of love"; and the author of the *Rougon-Macquart* series described his characters in such scientific jargon as the following: "Physiologically they are the slow succession of the nervous and corpuscular accidents declaring themselves in a race as a consequence of a first organic lesion, determining, according to the environment, all the manifestations, human, natural and instinctive, the products of which are known as Virtues and Vices." [14] In many of our contemporary novels this clinical experimentation with the feelings and impulses of men and women has led to a concern with mere physical sensations rather than with emotions and passions. Between such mere sensation and genuine emotion there is a vast difference; and the novelist who wishes to take advantage of his characters' fullest emotional life must recognize that difference.

In the laboratory there can be found no trace of the soul except certain rather undignified phenomena which give rise to the illusion that we have one, no sign of the will except that conditioned preponderance of one impulse over the other which leads us to feel as though we were exercising a choice, and no evidence of the existence of any such thing as morality except customs. . . [15]

Many of our present-day novelists fail to achieve much of the power they could achieve, merely because of their laboratory methods. Mr. Faulkner places his puppets on the dissecting table and with merciless scalpel picks at their live and quivering nerves. Mr. O'Hara's men and women not only mix like two bottles of chemicals that have an affinity for each other, but are, I think, just about as interesting. Mr. Farrell "packs" a rape into his pages with a scientific and mathematical regularity. Mr. Saroyan has reduced his portrayal of, for instance, brothel scenes to exactly that *"décolleté* photography of pleasure" that the Goncourts spoke of. Mr. Dos Passos' characters lead lives that can be followed, and anticipated, with a kind of clinical chart. And, to give but one further illustration, Mr. Caldwell has his puppets act always with this conviction, suggested by one of them: "God put us in the bodies of animals and tried to make us act like people." [16]

3

". . . act like people." Dealing as he does, with a world that is representative of life, it seems only fair to ask that the novelist let his characters act like people. "Formerly the imagination created saints for its legends, today it makes devils for its novels," said St. Marc Girardin. One does not ask, nor does one want, the novelist to create very many "saints" for his fiction. Neither does one mind how many devils he creates — if he creates the right kind.

A fallen angel is a splendid thing; a fallen simian is not. The one can topple from high heaven; the other, only from a tree.

Let men and women of fiction fall to any depths, but let them fall as men and women. For, as I say, to fall very far, characters *have* to be human — and even somewhat divine. Otherwise, it is rather difficult to think of them as having any place to fall *from*: to use the figure which Mr. Galsworthy once applied to some of his own creatures, they seem to be characters who are only falling off the floor.

This is one of the critical convictions which prompts me to write this book. Also, there are others. I believe that the writer who repudiates all responsibility toward his readers totally ignores the moral nature of man and the pattern of society itself. I hold that men live by a definite system of values, and that these values are absolute and objective.

I do not believe, therefore, in what is popularly understood by "art-for-art's-sake." I agree with Mr. Belloc that a writer who can evoke only reality is not a great writer: "No one sustains the culture of mankind, or bequeaths it a great thing because he merely registers an emotion or merely provokes one." [17] Finally, I reiterate my belief that man is more than a mass of protoplasm and that his instincts and appetites are not entirely those of the animal.

In all of which I am at one with the Humanist. I, too, find Naturalism, the materialism of John Dewey, the mechanism of Julian Huxley, the Einstein denial of free will, the Nietzschean will to power, determinism, and depressionism — I, too, find all of these unacceptable. But I go further, I think, than does the Humanist: in the long road through what is common to us both, I part company with him only when, at times, he can give me no satisfying reason for some of the signs along the way.

CHAPTER II

THEODORE DREISER AND THE RISE OF AMERICAN NATURALISM

"We do not call every book that moves us human. Some seem written with knowledge of the black art, set our base passions aflame, disclose motives at which we shudder — the more because we feel their reality and power ; and we know that this is of the devil, and not the fruitage of any quality that distinguishes us as men. We are distinguished as men by the qualities that mark us different from the beasts. When we call a thing human we have a spiritual ideal in mind. It may not be an ideal of that which is perfect, but it moves at least upon an upland level where the air is sweet ; it holds an image of man erect and constant, going abroad with undaunted steps, looking with frank and open gaze upon all the fortunes of his day. . ."— From "On Being Human," by Woodrow Wilson, in *The Atlantic Monthly,* for September, 1897.[1]

CHAPTER II

THEODORE DREISER AND THE RISE OF AMERICAN NATURALISM [2]

IT IS the year seventeen hundred and forty and in one of London's parks there walks a plump and lively little Englishman, dressed all in black, with one hand in the bosom of his coat, the other leaning heavily upon a cane, as he casts his eyes about in the hope of seeing some lovely lady to talk to. A few days before he had been only a moderately successful printer; today he is the lion of English letters and society. He has published his *Pamela;* he is prepared to bask in the warm popularity the book promises him; and he congratulates himself that his teeth are "not yet failing"— that the ladies will enjoy the covert glances and the smiles he intends to bestow upon them.

Samuel Richardson does not know it, but the ladies are already there, hiding behind the shrubbery to watch him pass: over-ambitious mammas who are seeing in him the answer to all their prayers for their marriageable daughters; servant-girls who have listened tearfully to installments of *Pamela* read to them behind pantry doors; young women of fashion who have been so moved by the more pathetic passages of the novel that they have had to retire to their bedrooms, at periodic intervals, to have their cry out. And even the men have been paying tribute. From their pulpits clergymen have been praising this smug and dapper little author; Horace Walpole tells us that his book has become, indeed, "the universal, and only theme" of all conversation and correspondence; and one critic is to hail Richardson as a modern Homer and Sophocles. A crowd of men who had gathered in a smithy to hear portions of the novel read, have become, indeed, so enthusiastic about Pamela that they

17

have hunted up a sexton and made him ring his church bells to show their joy!

How sentimental people were in those days, and how extravagant they were in praising their more popular authors! Thank Heaven, I am about to say, thank Heaven, our judgments are today a little more critical! But—are they? Take Theodore Dreiser as an example. Our critics have not only rung bells for him; but they have almost torn down the steeple in the process.

Thus, even Stuart Sherman modified his early estimates of Theodore Dreiser sufficiently to observe that *An American Tragedy* made the books of all rival authors "look like capering accomplishments of rabbits and squirrels." One of our most conservative magazines has declared that the same novel is comparable "in power and understanding to *Jude the Obscure,* or *The Brothers Karamazov.*" A fellow-novelist has assured us that Dreiser is "the most important American now writing"; when the Nobel Prize was recently bestowed on Eugene O'Neill, he was quoted as saying he thought Dreiser more entitled to it; and a well-known critic has compared him to Zola, only to have his voice muted by a second critic who immediately added: "Comparable to Zola?" Why, Dreiser is a "greater realist than Zola." And so the race has gone, until by this time most of us are ready to believe (with Mr. Dreiser's former publishers) that Theodore Dreiser is "the rock on which the future of American letters must be raised."

In his achievements Theodore Dreiser does represent something colossal; there is an intense honesty about his work, and no small degree of compelling power; and he is capable of humanitarian impulses that give warmth to many of his pages. But, although he has all of these qualities to recommend him to us—and many more—I doubt very much if the enduring values which I am confident our literature is capable of finding, are going to spring out of that barren rock of Naturalism upon which we are assured Mr. Dreiser has so unassailably taken his position.

1

There were to be three shows in St. Louis on one particular evening several years ago and surely the great McCullagh of the *Globe* might have let Theodore Dreiser, his young thirty-dollar-a-week dramatic critic, attend at least one of them! But McCullagh had other plans : a street-car strike in a remote section of the city made him send his reporter out there instead of to the theatres. Dreiser was determined, however, to review those plays ; and so he wrote them up, from advance press clippings on hand, as if he had actually seen them.

They were very good reviews. As a matter of fact, McCullagh, with all his fault-finding, was able to discover only one thing wrong with them. They were glowingly vivid descriptions of shows that, because of severe wash-outs in several states, had not even managed to reach town! And, although Mr. Dreiser's accounts of the "enthusiastic" and "top-heavy" audiences at the three plays amused Mr. McCullagh's rival editors very much, they failed to amuse Mr. McCullagh.

Dreiser needed a new job. He finally found one under H. B. Wandell of the *Republic,* an editor who could never quite decide, as Dreiser himself tells us, whether "the Christ theory or that of Zola" was the correct one. But on all questions relating to the interpretation of news, he leaned, as he explained to his new reporter, considerably toward a preference for Zola. And so he warned his young disciple, above all, to master Zola and Balzac.

Dreiser learned his lesson well — so well that I trust I may be permitted to digress here for a moment while I suggest briefly that method used by Zola and the other great exponents of Naturalism — a method which must be made clear for any plenary consideration of Dreiser's own point of view.

For one thing, the Naturalist novelist tends to emphasize the animal impulses in man. There is a story told to the effect that Zola had constructed a large gallery in his stables, and that he used to walk around this, secretly watching the stock below. In his own novels, Zola himself tended to treat men — their intimate relationships, physical lives, and motives — from the point of view of an observer watching horses and rabbits in his barn.

But the Naturalist novelist, as Zola argued in his *Le Roman expérimental,* is much more than an observer. He is also an experimenter. Men and women become his horses and his rabbits and his guinea pigs, not only that he might observe them, but that he might explore the animalistic behavior of each with a clinical concern. Also, he is likely to choose his characters from the lowest stratum of society, to be largely interested in imbeciles, idiots, degenerates, and maniacs, to find in such types the most absorbing material for his experimentation, to think of himself as an anatomist and an analyst.

In one of his prefaces, for example, Zola admitted that he had had but one aim in doing a certain series of his novels: to imagine a strong man and an "unbridled" woman together, that he might carefully note their every sensation and reaction. One of the Zola novels is a clinical study of a maniac with a desire to murder all the women he meets; another concerns a deranged physician who offers a repulsive account of his own disease up to the very moment of his death; and still another is a portrait of a courtesan treated in the manner suggested by Claude Bernard when he insisted that the novelist "take men from the hands of the physiologist solely."

The Zola technique was inclined, of course, to push to the extreme those beginnings of Naturalism which can be discerned in such other French writers as Balzac, the Goncourts, and Flaubert. It tended to establish a *milieu* that cannot possibly be entirely representative of real life; it focused attention upon human rabbits — many of them badly diseased; it portrayed man as a creature without free will and struggling against insuperable odds in a world of grim hardships and irresistible physical compulsions. It pictured man as a horse, tied in his stable and chewing upon his hedonistic oats.

Let us not forget, said Meredith, that Nature, when she is "at her best," reaches "to the footstool of the Highest." But the Naturalist seldom recognizes Nature at her best. Most often, as Meredith warned us, he "sees the hog in nature, and takes nature for the hog." [3] Most often he becomes the type of realist Robert Frost must have had in mind when he spoke of the writer "who offers a good deal of dirt with his potato to show that it is a real one."

2

The seeds of French Naturalism spread rapidly to America in the latter part of the nineteenth century and found receptive ground in the work of such writers as Henry B. Fuller, Harold Frederic, Frank Norris, Stephen Crane, and Jack London. As a sort of protest against the bland and overgenteel realistic method of William Dean Howells, Naturalism seemed at that time tremendously effective. It took the lank New England skeleton of Silas Lapham and put real flesh upon it — or, as others thought, a good deal of raw meat. For the decade that enjoyed such books as Mary Johnston's *To Have and To Hold* and Charles Major's *When Knighthood Was in Flower,* was at first somewhat fastidious about the new method. Nevertheless, the tendency was firmly entrenched in our literature even before the turn of the century. Let me suggest just a few of the better examples.

Blossoming "in a mud puddle." Crane's *Maggie : A Girl of the Streets* (1893) is one of our first examples of Naturalist fiction. This novel is the story of Maggie Johnson who manages somehow to blossom in the mud puddle of the Bowery, is seduced by a bar-tender and, after having been abandoned by him and trying unsuccessfully to become a prostitute, commits suicide. The heroine herself should be compared with the later ones of Dreiser; and the whole background of the book studied for the way it anticipates the realistic atmospheres of novels by such modern writers as Dos Passos and Farrell.

The doorways of the slums in which Maggie lives give up "loads of babies to the street and the gutter." Her tenement creaks from the "humanity stamping about in its bowels." The bar-tender, Pete, shows his lordly nature by the way in which he spits; and refuses to believe himself responsible for Maggie's downfall: "If he had thought that her soul could never smile again, he would have believed the mother and brother . . . responsible for it."[4] Jimmie, Maggie's brother, curses until his body "writhes"; small youngsters swear in "barbaric trebles." Maggie is pictured as a will-less creature betrayed by cruel environment and heredity.

When her mother hears of her suicide she calmly finishes drinking her coffee before she begins to weep; Jimmie falls into his father's habits of drinking and stumbles up the stairs "as his father had done before him." And though Maggie's mother realizes that her daughter is "gettin' t'be a reg'lar devil," she does nothing about it except to use the story in court, so often, by way of condoning her own faults, that the magistrate finally reminds her that the records show her the mother of forty-two ruined daughters!

"Animals tossed for a death struggle into a dark pit." Crane's second novel, *The Red Badge of Courage* (1895), tells of how Henry Fleming, crazed by the "iron laws" of war, and fleeing from its horrors, wanders back of the lines, where

he meets the wounded and dying, and is ashamed that he, too, cannot boast of a wound — a red badge of courage. He tries to condone his cowardice by telling himself that, after all, the first law of Nature is self-preservation. He throws a pine cone at a squirrel, sees that the animal flees instead of "baring his furry belly to the missile," and finds in this incident a confirmation of his argument : Nature herself "was of his mind" on the question of self-preservation. And so Fleming resolves "not to be badgered of his life, like a kitten chased by boys." Later, however, he throws himself recklessly into the great machine of war, survives like one of Darwin's "fittest," and finds himself distinguished for bravery.

The emphasis throughout the book is upon man caught inextricably in the net of a relentlessly cruel Nature. The soldiers "resembled animals tossed for a death struggle into a dark pit" ; [5] Fleming, we are told, was "an animal blistered and sweating in the heat and pain of war" ; the battle is an "immense and terrible machine" producing corpses out of the "methodical idiots" and "machine-like fools" sucked into its cogs. Nature drives man into a "final corner" : it is because of this that he cannot help developing teeth and claws.

"A kind of an adverb." None of Crane's stories illustrates his conception of man's helplessness in a deterministic world more than "The Blue Hotel." The tale describes a Swede murdered in a Nebraska saloon as a result of a series of events arising out of his own belief that he was *fated* to be killed. Dandled on the lap of Mother Nature, the Swede could not help it if, in a moment of caprice, she throttled him.

He was not responsible, it is hinted, for his own death ; and the gambler who commits the murder is exculpated by these words of one of the other characters : "The poor gambler isn't even a noun. He is a kind of an adverb." [6]

He was simply the "apex of a human movement" which Nature had ordained. This story should be compared with Hemingway's "The Killers."

"An old hen who knows not her intention." Crane's ironic "The Open Boat" describes four men who have been shipwrecked; and who have made their way to a coast, in an open boat, only to find such difficulty in landing that one of them is drowned almost upon the shore. That "old ninnywoman, Fate" could do no better than this for them! Nature is serenely symbolized by a great windmill on the shore "standing with its back to the plight of the ants." [7] Nature with her "iron laws," cruelly indifferent to poor, insignificant man!

The naked man on all fours. While at the university, Frank Norris always carried a Zola novel around with him. His own *Vandover and the Brute,* a first novel, though not published until 1914, pictures, in the Zola manner, a young man who by a series of sordid dissipations, finally reverts to his animal instincts and becomes a lycanthrope, crawling up and down his room on all fours! Vandover sees life as a great force that drives before it "the infinite herd of humanity"; he thinks of it, in a manner suggestive of Darwin and Nietzsche, as crushing those who lag behind or fall from exhaustion. God, if He exists, is powerless to "stay the inexorable law of nature" who is herself merely an engine hurling us into "the unbroken blackness of an eternal night." [8]

"The foul stream of hereditary evil, like a sewer." Norris' *McTeague* (1899) is the story of a San Francisco dentist who, in a drunken spell, murders his wife. Pursued by a sheriff's posse across a desert, he is overtaken by his wife's cousin, Marcus Schouler. McTeague kills Schouler; but before the victim dies he manages to handcuff himself to the murderer

and thus trap him. McTeague is a Nietzschean superman, with his brute instincts always close to the surface. Note some of the phrases used to describe him: "strong and brutal," "crude, untutored brute force," "irresistible, virile power," "obscure brute instinct." [9] He can crack walnuts between the muscles of his arms, kill a heifer with the fists he uses also to crash into his wife's face.

Norris says of McTeague: "Below the fine fabric of all that was good in him ran the foul stream of hereditary evil, like a sewer. The vices and sins of his father, to the third and fourth and five hundredth generation, tainted him. The evil of an entire race flowed in his veins. Why should it be? He did not desire it. Was he to blame?" [10] Note carefully the emphasis upon animal impulses, and the attitude toward man as a puppet, a mere product of heredity.

"A whole congeries of forces." In his trilogy entitled *The Octopus* (1901), *The Pit* (1903), and *The Wolf* (the last volume only projected) Norris planned an epic of the production, distribution, and consumption of wheat. The first novel deals with the rich fields of the San Joaquin valley into which corrupt railroad corporations stretch their vast tentacles to seize the helpless ranchers: "mere ephemerides that fluttered and fell" as they found themselves seized in this cruel grasp. The picture of Behrmann choked to death in the hold of the ship under the mountains of his own grain, is a symbol of this "congeries of forces" [11] that kill men as the railroad killed the herd of sheep.

In *The Pit* Curtis Jadwin is ruined by the wolves of the grain market; and Laura, his wife, reflecting upon the way in which the wheat had killed Cressler and ruined her husband, wonders upon all of these irresistible forces of life: "the Wheat that had intervened like a great torrent to drag her husband from her side and drown him in the roaring vortices of the Pit . . . like a vast Titanic flood . . . leav-

ing Death and Ruin in its wake . . ." [12]   Like the canvas
of Nature herself, Norris' novels are epical, sweeping, in-
clusive, indiscriminate.

There must be moles and dwarfs to serve the nimble.   Jack
London, who dipped the beam of our scales of fictional values
by piling on more red meat than any other early American
novelist, was a great admirer of Haeckel, Nietzsche, Spencer,
Huxley, Tyndall, and their school.   In *The Sea-Wolf* (1904)
he created one of the best examples of Nietzschean supermen
in our fiction.   On a ferry trip to visit his friend, Charley
Faruseth — who reads Nietzsche and Schopenhauer for relaxation — Humphrey Van Weyden is tossed overboard in a
collision and is picked up and pressed into service by the
crew of the sealing ship *Ghost,* whose captain, Wolf Larsen,
is a beast with all the strength of "the primitive" and "our
tree-dwelling prototypes."

Van Weyden sees Larsen for the first time as the latter is
cursing a corpse because the man had thoughtlessly died and
left the crew short; a few moments later Larsen crashes his
fist into the pit of the cabin-boy's stomach; and thus opens a
series of nightmare brutalities and cold-blooded cruelties
(among them choking Van Weyden into unconsciousness
just to prove his theory of the survival of the fittest) which
last for the rest of the voyage — until Van Weyden and his
"mate woman," Maud Brewster, find a romantic refuge on a
desert isle.   No ordinary brute is Larsen: he has read
Nietzsche, Proctor, Darwin; and he even enjoys "Caliban
Upon Setebos" — when that poem is explained to him.

He declares that life is only a ferment and a mess, with the
big pieces of yeast consuming the little ones.   Cruelty, he
believes, is only like seasickness: some men are affected by
it; while others are not.   Human life is as cheap as that of
fowl or fish.   And Larsen has also read his Spencer for he has
learned that "First, a man must act for his own benefit — to

do this is to be moral and good." [13] Van Weyden he considers only a "little rag puppet" and an "echoing mechanism."

The world is weary of invalids and decrepit creatures and my arch-enemy is "the spirit of gravity, and all that it created: constraint, law, necessity and consequence and purpose and good and evil." [14] Thus spake Neitzsche's Zarathustra. "My own doctrine is the doctrine of expediency, and it makes for surviving." Thus spake Wolf Larsen, demonstrating the doctrine by kicking and beating his victims into a livid unconsciousness.

3

During my rapid survey of the rise of American Naturalism I have meanwhile left Theodore Dreiser working in the office of the St. Louis *Republic* under the solicitous eye of Mr. Wandell who was advising his young reporter to study Balzac and Zola. It is fitting that I should continue my discussion of Dreiser at this point for to understand his work thoroughly we must bear in mind the fact that most of his attitudes and philosophies were shaped according to the fashions of that small part of the world which he was permitted to behold through a reporter's eye. It was during these early years as a journalist, for example, that he was rejoicing in his discovery of such "bibles" as Spencer, Huxley, and Zola; and that he was congratulating himself upon his privilege of associating with reporters — with whom "One can always talk . . . with the full confidence that one is talking to a man who is at least free of moralistic mush." [15]

However, before suggesting in greater detail the philosophy which he assimilated from the copy desk, it might be well to inquire a little more closely into the way in which Dreiser's life prepared him for the enviable position of being "the rock" upon which our literature rests. In such of his volumes as *A Traveler at Forty* (1913), *A Hoosier Holiday* (1916), *Twelve Men* (1919), *Hey Rub-a-Dub-Dub* (1920), *Newspaper Days*—formerly called *A Book About Myself* (1922), and *Dawn* (1931) he has, fortunately, told us enough about himself to permit the collation of such facts as may be necessary for this background. With the publication of *Dawn* we were told, also, that he was projecting a whole new *series* of autobiographies. Think of the possibilities! *Dawn, Sunrise, Lunch Time, Tea Time, Dusk, Twilight, Darkness*—bound in calf, with gilt tops, and autographed, what admirable collectors' items these will be!

Theodore Dreiser was born in Terre Haute, Indiana, in 1871, one of a family of thirteen children, largely under the domination of their father—"a Catholic and a bigot." "I never knew a narrower, more hidebound religionist nor one more tender and loving in his narrow way," [16] the son was later to say of him. Poverty haunted the family always; when fire destroyed their small woolen mills, this poverty was aggravated almost unbearably. "I recall being sent to the distant mill to buy fifteen cents' worth of cornmeal, because it was cheaper there and one got more of it," says Dreiser.

In Warsaw and Evansville (Indiana), to which his mother moved the family, Dreiser attended elementary schools. But he remained a dreaming, somewhat lazy and egoistic youth who was later to declare that he had never been given a real opportunity to learn the "mental A B abs of life"; and to lay much of the blame for his stifled dreams upon the narrow culture of his home: a home in which only good books were supposed to be read—Dickens, Scott, Irving, Hawthorne, Goldsmith, Kingsley, Macaulay, for example—and a home in which pictures of nude women were prohibited.

After such a disadvantageous home life—and amidst other constrictions of culture which were, no doubt, more justly to be condoned—he found his way into Chicago, a lad of sixteen, forced to wash dishes, work for a hardware concern,

paint scenes, and work at any other job that would enable
him to keep his foot on the bottom rung of the ladder. A
year at Indiana University only served to make him realize
the hopelessness of a college career; he returned to Chicago
to drive a laundry wagon and become an installment collec-
tor for a furniture firm. Eugene Field's newspaper column
inspired him, however, to seek a post in journalism; and
Theodore Dreiser spent the next weeks — like a homeless cat
on a doorstep, as he says — hanging about newspaper offices,
lost in the "seething maelstrom" of the newspaper world,
while he waited for a job. He landed one, finally, on the
Chicago *Daily Globe,* at fifteen dollars a week; and was sent
out to cover the hotels for convention news — an assignment
which reflected that thoroughness, zest, and insatiable thirst
for the colorful which, it must be conceded, he has always
possessed.

It is true that he made the unforgivable reportorial mistake of doing it on both sides of the paper; and that he pursued Senator Tillman until the latter damned the *Globe* and
told the young reporter he insisted, at least when he was going out for his laundry, upon his right to privacy! Maxwell, back in the *Globe* office, however, praised Dreiser —
though he modified his praise by calling him one of the
"damnedest crack-brained loons" he had ever seen. But he
resolved to keep his thumb on his young charge, and so he
got him off on the right foot with a bit of sage advice to the
effect that life is nothing more than "a God-damned stinking,
treacherous game, and nine hundred and ninety-nine men
out of every thousand are bastards." [17] Theodore Dreiser
was launched on his career.

This career was to include jobs on the St. Louis *Globe-
Democrat* and *Republic,* on the Cleveland *Leader,* and fi-
nally on the Pittsburgh *Dispatch* where the final stages in
Mr. Dreiser's interesting liberation were to be effected.
Hitherto, he had been a somewhat wistful young man whose

urge for philosophizing had not led him much beyond a vague feeling that "somewhere there was a screw loose in the 'Fatherhood of Man — Brotherhood of God' machinery." [18]

In Pittsburgh he delved more deeply, however, into the writings of Tyndall, Huxley, and Spencer, and found a new conception of the universe that "blew me, intellectually, to bits." Before reading Huxley some "lingering filaments of Catholicism" had still trailed about him : he had believed, for instance, in the existence of Christ, in the moral teachings of Christianity, and in the brotherhood of men. But Huxley and Spencer left him convinced that both the Old and New Testaments are no more than mere records of erroneous religious experiences and that man moves only "unconsciously as an atom" that is blown about the world by forces we are powerless to understand.

Dreiser came on to New York in 1894. He served as Editor of *Every Month* from 1895 to 1898 ; held editorial positions on the *Century, Cosmopolitan,* and *McClure's ;* and finally, served as editor-in-chief of the Butterick Publications from 1907 to 1910. Upon the recommendation of Frank Norris, his *Sister Carrie* had been published in 1900, and issued privately to the critics before its public release ; but upon the immediate disapproval which followed, the book was buried in its publisher's cellars.

His next three novels — *Jennie Gerhardt* (1911), *The Financier* (1912), and *The Titan* (1914) — met with only a modicum of success ; but the censorship imposed upon *The Genius* (1915) "did much to pave the way for his subsequent career as the bed-rock of American literature during the 'twenties — besides establishing the tradition, so well maintained throughout the decade, of a brush with the censor as the inevitable sign of a new genius." [19] His most artistic novel, *An American Tragedy,* appeared in 1925, to be followed by *Moods, Cadenced and Declaimed* (1926), *Chains*

(1927), *Dreiser Looks at Russia* (1928), *A Gallery of Women* (1929), *Dawn* (1931), and *Tragic America* (1932). So much for his life. And of his personality and appearance? This man with the large and loose frame, thick cheeks and lips, overhanging eyebrows, staring look, ungainly and shambling walk, and serious massive face — this man refuses to be classified. Miss Dudley, in her *Forgotten Frontiers: Dreiser and the Land of the Free* (1932), tells us that there are really three Dreisers: the brusque Dreiser; the companionable Dreiser of the Greenwich Village and Floyd Dell days; and the solitary, or original, Dreiser. Perhaps this is as close as one can come to suggesting the various facets of his personality.

Before the publication of *An American Tragedy* he seldom came into his publisher's office; but his impressive bulk, disputing over royalties and commissions and investments, was, after 1925, to become a more familiar figure to his associates. We have pictures of him in the Liveright offices, talking about stocks and bonds; or priming himself with a drink before entering into discussion with Mr. Pell, the Liveright treasurer. As Mr. Pell did not drink and Dreiser "did not like to drink alone, someone had to be summoned from upstairs to toss off, in silence, a glass with Dreiser, and then march out, carefully shutting the door."[20]

Mr. Burton Rascoe had another portrait of the man in his New York *Tribune* "Bookman's Day Book":

Dreiser kept rolling up his handkerchief and letting it unfurl again, trying very hard now and then with some gibe to get Mencken's goat, and altogether having much more fun than I have ever seen him have before. . . Mencken allowed that "Say what you will, fellows, the greatest living poet is Kipling," and Dreiser chimed in, "And he wasn't such a slob as a short-story writer. What about his Indian stories, and what about *Kim?* Where do you find fiction any *better?*" . . . Fields entertained us with anecdotes until tears of laughter streamed down Dreiser's cheeks.[21]

And Sherwood Anderson's portrait in the foreword to *Horses and Men* is well-known :

> Theodore Dreiser is old — he is very, very old. I do not know how many years he has lived, perhaps forty, perhaps fifty, but he is very old. Something gray and bleak and hurtful, that has been in the world perhaps forever, is personified in him. . .
>
> Long ago, when he was the editor of the *Delineator*, Dreiser went one day, with a woman friend, to visit an orphan asylum. The woman once told me the story of that afternoon in the big, ugly gray building, with Dreiser, looking heavy and lumpy and old, sitting on a platform, folding and refolding his pocket handkerchief and watching the children — all in their uniforms, trooping in.
>
> "The tears ran down his cheeks and he shook his head," the woman said, and that is a real picture of Theodore Dreiser. He is old in spirit and he does not know what to do with life, so he tells about it as he sees it, simply and honestly. The tears run down his cheeks and he folds and refolds his pocket handkerchief and shakes his head.[22]

We have portraits of him, I say. But, for the most part, he still retains, as a man, many of the contradictions and much of the dark inscrutability which he himself has found in the world.

4

The world which Mr. Dreiser reflects in the more than a score of books which he has written, is a world, let me repeat, which he has seen largely through the windows of city rooms, across copy desks, and in those assignments which occupied him as a newspaper man. It is now time that our study first examine this world a little more closely, and then see how it is reflected in the method and material of the novels themselves.

The "harp on which nature idly strummed her melodies." [23]
At the outset it should be noted that Theodore Dreiser has

an honest and comprehensive sympathy for mankind and a nature so generously sensitive to the ills of humanity that we ought, in all fairness, to make a serious attempt at understanding the reasons for his bitterly skeptical attitude toward life.

From the early days in which he and his brothers were forced by poverty to pick up coal along the railroad tracks, and all through his experiences in the "seething maelstrom" of his newspaper days, the vision of life presented to Dreiser was chiefly that of great suffering — a world of rank favoritism in which the strong always prevailed and the weak suffered. He tells us himself that he suffers for things which would not cause another person a single ache or pain : that he is as sensitive as a harp on which nature idly strums her melodies :

. . . I was filled with an intense sympathy for the woes of others, life in all its helpless degradation and poverty, the unsatisfied dreams of people, their sweaty labors, the things they were compelled to endure — nameless impositions, curses, brutalities — the things they would never have, their hungers, thirsts, halfformed dreams of pleasure, their gibbering insanities and beaten resignations at the end. I have sobbed dry sobs looking into what I deemed to be broken faces and the eyes of human failures. A shabby tumble-down district or doorway, a drunken woman being arraigned before a magistrate, a child dying in a hospital, a man or woman injured in an accident — the times unbidden tears have leaped into my eyes and my throat has become parched and painful over scenes of the streets, the hospitals, the jails ! [24]

He saw around him, as he went about his duties as a journalist, "men low-browed, ill-clad, rum-soaked, bodyracked ! Mere bags of bones, many of them, blue-nosed, scarlet-splotched, diseased . . ." [25] And when he was not out on one of his assignments, his favorite pastime was to walk about city streets, viewing the lives of others, and pouring out his sympathy for the poor. Everything he saw was a reminder of suffering — even the butcher shop at every corner: "You do not *see* the abattoirs scattered throughout the world, but hourly they serve you, by murder, even though you dress in silks, sniff bouquets, and perfume your hands." [26]

Life is intended to sting and hurt. Despite the misery of life, its spectacle filled Dreiser with the greatest wonder and with what he calls the "sting of existence." Attracted always by the spectacularly wild and horrible and strong, he has never failed in his willingness to testify to the "aesthetic perfection" of living — to the fact that the world is stronger, wilder, more horrible and more beautiful than anything we can know. This sting of existence, Dreiser believes, serves as a sort of bait to drag man into the "internecine contest" of life. And in this contest quarter is neither taken nor given: for it is only when we are more or less successful that we are likely to feel warm-hearted toward "the brigandage of the world." Thus spake Zarathustra!

The tapestry of life turned on the wrong side and showing no pattern. Dreiser's world is one of denials rather than affirmations. He has pushed Naturalism to the point of Nihilism. The world he sees may be colorful; he may admit that people suffer; but nothing in his work presents, to use Newman's idea, either a history or a promise.

Life is a good show; its lunacies, illusions, and anachronisms make it, however, *only* a show. And even before the final curtain has fallen, we wonder what it is all about. ". . . I do not understand life, although I like it," [27] Dreiser tells us; and upon another occasion he remarks that the best we can do is to hobble along responding to our dreams and lusts and making the most of them. How is it possible, he wants to know, that any sort of Deity could permit a world in which both saints and devils, good and evil, are tolerated at the same time?

Mr. Dreiser, as a matter of fact, hasn't "the faintest notion of what it is all about." When the Editor of *The Bookman* sometime ago invited him to prepare a brief credo for the issue of September, 1928, he responded with this astonishing admission : "I can make no comment on my work or my life that holds either interest or import for me. Nor can I imagine any explanation or interpretation of any life, my own included, that would be either true, or important, if true. Life is to me too much a welter and play of inscrutable forces to permit, in my case at least, any significant comment. One may paint for one's own entertainment, and that of others — perhaps. As I see him the utterly infinitesimal individual weaves among the mysteries a floss-like and wholly meaningless course — if course it be. In short I catch no meaning from all I have seen, and pass quite as I came, confused and dismayed." [28]

I have said that this admission is "astonishing" because, for one thing, it totally fails in explaining why Mr. Dreiser has written so many autobiographies — why he has bothered to write at all !

God is a bootblack "Eager to earn a dime." Those interested in Dreiser's Bergsonian conception of a "restless," "changeful," and "moody" God, will do well to turn to his short poem "All in All" which can be found in *The Forum* for November, 1929. But the same attitudes toward the Creator and His creatures are to be found in most of this novelist's books. God, if, indeed, He exists at all, does not know His own Mind. Religion, of course, tells us that a God created us in this misery that He might ultimately save us. But why would any God trouble to create us only to have the further trouble of "saving" us? "For if God, or Good, as so many have already pointed out, can do no better than produce the quarreling, eating, seeking, spewing thing we know as man," [29] then He Himself cannot be very great.

"Presuming Him even moderately intelligent, how unimportant His little mannikins must be to the ultimate scheme of things, the giant forces through which He manifests Himself and which grind, helplessly create, helplessly control."[30] Such a God would no more think of listening to the protests of man than man himself would think of taking advice from a gingersnap he had baked! And some day, perhaps, man himself will be able to invent "crawling and winged things" which will serve him as he himself now serves a higher power.

For God uses man only as a painter would his brush, a carpenter, his tools. An "avatar" or a "devil" is simply doing its will with us. We cannot tell whether the vision God has for us is good or not: all of us are "crazy and He is crazy." God's performance, for all we know, may be as bad as that of a cheap vaudevillist "clowning it before a hoodlum audience." And Christ, Himself, was only a "humanitarian poet." Such are some of Mr. Dreiser's feelings toward religion.

Watery, bulbous, spewing, puling man. Life is a brilliant lamp sucking into its autogenetic flame the moths that we mistakenly call men. Humanity itself is but an "accompanying welter of animals and insects," bees in a great hive, cogs in a machine.

How could there possibly be success for a watery, bulbous, highly limited and specially functioned creature, lacking (in the case of man, for instance), many of the superior attributes of other animals — wings, a sense of direction, foreknowledge and the like — and manufactured every forty years by hundreds of millions . . . made apparently not in the image and likeness of anything superior to himself but in that of an accidentally compelled pattern, due to an accidental arrangement of chemicals, his every move and aspiration anticipated and accounted for by a formula and an accidentally evolved system long before he arrives, and he himself born puling, compact of vain illusions in regard to himself, his "mission," his dominant relation to the enormous schemes of Nature, and ending, if "life" endures so long, in toothless senility and watery decay, dissolution. . .[31]

We are merely "insects with an appointed task." Furthermore, we respond to stimuli mechanically; our conduct is limited by our senses, by biological impulses, and chemical necessities. The stimuli of sex form the basic reasons for a disproportionately large part of human activity. And man cannot resist these stimuli.

Some asinine moralist prepares to rise. Mr. Dreiser is extremely bitter against any critic who becomes "an asinine moralist," and against that "frozen, perverted religiosity" which would make a sin of sex. We are — or ought to be — only healthy animals! Since self-immolation has come to be considered a virtue, he reflects, think of the misery, torture, and pain which we have had to suffer!

As a boy, Dreiser searched through old books to find the passages dealing with sex. "My body," he confesses, "was blazing with sex. . ." [32] Most of the bodies of Dreiser's characters burn with the same fire : and their creator usually sees to it that they do not suffer the torture of blazing very long. The aspects of life in which he is most interested are primarily physical and biochemical : his characters resolve themselves into ducts, glands, and chemical tissues which, in the words of Carlyle, are thoroughly "probed, dissected, distilled, desiccated, and scientifically decomposed." We are "bottles of fluid dynamite" always ready to explode!

Man cannot add a single cubit to his stature. If Christ Himself had lived up to His own utterance on the question of adding cubits to our stature, Mr. Dreiser tells us that He would have seen how illogical are both the Sermon on the Mount and the Beatitudes. For conscience is "little more than a built-up net of social acceptances and agreements." [33] If the fortuitous forces of life will otherwise, who can possibly advance himself with mere honesty, sobriety, and industry?

Moral progress is thus entirely impossible. "Life is above these petty rules, however essential they may be to the strong in ruling the weak, or to a state or nation in the task of keeping itself in order." [34] Slave morality and Master morality.

There is always in life, moreover, an inexplicable conflict between instinct and reason, between our impulses and the conventions. But it is the conventions which are wrong: neither convention nor law, neither the moral code nor religion, must ultimately prevail upon the man of successful experience. For the "various statements concerning right, truth, justice, mercy are palaver merely . . . small-change names for a thing or things of which we have not yet caught the meaning." [35]

Religion is a game of checkers. Together with all its abstractions and theories, religion can at best divert our minds; and, at its worst, narrow our vision. It can serve, perhaps, as a make-shift, a shield against the avidity and treachery of life; but this shield is so full of holes as to be no real guaranty of safety — real safety is insured only by the pragmatic fact that our fellow-mortals *"dare not do unto us for fear of what we will do to them. . ."*

Mr. Dreiser has always had a violent antipathy for all forms of "organized" religion: he congratulates himself for having escaped the constricting points of view which it imposes upon one; and looks back with great regret upon the time when his mind, "although largely freed of Catholic and religious dogma generally and the belief in the workability of the Christian ideals as laid down in the Sermon on the Mount, was still swashing around among the idealist maxims of Christ and the religionists and moralists. . ." [36]

In 1927 Mr. Dreiser made an official visit to Russia; since
then his interest in that country has influenced his writing
in many ways but perhaps in nothing more than in his belief
that Russia did wisely "to rip out root and branch" the "ser-
pentine organization" of the Church.

But why should Mr. Dreiser so selfishly refuse to concede
any people their harmless game of checkers?

The real rub in Hey Rub-A-Dub-Dub. The volume of
philosophical essays and phantasmagoria which is entitled
Hey Rub-A-Dub-Dub should be read by every careful student of Dreiser for its indication of the "mystery and terror
and wonder" which its author finds in life; and for the way
it reveals the limitations which somehow have been imposed
on his *understanding* of life.   Back in the office of the *Daily-
Globe* Maxwell had reminded his struggling young reporter
that over in the *Tribune* they had a sign which read:

WHO OR WHAT? HOW? WHEN? WHERE?

Tribune reporters were to see to it that their "stories" gave
the answer to each of these questions.

Theodore Dreiser learned the value of these five interesting little pronouns; and in color, news value, and interest
almost all that he has written proves that he learned that
value well.   But one still more interesting — and important
— pronoun was not above the *Tribune* door: the pronoun
WHY.   And one of Mr. Dreiser's greatest deficiencies lies in
the fact that all the rich material he has absorbed has failed
for him to resolve itself into any sort of pattern and has left
him merely surly and dismayed.   He has not been able to
strip the "welter" of life to any kind of form.   Thus he tells
us that from a daily reading of the papers — "to beguile my
loneliness" — he notices certain items:

(1) A group of Newport millionairesses give a lavish dinner
for their dogs.

(2) A politician erects a fifteen-thousand-dollar monument to a horse.

(3) A negro ironically freezes to death after he has made his way north on the rods of a Pullman.

(4) A wealthy Staten Island brewer dies of heart disease brought on by news that he has been appointed snare drummer in a shriners' lodge.

(5) Several people die in a line while they are waiting for cast-off clothing.

(6) Mr. Ford announces that he can reform any criminal by giving him healthy and promising working conditions.

(7) Mr. Belmont and Mr. Morgan, Jr., decide, upon noting the preceding item, that they cannot help any one.

(8) An attendant in an old folks' home chloroforms all his patients.

(9) A New York murderer is sentenced to only one year, while a Southern family of colored people is "strung up and riddled with bullets" because one of them had fought with a sheriff.

(10) After twenty years of imprisonment a man is found totally innocent of the crime for which he had been imprisoned.[37]

Where, Mr. Dreiser wants to know, can we locate in all of this, any evidence of "Divine Mind, Light, Wisdom, Truth, Justice, Mercy?" The WHO? WHAT? HOW? WHEN? WHERE? are each above the door; the WHY he does not see, though it is probably written in larger letters than any of the others! At least all greatest writers have found it there.

5

Let us now turn to the novels. Despite their solecisms, excessive detail, and at times somewhat tedious use of auto-biographical material, they nevertheless loom significantly large on our literary horizon for their verve, color, robust-ness, gigantic character drawing, and intense effort at assimi-lating their material. For the most part they have a com-mon theme: the struggle of a man or woman who is prompted by the desiderata of sex, power, fame, or money to fight against cruel and tragic forces which prove insuperable.

In *Sister Carrie,* Caroline Meeber boards the Chicago train at Columbia City, with her small trunk, cheap imitation satchel, lunch box, and yellow purse, to become the first of the heroines — the first bottle of fluid dynamite that Mr. Dreiser interestingly upsets. Sister Carrie arrives in Chicago, tires of her Van Buren Street relatives and, seeking consolation in the open arms of a drummer whom she had met on the train, finds that he has not only his arms open for her, but also an apartment.

After she has tired of Drouet, she surrenders to a bar manager by the name of Hurstwood, who soon involves himself in a theft to get money he needs for her. Carrie becomes successful as an actress but while she is achieving that success, Hurstwood proves to be a failure; and after detailing his moral disintegration in several chapters that are conspicuous both for their masterful awareness of personality and for their use of incidents from Dreiser's own life (the streetcar strike, for example), Mr. Dreiser lets his hero quietly go to a cheap hotel, take off his shoes and socks, and turn on the gas.

Jennie Gerhardt who is Mr. Dreiser's "pet heroine" and who gives the title to the next novel, is seduced by a Senator before he dies, leaving her with child, and ready to become the mistress of the scion of a wealthy manufacturer's family. This lover, in turn, is persuaded by Jennie herself to abandon her in favor of a woman of his own class.

The amours of Eugene Witla in *The Genius* are multiple : his infidelities are chronicled with the accuracy of a clinical report; when he finally marries Angela he does so chiefly to prevent her from killing herself; and in the end, after a nervous break-down and a phenomenal interlude as director of a corporation at twenty-five thousand dollars a year, Witla finds himself searching in Herbert Spencer for the answer to it all !

In *The Financier* and in *The Titan,* ambitiously projected volumes about the life of Charles T. Yerkes, the street-railway tycoon, Dreiser attempted a wider canvas. Frank Cowperwood, the chief protagonist, is a character of almost Balzacian proportions, a man of dynamic purpose and unscrupulous methods, whose every lineament and whose career are sketched from the countless newspaper items about Yerkes which Dreiser had digested in the libraries of Philadelphia and Chicago.

The son of a Philadelphia banker (he reminds one of the central character in Zola's *L'Argent*), Cowperwood has little to recommend him except an inborn capacity for finance and a determined desire to become affluent. Even at the age of thirteen, Cowperwood engages in a soap transaction with his neighborhood grocer which nets him a profit of thirty dollars for an hour's work. By the time he is thirty-four his meteoric success has brought him a business of almost two million dollars !

Cowperwood is one of Nietzsche's "blond beasts" : he is the best illustration that Dreiser has yet given us of his belief that the world is made up of a number of strong men who survive by preying upon the weak. Not far from Cowperwood's home there was a large fish market with a great tank of fish ; it was here that young Cowperwood spent many of his hours watching the sea life in that tank :

One day he saw a squid and a lobster put in the tank, and in connection with them was witness to a tragedy which stayed with him all his life and cleared things up considerably intellectually. The lobster, it appeared from the talk of the idle bystanders, was offered no food, as the squid was considered his rightful prey. He lay at the bottom of the clear glass tank on the yellow sand, apparently seeing nothing — you could not tell in which way his beady, black buttons of eyes were looking — but apparently they were never off the body of the squid. The latter, pale and waxy in texture, looking very much like pork fat or jade, moved about in torpedo fashion; but his movements were apparently never out of the eyes of his enemy, for by degrees small portions of his body began to disappear, snapped off by the relentless claws of his pursuer.[38]

Finally, the lobster ate the squid; and Cowperwood learned from this incident that life is organized so that the stronger live on the weaker. Lobsters live on squids; men live on lobsters and other men. There were mobs and street-fights — men killing other men. That was the way of life!

Cowperwood lives on men. He bargains with corrupt city officials; they entrust public funds to him which he invests at great profit. But he lives on women, too. He seduces the daughter of one of his best friends, Edward Malia Butler, a powerful contractor (whose portrait, together with that of Jennie Gerhardt's father, is one of the most sensitive and human this author has drawn). As a result of this seduction, Butler refuses to lend Cowperwood money which he needs in a crisis; and so the crash comes, precipitated by the great Chicago fire, with its ensuing panic and the defaulting of the insurance companies. Cowperwood is sent to a prison, from which he later emerges as unscrupulous as before. For moral progress, a transition from evil to good, is, according to Dreiser, quite impossible.

The three witches that hailed Macbeth upon the blasted heath might in turn have called to Cowperwood, "Hail to you, Frank Cowperwood, master of a great railway system! Hail to you, Frank Cowperwood, builder of a priceless mansion! Hail to you, Frank Cowperwood, patron of arts and possessor of endless riches! You shall be famed hereafter." But like the Weird Sisters, they would have lied, for in the glory was also the ashes of Dead Sea fruit — an understanding that could neither be inflamed by desire nor satisfied by luxury; a heart that was long since wearied by experience; a soul that was as bereft of illusion as a windless moon. And to Aileen, as to Macduff, they might

have spoken a more pathetic promise, one that concerned hope
and failure. To have and not to have! All the seeming, and
yet the sorrow of not having! Brilliant society that shone in a
mirage, yet locked its doors; love that eluded as a will-o'-the-wisp
and died in the dark. "Hail to you, Frank Cowperwood, master
and no master, prince of a world of dreams whose reality was
disillusion!" So might the witches have called, the bowl have
danced with figures, the fumes with vision, and it would have
been true. What wise man might not read from such a beginning, such an end? [39]

I do not wish to underestimate the many merits which an
unbiased reader must notice in *The Financier*. As I have
already observed, the portrait of the brawny and generous
Butler indicates on Mr. Dreiser's part a consummate mastery
of at least certain aspects of the Irish character — a mastery
further suggested in *A Gallery of Women*. Further, in those
long scenes in which Butler plans for his family and pleads
with his daughter there is an undeniable commingling of
rich and fervent emotions; in the scope and breadth of the
narrative there is an effect of great cumulative power; and
in the weaving of countless incidents, carefully culled from
newspapers, there is evidence of an indefatigable mastery of
detail. All this — and much more — I grant.

But I do wish to call attention to the fact that the whole
book might have been cut in half without losing much of
its effect; that boring discussions of stock market procedures,
banking methods, and the descriptions of Cowperwood's
homes might have been omitted without loss to all readers
except those who wish a novel to be a manual of the stock
market or interior decorating. It must, indeed, have been
this novel which Miss Cather had in mind when in "The
Novel Démeublé" — that discerning essay later reprinted in
Not Under Forty (1936) — she asked if "the story of a banker
who is unfaithful to his wife and who ruins himself by specu-
lation" can be "reinforced" merely by long discussions of the
Stock Exchange and our system of banking. I should like

to ask the reader to notice how pitiably thin *The Financier* would often seem were it not for these reinforcements of literal detail.

And I should also like to ask the reader to notice how inadequate Dreiser's theories of chemical compulsion are in explaining the conduct of the characters in this novel. One bottle "of fluid dynamite," upset upon the shelf of human life, is very interesting; and many human beings do have the explosive qualities of dynamite.

Still, to make all human compulsions chemic ones; to set all people into neat rows of explosive bottles, and then let them topple over consecutively — may, while being good enough pyrotechnics, also be rather hard on the framework of the house — on the effect of a novel. It may likewise easily become mere burlesque. And the interesting *series* of explosions which we are offered in *The Financier* are often just this — nothing more than burlesques, mere parodies of themselves.[40]

I believe I can make this fact clear by asking my readers to compare certain of Cowperwood's own amours with the following lines in which Corey Ford parodies Theodore Dreiser in a game of "post-office":

I could only suggest the perturbation of spirit which seized upon me, therefore, as in the course of this sensual pastime I saw Gussie, my dream-girl, enter the room. What doubts assailed me as I waited with the rest, trembling alike lest she call my name and lest she pass me by for another. But at last, to my terror mingled with a strange thrill of anticipation, I heard my name called. "Something for Theo Riddell!" giggled the little girl next me. I rose blushing and entered the darkened room.

Within the door I saw her meaty form outlined against the shadow, and the next moment with a "Theo, dear!" she put her arms around me and led me to a sofa. In the dark, she leaned her head on my shoulder. I licked my lips nervously.

"Wh — what is it, Gussie?" I managed to inquire at length. "A stamp?"

"No," she murmured, her cheek against mine; and she commenced to stroke my arm gently.

"Well, then," I said, trembling a little with eagerness, "is it — a post card?"

"No," murmured Gussie, as she slid into my lap. Her breath was hot against my cheek, and I loosened my collar as I put the final question.

"Is it — a letter?"

By way of answer Gussie let down her hair all over me, and loosened a silken shoulder strap as she pressed her lips close to mine. "No . . . Theo . . ." she whispered passionately.

"Well," I said, sitting up indignantly and removing her arms, "if it isn't a stamp, and it isn't a post card, and it isn't a letter, Gussie, I don't see why you could have possibly brought me into this darkened room." And I rose disappointed and straightened my tie, while Gussie put up her hair again wearily; and that was the first and last time that I ever played "post-office." The meaning? Phfooey. The answer to it? Lordy, who can tell? Not myself, that's a cinch.[41]

As an illustration of the way in which mechanism and biochemistry are made to assume the full responsibility for the actions of the Dreiser characters, we might recall the manner in which this novelist justifies Aileen's career as Cowperwood's mistress. We are told that Aileen did not go outside of her temperament to do wrong: she had merely been poured into a mold shaped, beyond her control, by "time moods, and nation moods, and climate moods!" And this emphasis upon temperament and instinct is further brought out in another auctorial comment upon Cowperwood's *liaisons:*

How shall we explain these subtleties of temperament and desire? Life has to deal with them at every turn. They will not down, and the large, placid movements of nature outside of man's little organisms would indicate that she is not greatly concerned. We see much punishment in the form of jails, diseases, failures, and wrecks; but we also see that the old tendency is not visibly lessened. Is there no law outside of the subtle will and power of the individual to achieve? If not, it is surely high time that we knew it — one and all. We might then agree to do as we do ; but there would be no silly illusion as to divine regulation. *Vox populi, vox Dei.*[42]

Cowperwood had heard a good deal about honor but he preferred to think of it only as a figment of the brain, a quality allied perhaps with temperament but in no way associated with conduct. The "palaver about the sanctity of the home" he disregarded entirely. And, lest we be betrayed into thinking that Dreiser himself does not share his hero's opinions, listen to our author's own pronouncement on the matter :

It is a curious fact that by some subtlety of logic in the Christian world, it has come to be believed that there can be no love outside the conventional process of courtship and marriage. One life, one love, is the Christian idea, and into this sluice or mold it has been endeavoring to compress the whole world. Pagan thought held no such belief. A writing of divorce for trivial causes was the theory of the elders ; and in the primeval world nature apparently holds no scheme for the unity of two beyond the temporary care of the young. That the modern home is the most beautiful of schemes, when based upon mutual sympathy and understanding between two need not be questioned. And yet this fact should not necessarily carry with it a condemnation of all love not so fortunate as to find so happy a dénouement. Life cannot be put into any mold, and the attempt might as well be abandoned at once. Those so fortunate as to find harmonious companionship for life should congratulate themselves and strive to be worthy of it. Those not so blessed, though they be written down as pariahs, have yet some justification. And, besides, whether we will or not, theory or no theory, the basic facts of chemistry and physics remain. Like is drawn to like. Changes in temperament bring changes in relationship.[43]

The amours and adventures of Frank Cowperwood are continued in *The Titan,* where we trace his fortunes in Chicago, see him still the tycoon of a financial world, living with his mistress, and finally marrying her after his wife had divorced him. He is the Nietzschean superman, a briber of governors and councils; nevertheless he is ultimately crushed in the wreck of a city election which goes contrary to his plans. Call it destiny or fate; call it the result of his strange constitutional temperament; call it what you will. Cowperwood was *determined* by everything toward that particular and definite end :

It is one of the splendid yet sinister fascinations of life that there is no tracing to their ultimate sources all the winds of influence that play upon a given barque — all the breaths of change that fill or desert our bellied or our sagging sails. We plan and plan, but who by taking thought can add a cubit to his stature? Who can overcome or even assist the Providence that shapes our ends, rough hew them as we may? [44]

The Titan is not an easy book to read — a repetition of much ground of the previous book, it grows somewhat tedious. Cowperwood's amours as detailed in *The Financier* are at least novel; but by the time the sequel has been reached Cowperwood has become a robot. Assuming for the moment that man's technic *is* that of the mechanist, it still remains an incontrovertible fact that a mechanical made sin is not even a very interesting sin: nothing could be more dull, for example, than an automaton caught in adultery or a rape committed by a robot.

In *The Titan* there are, as a consequence, to be found almost none of the merits which the preceding novel possesses. Cowperwood has become a machine; the technique used to describe him is that suggested by the dictograph; and, by a mad sort of paradox, though intended as a large, looming figure on a great canvas, he so fills that canvas with the coloring of his "chemic compulsions" as to leave no room for any *human* figure upon it at all!

With the publication of *An American Tragedy*, Mr. Dreiser brought out what is certainly his best novel. The style, it is true, is not much more sustained than that of the earlier novels; and the story is lengthened disproportionately into two extremely bulky volumes that at times resemble a yearly news digest. But the book has merits which Mr. Dreiser's preceding books were conspicuously lacking in: an objectivity; a tremendously intense absorption, on the part of the author, in the truth of what he has to say; and a profound atmosphere of despair that at times remotely suggests the sombreness of some of our greatest tragedy.

The book tells the story of Clyde Griffiths, the son of evangelist parents in a midwestern town, who leaves home to accept a job as a bellhop in a city; falls into the loose habits of living of his associates; impresses a wealthy uncle and is given a job at Lycurgus in his uncle's factory; and becomes so involved with Roberta Alden, one of the employees, that when he learns she is pregnant, he willingly lets her drown and later is sent to the electric chair to pay for the crime. In outline, therefore, and as I have already said, in mood, the story has about it all the makings of tragic literature.

In the way, however, in which Mr. Dreiser has again fallen under the limitations of his methods as a Naturalist, it should be noted that the book is not in the truest sense, and despite the urgency of its theme, a true tragedy at all. When a man dies in the electric chair, that is a matter of tragedy; when an innocent girl is cruelly seduced and betrayed, the consequences are tragic. But when a bottle of fluid dynamite is capped with an electrode and shattered, there is only an explosion and a great deal of debris; and when a mere moth flutters a bit too near the "autogenetic flame" of life we can hardly be expected to shed many tears if it is crisped in that flame.

Dr. Robert Shafer in his illuminating and intelligent article on Dreiser in *Humanism and America* (1930) puts the matter quite nicely by calling attention to the fact that, because of the "chemic compulsion" theory of her conduct,

Roberta Alden is rendered so unimportant in the novel as to
make her distress take on, "under Mr. Dreiser's hand, the
same significance as the squirming of an angle-worm, im-
paled by some mischievous boy — no less, but certainly no
more." [45]   And then, by a deft comparison of Dreiser and
Æschylus, Dr. Shafer focuses the kleig light of his intelligent
logic upon the most egregious weakness in *An American
Tragedy:*

But it is not for his plots, nor because he was well acquainted
with Mr. Dreiser's view of life, that Æschylus lives on still
amongst us. His dramas have a perennial and deep value for
mankind because, rejecting the plausible notion of "chemic compulsion," he struggled with profound conviction to convey a very
different meaning through their form, characters, and action.
Without evading any of its difficulty, he asserted his faith that
Moral Law uncompromisingly governs the life of man, making
for an order which is divine, in the face of a chaos intrinsically
evil, and that men are fully, if tragically, responsible for the consequences of their acts, whatever their motives or compulsions, so
that ignorance and self-conceit are equally as criminal as violence. . .
Mr. Dreiser's difficulty is not that he has different facts of
experience to interpret ; — he has precisely the same facts concerning an essentially unchanged human nature. His difficulty
is that his mechanistic naturalism compels him so to select and
manipulate facts of experience as to deny, through his narrative,
that human life has any meaning or value. The attempt is suicidal, and the more consistently it is carried out the more completely is Mr. Dreiser forced to divest his creatures and their
actions of any distinctively human quality and meaning. The
more successful he is the more insignificant his work becomes.[46]

6

Suppose you go into a studio to have your picture taken.
The photographer may, perhaps, take one of two kinds of
portraits. He may snap an honest, though unflattering, picture of you in all the undefiled simplicity of your possible

disarray — your hair in your eyes, cravat loosely tied, and face in a scowl. At least, you say to yourself, this is an honest likeness.

Or he may, by carefully posing you and getting you properly prepared, flatter you with a portrait which improves a good deal upon the material he had to work with. Such a photograph will probably please you also.

But let us suppose that after you had sat for him he were to offer you a nicely mounted portrait which turned out to be one, not of yourself, but of your dog. You'd know there was something wrong somewhere : *somebody* had been tampering with the photographic plates!

Realism may not always flatter ; but it gives us a picture of life that we immediately recognize as *our* life — a human picture. Romanticism does the same, merely touching up the photograph a bit. But Naturalism, with its theory of animal behavior — manages, somehow, always to tamper with the plates. And our own experience — human experience — should be the first thing to tell us that either a trick has been played upon us, or that we are the victims of bungling incompetence and error.

A theory of animal behavior is an adequate one in explaining the conduct of the lower animals ; it is inadequate, and will always be inadequate, in explaining the conduct of the human animal. It does very well in explaining why a cat should hook a goldfish out of its bowl ; but it fails, from both a logical and a literary point of view, in justifying a man's strangling a woman in a bath-tub, or, let us say, Clyde Griffith's drowning Roberta Alden in a lake.

But — let me quote from René Bazin's *Questions littéraires et sociales.* No writer, I believe, could furnish me with so terse a list of the inadequacies of Naturalism :

Si j'avais à juger l'école naturaliste française, non dans son formule, *ou il y a beaucoup de verite,* non pas même dans l'œuvre de tel et tel auteur, mais dans l'ensemble des livres qui se réclament du nom de naturalisme, je dirais que son principal défaut litteraire a été de méconnaître la réalité : je montrerais ce qu'il y a de *contraire aux règles de l'observation* et de la sincerité, dans le procédé qui consiste à ne peindre de l'homme que les instincts, à supprimer les âmes, à expliquer le monde moral par les causes inégales aux effets, à murer toutes les fenêtres que l'homme, accablé tant qu'on le voudra par la misère, le travail, la maladie, l'influence du milieu, continue et continuera d'ouvrir au ciel. Car il y aura toujours de ces fenêtres — là, par òu la prière monte et l'espérance descend. . . Je trouve (dans l'œuvre naturaliste) un parti pris de denigrement, voisin de l'orgueil, une manière dure de parler de la misère, une brutalité de touche dans les portraits des pauvres gens, toujours représentés comme des êtres d'inpulsion, escalves des instincts, des herédités et des passions, une tendance à considérer l'ouvrier comme une machine à boire et à faire des révolutions, qui dérivent d'un mepris foncier de l'espèce humain, à moins qu'ils ne relevent la plus certains des conprehensions.[47]

Mr. Dreiser fails to recognize that the human race has been endowed with refinements and sensibilities, and with a certain moral nature, which distinguish it from the rest of the animal creation. *He is a humanitarian who has inconsistently retained an un-human point of view.* He professes a great sympathy for us as human beings who suffer ; and then he proceeds to tell us that we are not human beings at all ! Why sympathize with a mere "moth fluttering about the autogenetic flame" of misery ?   Such solicitude is worse than that of the man who told his wife : "Be careful, darling, or you'll slip and break your damned neck."

Nor is Mr. Dreiser, I am sorry to say, a very logical or a very penetrating thinker in certain other matters.   If, as he holds, men are "too minute and too brief to be discussed" why should he take the trouble, as I have previously suggested, to discuss his fellow-men in long novels and, more especially, his own life in such unconscionably long autobiographies ?

We are told, however, that he is a powerful writer and

that he is, beyond contradiction, very earnest and very sincere. But do these qualities alone make a great or an enduring writer?

A man is in earnest when he is trying to catch a train, sincere when he asserts that he detests spinach, painstaking when he manufactures a powerful motorcar, feels deeply when his wife dies, communicates emotion when he waves a flag, makes us think when he demonstrates a theorem in geometry, makes us laugh when he clowns, makes us prayerful (perhaps) when he preaches a sermon. Yet in doing any one of these things or all of them he does not necessarily create a work of literature.

The writer, great or small, who produces a work of art follows Hedda Gabler's advice, "Do it beautifully." We have no literature where there is no beauty. You and I argue about what constitutes beauty, we may differ as to whether a given object is beautiful or not, we may and should find that our conception of what constitutes beauty widens and deepens with our experience of books and life; but we know that certain things, certain moments, certain events appeal to us because in some way or other they evoke our appreciation of the beautiful, that they please us because they gratify our hunger for beauty. This is a matter of common knowledge, which philosophers may rationalize, which scientists may analyze and about which teachers and critics may dogmatize.[48]

In *A Hoosier Holiday*, Mr. Dreiser describes one of his old school-teachers who sometimes kept him after school to help him with his grammar — a "profound mystery" which he admits he could never master. The school-teacher herself must have finally realized this, for one day she pinched his cheek and said: "Well, don't worry; you can get along without grammar for awhile yet."

Mr. Dreiser never has worried about his grammar. As a matter of fact, he writes so very badly that not long ago the editorial columns of one of our biggest newspapers suggested using his lumbering, clumsy, ungrammatical sentences as drill exercises to teach classes just how badly the King's English can be written. His style, it should be observed, is far below the standard set by our better newspaper men who, despite his own long years of newspaper work, could teach him much about effective writing.

Of this defection Mr. Dreiser must himself be aware, for he has remarked: "I did not think I could write anything beyond newspaper news items, and with this conclusion many will no doubt be glad to agree with me even unto this day." [49] I hope, indeed, that many people will.

CHAPTER III

SOMETHING MORE ABOUT CABELL

"You are too fond of juggling phrases with no better end in view than to get pleasure from your own dexterity."— Branch Cabell, in *Straws and Prayer-Books*, p. 6.[1]

CHAPTER III

SOMETHING MORE ABOUT CABELL

AND there he stands, a fat lad of about twenty-two, with thick, sleeked hair, coat lapels fastened with a coat spring, high collar, Ascot tie, sparkling sword-hilt tie pin, and flushed with the success of just having sold three magazine stories and his first novel. There stands the young Branch Cabell.

He is being interviewed by the older Cabell — the Cabell who had written *Jurgen;* and Mr. Cabell's own account of the interview, to be found in *The Round Table in Poictesme*,[2] is, indeed, a delightful one. The young man asks his older self's advice about becoming an author. Ah, muses the older man, I can only say that "there is a great deal to be said upon both sides."

You are but making fun of me, says the younger man. I know it, replies his older self. But I cannot resist doing so. For, with one exception, you are the most ridiculous person I have ever seen. That one exception, I must tell you, is myself!

But Branch Cabell is in no sense a ridiculous person. I grant that neither time nor the persecution of his critics has served to improve his temper. They have at times ruffled his urbanity; but they have scarcely disturbed the high eminence of his literary achievements. On the contrary, to his leading position among our American romanticists, Cabell brings a style that is brilliant and a craftsmanship that is well-nigh perfect. In a day when our literary tastes are guided by the gutturals of Theodore Dreiser, or the inchoate phrases of William Faulkner, here is a craftsman who consistently refuses to compromise with the King's English. Further, here is a craftsman who refuses to relegate writing

57

from an art to a business: a romanticist who by years of
painstaking work has managed, almost phenomenally, to become successful in a period of crass realism; a classicist of
culture and rare charm working late into a night that has
seen the abandonment of literary form.

Make no mistake about it: Branch Cabell knows how to
write. His apprenticeship to his craft has not been, of
course, without its travails and troubles. He confesses that
even with a microscope nobody but himself can decipher his
own calligraphy. Thus he has had to do most of his own
typing. But he has consoled himself by reflecting upon the
money and profanity he has saved!

Some of his trials have not been so amusing. Try as he
will, he assures us, he gets the carbon in his typewriter
upside down seven-tenths of the time! Consequently, he
long ago gave up making carbon copies; and on one or two
occasions the results have been almost disastrous. There
was the time, for example, when his manuscript of *The
Silver Stallion* fell out of the torn mail bag and lay in the
ditch beside the railroad tracks at Dumbarton for thirty-six
hours before being discovered.

And there was the time that the precious bundle containing his typescript of *The Certain Hour* was lost in the
charred wreckage of a burned down express office. Weeks
went by; the express company finally notified Mr. Cabell
that they had found his package. But when it was finally
sent on to him, and when he opened it with relief, he found
that the manuscript which had been forwarded was not his
at all — but another poorly typed one, by some embryonic
novelist, and titled *My Seven Husbands!*

The express company failed to understand Mr. Cabell's
further objections. He had lost *a* manuscript; they had
delivered *a* manuscript to him. And moreover the one he
had was a bit thicker than his own. What was he com-
plaining about? The express company was not interested

in the nice distinctions between two different books; and when he did at last get back his own copy, the agent who wrote him was still of the opinion that Mr. Cabell had better be more careful about his dishonesties from then on!

With all his troubles, there are few American writers who have been more completely dedicated to their art. And none, I think, know better how to write than Cabell does. He knows how to handle the English language, indeed, as few of his tired younger contemporaries know how to handle it; and I can say without qualification that I know of no other American novelist whose work so sparkles with the swift interplay of fancy and imagination, with such daring diction, with so much verve, urbanity, and neat irony. To read certain passages in Branch Cabell is to lose oneself in the word witchery of Spenser and Keats, Swinburne and Synge, Malory and Moore. And then it is to find oneself again in the midst of a glorious fugue with a perfect orchestration of rhythm and cadence, color and symbolism and tone, all united into one great symphony of style.

I have said you will find yourself in *the midst* of the fugue. For Cabell can be dull; and unless you are a very patient person, indeed, you will nod a great deal through the first part of his work — through such books as *The Eagle's Shadow* (1904), *The Line of Love* (1905), *Gallantry* (1907), *The Cords of Vanity* (1909), *Chivalry* (1909), *The Soul of Melicent* (1913), *The Rivet in Grandfather's Neck* (1915), *The Certain Hour* (1916), *From the Hidden Way* (1916), and *The Cream of the Jest* (1917).

Your attention will pick up a bit with the volume of philosophical essays entitled *Beyond Life* (1919), and perhaps, if you enjoy a disguised sort of phallicism, with *Jurgen* (1919). And then, as Mr. Cabell continues playing the same scales over again, you will be tempted to go to sleep entirely through *Figures of Earth* (1921), *The Lineage of Lichfield* (1922), *The High Place* (1923), *Straws and Prayer-Books*

(1924), *The Silver Stallion* (1926), *The Music from Behind the Moon* (1926), *Something About Eve* (1927), *The White Robe* (1928), *The Way of Ecben* (1929), *Some of Us* (1930), *These Restless Heads* (1932), *Special Delivery* (1933), *Ladies and Gentlemen* (1934), *Smirt* (1934),[3] *Smith* (1935), *Preface to the Past* (1936), and *Smire* (1937). You should, however, awake at the end long enough at least to make a thorough study of *Preface to the Past,* for it contains some interesting commentaries and notes on Cabell's own books and literary theories — comments which, for the most part, comprise the prefaces to the famous Storisende edition of his books.

Dean Chubb, of Ohio University, refers to certain lectures as "stirring, soothing, and satisfying" : stirring, because half of the class walks out of the lecture hall at once ; soothing, because the other half falls asleep ; and satisfying, because the half that has walked out never comes back for more.

You'll be tempted, unless you belong to a very exclusive coterie of his admirers, to take a walk on Mr. Cabell. You will be tempted to do so for the very simple reason that you will find this author in many ways really a great literary impostor : he poses as a novelist, you will soon discover, when he is actually trying his best to be a philosopher : the images and pictures which are the province of the novelist, and which give to the novel its sustaining quality of interest, he insists upon tagging with concepts and ideas which by every right of prior possession belong to the philosopher. And there can be nothing more annoyingly dull than a concept — that is, when it is an illogical one and when you meet it face to face on every page of a novel in which you are trying with your most dispassionate might to find a story of some kind. Frequently, in Mr. Cabell's work you cannot see the forest because of the trees. Lost in the woods of speculative thought and bad philosophy, furthermore, there are times when you cannot even see the trees.

When you go down a dark alley and come upon some figure, hunched in the darkness, with a strange story to tell and some curious adventure to lead you into, you do not mind. You're in the company of a romanticist. But when you go down a dark alley and find there the proverbial metaphysician hunting with a dark lantern for the black cat that isn't there, you are likely to be just a little bit annoyed.

In the final analysis, therefore, it is neither Branch Cabell's style nor his craftsmanship which will one day have distinguished him from our more innocuous romanticists remembered only for their prolixity. The "muzzy" virtues of fiction hold little appeal for him. Writing, in *Special Delivery,* a whimsical and yet sharply ironic reply to a woman who is to be imagined as having asked him for a "blurb" for one of her novels, he wishes the woman success with her edifying novel and goes so far as to concede the sincerity which gives it birth. He even tells his correspondent that, though the staleness of her virginity is on every page of her book, he can forgive her when he remembers that the "delinquencies" of certain men are responsible for it. But the fiction itself? He will have none of it!

Rather does he prefer fiction which has a message and a meaning. He has, like one of his own characters, ridden a silver stallion to the moon; like his own Felix Kennaston in *The Cream of the Jest* he has gazed at certain silver sigils of magic; and by the strange necromancy of his imagination he has escaped with beautiful Ettarre into worlds of wisdom beyond the reach of men. Like Florian he has gone with charming princesses to some high place to discover there a sleeping beauty which no man but himself has ever yet beheld. He is a writer who has wandered about on these high places; he has convoked Olympus, enjoyed the nectar unknown to mortals, and put a piece of the cake in his pocket for those of us not invited to the party.

"Quid licet Jovi, non licet bovi." What is permitted to
Jove, is not permitted to the ox. What it has been permitted
to Mr. Cabell to see, has sometimes been denied to us to
understand.

Also, his diagnoses of the ills of humanity are frequently
at odds with common sense. The little fiction-coated pills
which he prescribes are usually pleasant looking enough.
But they do not always contain the right drugs: not only
are they often hard to swallow; but too often they even choke
in the throat of a person who is trying, like most of us, to be
logical about this whole business of living. What is worse,
because the doctor has been plagued so much of late by his
critics, he is beginning to force those pills upon us with a
surly grace. At least one patient has been led into ex-
claiming: "such puerile damned nonsense, without humility
and without a smile, could, in the present year of grace, come
only from the ill-tempered and priggish." [4]

But, is he really priggish? Certainly one would not guess
as much from the following self-portrait. A man in his late
fifties — just old enough to remember the time when cows
wandered about the streets of Richmond. Especially fond
of mushrooms — when they are prepared in a certain way.
With no preference whatsoever regarding the color of his
garters. No liking for outdoor exercise in any form. Never
carries a watch and has never had to pawn one. Thrifty
in the matter of saving every piece of string and all wrapping
paper from the packages he receives. Very low blood pressure and metabolism — low enough, as a matter of record, to
alarm any family physician.

He has never read *Ulysses,* and probably never will read
Ulysses. Once went so far, however, as to renew his sub-
scription to *Vanity Fair.* Partial to the operas of Gilbert
and Sullivan. Refuses to argue with anyone except upon
the occasions of his being served peach ice cream or chipped
beef. Prefers women who are illiterate and likes sunsets,

china figurines, genealogy, and Benedictine. Wears a turn-down collar even with his dinner coat.

Does most of his own typing with his two forefingers. Since Woodrow Wilson's death, has found it possible to hate nobody. Dreadfully afraid of thunderstorms. Wishes that he had written *Henry Esmond*. Finds a great deal of comfort in waving his feet in the air while the dentist is drilling his teeth. Owns twenty-eight goldfish — each of which has its own appropriate name. . .

Surely, the foregoing self-portrait — which is, I ought to add, one that I paraphrase from Mr. Cabell's "Ruth Universal" in *Special Delivery* — surely, the foregoing self-portrait does not picture Mr. Cabell as being ill-tempered and priggish. As a matter of fact, the portrait does not reveal Mr. Cabell at all: for a complete and satisfying revelation of the man we shall have to turn to his books in more careful detail, and to the world which those books reflect.

1

As seen through the Cabell lens, the actual world of man is far from satisfactory; and so his ingenuity has prevailed upon him to create one of his own : a fictitious world of his imagination in which the artist and dreamer are not forced to rub their elbows against those "loose ends" of futility and waste which God, in a nodding moment, left hanging on the fringes of our own sphere. Life in the actual world, Mr. Cabell believes, can never really "engross" the true dreamer, who must, perforce, find some nobler exercise for those faculties and impotent yearnings which this real world denies him. The only thing for such a dreamer to do is to create his own universe. This, Mr. Cabell proceeded to do early in his career as a writer.

To be sure, new worlds have been created in literature before. Anatole France created one. So, too, did Spenser,

and Samuel Butler, and Howells, and a number of others.
But Mr. Cabell's imaginary world — which he calls Poictesme
— is more clearly drawn than any of the rest.   He has even
prepared a careful map of it to show us its exact location!
Further, in an illuminating essay which is entitled "A Note
Upon Poictesme" and which is to be found in his *Preface
to the Past,* he has given us an interesting commentary upon
the geography of this country, and upon the convenience
in not having to bother at all about the somewhat more
difficult geography of Mother Earth.

His invention of Poictesme struck him, he says, as being a
particular coincidence when he came a few years ago to
write a preface for the new Storisende edition of *The Silver
Stallion.*   While he was then contemplating the illustrations
being done for the edition by Mr. Papé of St. John's Road
in Tunbridge Wells, England, he recalled how back in
Gallantry his own characters had landed in the same Tunbridge Wells from which Mr. Papé was now sending forth
his designs.

And what a time, Cabell recalled, had he not had with that
book, simply because he had known so little about the
Tunbridge Wells of two centuries ago!   What were its
suburbs?   Its hills?   Its inns?   Five hundred problems had
presented themselves when he had written *Gallantry;* and
he had sworn that never again in his auctorial career would
he bother himself with any real scene.   He would make
his own hills and construct his own inns from that time
forward.   He would be the demiurge to shape his own world.

Thus did Cabell invent Poictesme.   In this country
(which gets its name from a supposed union of Poictiers
and Angoulême) he built his own Bellegarde chateau; he
raised the Taunenfels; he established towns; and he set the
castle of Storisende, in the midst of this rolling land of grain
and forests and streams, towering high above the leaded roofs
of the fortresses below.   Its people were to be, above all,

human — with all the weaknesses and passions of humanity. Furthermore, the characters were to follow the best tradition of faëry literature: though they were, as Chesterton put it, to be in the midst of a mad faëry world, they were never to go mad themselves. They were never to lose the lineaments of men. Thus Jurgen, as Mencken has observed, chases dragons in the way that a stockbroker would play golf; he is as real as a Rotarian.

To help our imaginations, then, let us get this land of Poictesme clearly in mind. It is a medieval country, occupying a tract of land along the Mediterranean, between the fictitious cities of Aigues-Mortes and Cette. Its western frontier is the city of Nimes and its eastern boundary the town of Castres in Languedoc. Into this world — created as a convenience, but more especially, it is to be remembered, as an improvement upon the poor job that God did with the earth — Cabell has placed all of the earlier characters of his books: characters whose lineage is first established by one Dom Manuel, the Count of Poictesme, and then extended down through twenty-three generations to Lichfield, Virginia, the home of Dom Manuel's descendants.

As distinguished from such of his commentaries and critiques as *Special Delivery, Smirt, Some of Us, These Restless Heads,* etc., we might then note that Mr. Cabell's novels constitute what he is pleased to call the Biography of Dom Manuel, of Dom Manuel's sixteen children, and of their very numerous progeny. But lest the reader become too confused by this highly ramified genealogy, in *The Lineage of Lichfield* we are given a very sturdy, though not any too helpful, family tree of their complicated descendance. And in 1929 the "colophon" to *The Way of Ecben* announced that the author had completed this life of Manuel and the Manuelites; to mark a distinction between the biographer of Manuel and the later commentator, moreover, Mr. Cabell changed his name from James Branch Cabell to the simpler

Branch Cabell. The surname is pronounced — I mention this to save your writing to him and getting back one of those saucy letters from *Special Delivery* — to rime with "rabble."

The author looks upon *Beyond Life,* I ought further to add, as a sort of prologue to the Biography; and he considers his *Straws and Prayer-Books* its natural epilogue. It might clarify his whole grandiose conception of Poictesme somewhat if I mention also the fact that the Biography taken as a whole is meant to suggest the three attitudes toward life which are held by the Manuelites : the chivalrous, the gallant, and the poetic : or, in other words, a conception of life as "a testing," as "a toy," or as the "raw material" for man's dreams.

The daughters of Manuel illustrate this three-fold conception (with which I shall later be at some pains to disagree) in a clear enough way : Ettare is to be associated with the poetic dream ; Dame Melicent, with the chivalrous attitude ; and Dorothy la Désirée, with the gallant attitude — that which holds that all fine literature has a wanton as its mother. And Manuel is himself supposed to be a type of the man in action, in contrast to such characters as Jurgen who live chiefly in the mind. Finally, to cut short my already long but necessary remarks on the Biography, the whole series of these novels is intended to illustrate the old idea that humanity is just about the same wherever you find it : that Lichfield and Storisende are, in the way they illustrate human nature, as much twin cities as are Minneapolis and St. Paul.

Because of their highly allegorical and complicated nature it is impossible for me to give here a detailed summary of many of Mr. Cabell's novels. But as a preparation for our later incursion into the real Poictesme, I wish to suggest at least the nature of a few of them when they are stripped of their symbolical significance. One central theme is common to them all : their characters always set out in pursuit of some glittering fancy and then realize at last how ultimately unattainable and elusive all our dreams really are.

Figures of Earth, though not the first novel in the Biography, introduces us most vividly to Dom Manuel, the pig-herder, fashioning his little figures of clay, until he is lured on by flattery to rescue Gisele from her captor, Miramon Lluagor. He rescues her, however, only to marry the more alluring Niafer whom, in turn, he gives up to the mysterious owner of the Pale Horse. After a further series of adventures, colored largely by Mr. Cabell's erotic imagination, Dom Manuel wins the aid of the Head of Misery in bringing Niafer back to life and then surrenders himself to Grandfather Death.

In his armor of gold and upon his black horse, Dom Manuel rides against the yellow sunset behind the jet-black figure of Death, who is upon a white horse and who is carrying Manuel's graveclothes packed into a neat bundle. But before the Count of Poictesme dies, he perpetuates a progeny which extends down through other novels. *Domnei* ("Woman-Worship") — or, as it was originally titled, *The Soul of Melicent* — tells, for example, of how the Count's daughter, Melisande, and her lover, Perion de la Forest, are both captured by the pagan Demetrios. Melisande pays for Perion's freedom with a price which always has a rather low and easy rate of exchange in the Cabell books : namely, with her body. But Demetrios soon tires of her ; and so, too, does Ashaverus, her next lover. All men tire of the dream of woman once they have possessed the object of the dream ! Such is the curse of the *domnei !* Christian, pagan, Jew — Perion, Demetrios, Ashaverus — all find woman no longer worthy of worship or pursuit when once they have won her. For the *domnei,* though a world-controlling force, merely heaps disillusion upon mankind.

Again, in *Jurgen,* the central character, this time a pawnbroker, sets out upon his journey : one which differs little

from the other Cabell excursions except in those matters of
an intenser eroticism which the censors have already observed. As a reward for Jurgen's praise of him, the devil
rewards his devotee by snatching off Jurgen's garrulous wife,
Dame Lisa. But Jurgen's conscience troubles him: after
he has conversed with the God of his Grandmother, tired of
Anaïtis and several other women, and married a hamadryad,
he bargains with the great Koshchei and is permitted to
return to his pawnshop and the garrulities of his wife.

The quest of Florian de Puysange, in *The High Place*,
leads him to dream first of meeting the beautiful Melior;
and then to plan the killing of his four earlier wives that
he might marry his fifth, Mademoiselle Louise de Nerác!
But Janicot, the devil, dissuades him from this woman;
and he accepts Melior until, in turn, he tires of her.

Like his creator, Felix Kennaston of *The Cream of the
Jest*, evades life by dreaming and writing. One day he
finds a glittering disc in his garden; and by the magic of
this sigil he escapes with the alluring La Belle Ettare into
a world of dreams. He finds that he can summon the dream
at will by holding the disc in his hand at night until he falls
asleep as the candle by his bedstead sputters out. But he
is never allowed to touch Ettare: whenever he tries to do so,
she disappears, and he awakes from the dream. And at the
end of the book, Kennaston's wife, Kathleen, throws away the
sigil and he learns for the first time that it is nothing more
than part of the cover to a jar of his wife's cold cream! Like
his counterpart, the character Horvendile, Kennaston had
learned that in one's own country there is no woman whom
we can love. Such a woman must remain always in our
dreams.

The real cream of the jest? That even dreams cannot
serve as a satisfying escape from reality. No man can ever
touch upon this thing called reality: he cannot trust his
five senses; and his dreams, it is just cruelly possible, may

be no escape either. But though he may be doomed to disappointment and though he may know it, the wise man will still subscribe to the salutary effect of dreaming, and hoodwink himself into believing that some day his dreams may come true.

Such, in a very general way, is the whole philosophy underlying the invention of Poictesme—the fictitious country to which Mr. Cabell has fled because he has wished to escape from that actual life which he feels is so painful a one. Such is the atmosphere of egoistical mist in which Mr. Cabell has enshrouded himself because he sees in this everyday existence only tedious routine and boredom : because he wishes to find a mouthpiece to tell us what is wrong with God's world ; and then help Him just a little bit in improving it.

Cabell has, it is true, emphatically refused to admit that the opinions of John Charteris and certain of his other characters are necessarily his own. But no reader should be misled by this insistence. The dizzying succession of Manuels, Musgraves, Kennastons, and other characters who parade before us in the colossus of the Biography speak for their creator in unmistakable accents. They utter, not so much their own opinions, as those of Branch Cabell.

For it is to be remembered that here is a writer who looks at the world with the eyes of disillusion. Life, he tells us, has damaged him, scratched him, banged him, and mauled him. It has bored him. And he insists that though he does not like to quarrel with living, he does wish to escape from it, even if his evasion must be found in dreams. So it is that Cabell escapes to Poictesme—not quite so much the world of the Manuelites as it is a world populated by the puppet ideas, the progeny, of Cabell's own mind.

2

Let us now enter Poictesme.

Checking conscience at the customhouse. To secure a passport to this very interesting country, Cabell himself tells us that it will first be necessary to give our consciences a "half-holiday" : to check them for the duration of our visit at the customhouse where we must also deposit whatever "impedimenta," in the way of altruism, ideals, ethics, scruples, or religion, that we have encumbered ourselves with.

There may be some of us, of course, who will be inclined to reflect that conscience, when once given a *half*-holiday, is quite likely not only to want the rest of the day off, but also to wish to retire on some permanent pension fund.

However, our visit among the citizens of Poictesme is to be so pleasant that we may be willing to risk that danger. For we are there to associate with a people whose incomes are not limited and who are never bothered by the police. We are bidden only to have a good time ; and the guide furnished us for our journey is a nice old fellow, trained in the ways of hedonism, who will be quite satisfied if we but have that good time. Let it be clearly understood, however, that he will tolerate no nonsense in the nature of moral restrictions ; and that he will look with disfavor upon anyone who has managed to sneak in with his conscience shamefully hidden about him. For conscience, as Jurgen hints, belongs only to the damned. Besides, what we call evil is really impossible : in *Beyond Life* does not John Charteris tell us that there is no such thing as wickedness outside literature?

Vice but not vulgarity. A kind of insidious distinction, I hear you say? But it prevails in Poictesme, where no form of gross voluptuousness is to be tolerated but where refined sensuality is to be encouraged in every way. Subtle insinuations of a phallic symbolism are to confront us as sign-posts along the way; politely worded perversions are to beguile our journey.

We are to read no writings scribbled on latrine walls; but we are to hear spoken the language of Fescennia as the native tongue of the exhibitionists on the high-roads of fancy leading through the kingdom. . . Madame Elizabeth Charlotte d'Orleans is to give us the key to this language in such of her remarks as those in which she hints that in the Regency, men not common no longer make love to women; and in the towns through which we pass we are to get a reminder of certain fallen cities of long ago. Furthermore, the books that entertain us are to justify their own morals. We are to be told, for example, that if *Jurgen* survives, it will prove itself exonerated; if it does not survive, it cannot be objected to for its offensiveness. And we are to hear, all along the road of the Cabell books, a large number of critics lending a smirking support to this doctrine.

Silent naked frozen clod. Christ and Pan are the two "scapegoats" of this country — the one, the "savior" of religion; and the other, the "savior" of art. But it is Pan who gazes upon the "divine handiwork" and sees at once that the world in no way reflects credit upon its Maker. It displays little harmony or order; the spheres of the universe, frozen or flaming as the case may be, are governed by chance alone. Water and land are, unfortunately, not balanced upon the earth; mountains are stuck upon it like "pimples" or "welts." It is a great prison house, of little importance, and destined to be only a "silent naked frozen clod." Such is the Cabellan attitude toward the earth.

Huxley's Clock. You will recognize in the great timepiece that ticks the moments in Poictesme, the famous Huxley Clock. This illustration, you may recall, Huxley used to suggest the insignificance of men. Allowing all the minutes of the day to stand for the years of the earth, Huxley suggested that man does not appear upon its surface until a few minutes to twelve. How unimportant man is!

The wet sponge inside our skulls. For, in arguing that the world does not reflect much credit upon its Creator, Mr. Cabell allows such of his characters as John Charteris to imply also a great deal of dissatisfaction with the creatures who inhabit that world. Man makes, indeed, a very sorry blotch upon the epidermis of the Cabellian earth. His brain is a wet sponge; he, himself, seems destined to play the part of the fool in the gigantic comedy of life; the most that he can do, we are told, is to wear his motley with some show of bravery.

He is an "ape reft of his tail, and grown rusty at climbing"; [5] the optimist, Mr. Cabell assures us, will rank his kind as "lice" though the pessimist will perhaps prefer the more poetic way of putting it, and call us "maggots." In either case, however, there is little consolation to be found in this animal who prefigures himself as the hero of the universe: "For it was unpleasantly apparent that man did not excel in physical strength, as set against the other creatures of a planet whereon may be encountered tigers and elephants. His senses were of low development, as compared with the senses of insects: and, indeed, senses possessed by some of these small contemporaries man presently found he did not share. . . The luxury of wings, and even the common comfort of a caudal appendage, was denied him. He walked painfully, without hoofs, and, created naked as a shelled almond, with difficulty outlived a season of inclement weather. Physically, he displayed in not a solitary trait a product of nature's more ambitious labor. . . He, thus, surpassed the rest of vital creation in nothing except, as was beginning to be rumored, the power to reason; and even so, was apparently too magnanimous to avail himself of the privilege." [6]

And what of man's accomplishments and inventions? This "amiable and shatter-pated" being, who in his progress through the protoplasmic, fish, batrachian, reptilian, and mammalian stages still remains unproportioned, with his viscera jumbled, his heart not in the center of his body, his brain not correspondingly divided — this "maggot" achieves things only by accident. He is, in short, but one of billions of parasites crawling about the "big barren studio" of the world. And no Artist has planned that studio, though He tries to do the best He can by occupying it.

The owl or the ostrich? As a symbol of wisdom, therefore, Mr. Cabell insists that the ostrich, rather than the owl, is the *rara avis,* the rare bird. In his *Preface to the Past,* he gives illustration to this point by asking us to note how Florian de Puysange inevitably learned the same lesson and then settled down contentedly to become a "pattern of the best-thought-of vices" instead of trying to fly above the earth. So, too, does the romanticist come sooner or later to regard art as allegorical and fiction as an anaesthesia, an opiate for humanity's gout. The novelist, in an attempt to forget that life is but the "restlessness of a prolonged demise," can find his only hope in diverting himself and his fellow-men.

Writing as a game: a tête-à-tête with the typewriter. To carry out further this romanticist's theories of evasion, it follows that self-diversion should be the first motive of the writer; and the artist who thinks of anything but playing with his ink and paper, or who considers himself responsible to anyone — is really only committing an undignified form of suicide!

Mr. Cabell's style both suffers and gains from this conception of art. He knows his game; and he plays it with the skill and suave confidence of a man certain of the moves. But his very proficiency makes him, at times, a damnably disagreeable player : when you know all the advance moves you are likely to be a bit impatient while your opponent fidgets with the chess-men. And you may not play the game with zest ; but rather like an old man who waits to stalemate his grand-daughter's king, and amuses himself, meanwhile, with artificial mannerisms and poses, and with diverting comment on his rheumatism.

Mr. Cabell talks with uninvited garrulity about all his aches and pains ; he amuses himself with mannerisms such as the following : "Meanwhile you went about the one thing you, nowadays, knew how to do, typing, always typing, in a continuous tête-à-tête with this indeterminate tapped-out tattoo of ticktocking types and tinklings." [7] He plays with such acrostics as those in the dedication to *Jurgen, Beyond Life,* and *The Silver Stallion.*

He makes a cabala of the commonplace, employing such anagrams as Lytreia and the Land of Dersam instead of saying Reality and the Land of Dreams. He "invents" textual references and hoodwinks us into believing him learned by creating authors for these references. He mystifies, and proves tedious, with mannerisms of sentence structure, connectives, ellipsis, etc. ; and his fondness for the orotund clutters up his pages with such words as imauns, mundicidious, mundivagant, bruice, orgulous, siccative, arietin, and epigoni.

Further, in his experiments with "contrapuntal" prose he forgets to preserve that main theme which should unite all stylistic melodies into some sense. In short, he is a decadent, representing one of the last high notes of beauty which our stylists struck before surrendering their voices to the raucous voices of the new generation of "realists." "There is no power in his prose to move us to anything but a vain regret, pity that so much loveliness should be without life and without hope—as when we look on the dead face of some once lovely girl. It is a reminder of things past and done with. The quiet and peace that enthralls us is the peace and quiet of the grave. It is English written (as Max said of the English of Walter Pater) as though it were a dead language." [8]

Escape or Evasion? The true romanticist may, for any number of reasons, wish to *escape* from life. But he does not, for any reason, try to *evade* life; and, least of all, does he ever attempt to evade it in favor of some Mispec Moor of a miasmic fancy. Charles Lamb—to draw a comparison odious to those who may think our literature began in 1904 with the publication of *The Eagle's Shadow*—Charles Lamb, for example, refused to evade life though on one occasion it even sent him, insane, over the hill to the asylum.

Literary escape may thus be a matter contrived even with bravery and courage; evasion—hiding one's head in the shifting sands of disillusion—is almost necessarily attended by ignorance and cowardice. To run from a fire while a building burns down is to escape; to evade the holocaust, or to attempt to, by hiding one's head under the blankets, is to fail signally in coping with the situation. And long after the strictures imposed upon Branch Cabell for his many other faults have been forgotten, we will still remember what is one of his greatest shortcomings—he has buried his head in disillusion : he has refused, in his whole ambitious comedy of humanity, to meet the challenge of one single problem which confronts that humanity. Even when he does manage to pose the problem, he has neither the courage nor the patience to wait for the answer.

The Cabellian castles. Just as, in architecture, there could be no more gigantic a monstrosity than a Gothic building with modernistic furniture inside it, so in Mr. Cabell's medieval world there is a series of hideous anomalies which

result from his real lack of sympathy for the medieval temper.
The turrets of Storisende castle, the moon over it, the colorful silks of the ladies on its balcony, the doublets and jerkins
of the men upon its walls — all this seems faithful enough.
But when you enter the castle you immediately stumble
against certain embodiments of thought that in their sharp
angularity belong, most certainly, to the furniture of the
twentieth century.

The medievalist kept his gargoyles — his distortions — on
top of the castle ; and, even in fashioning them, knew that he
was not fashioning a man.

The medievalist knew, when he went upon a journey, just
where he was going; Mr. Cabell's characters follow their
erotic aberrations without purpose or direction.

The medievalist saw not only the color, but what is more,
the pattern, in life, just as surely as he recognized it in the
tapestry on his walls.   He had a high regard for man, whom
he saw as a significant part of that pattern.

He went, at times, upon a pilgrimage ; and often he knelt
in prayer or paused in silent admiration of some beauty in
the rolling and ordered countryside.   He wore certain colors
upon his sleeves and was loyal to them ; Branch Cabell has
few loyalties or compelling admirations.

The medievalist saw the world as good : it did not bother
him that water and land are unequally divided, or that the
mountains are placed like pimples upon the earth. . . I
wonder if it is not significant, perhaps, that Howard Pyle
refused to continue to illustrate Mr. Cabell's books because
he believed them true neither to real fancy nor to real
medievalism ?

"Women go to the devil in search of congeniality."
But none of Cabell's conceptions of the medieval temper
offer quite the anomaly that is to be found in his whole
attitude toward woman, an attitude which he refers to as

"domnei," or "woman-worship." Conceived as a world-moving force which seems both to bemuse our author and give him cause for lamentation, this *domnei* is the basis of conduct for most of the Manuelites. Like Jurgen they leave their pawnshops, or like Kennaston they play with their sigils, always in an attempt to pursue the dream of some inaccessible though tantalizing woman ; and, then, they awake to find out just how evanescent the dream was — how futile the worship of woman seems to be.

In "A Little More About Eve" — an essay to be found in *Preface to the Past* — we have a cynical account of the progress of man's feeling for woman, as the author sees it, up to medieval times : First, she was merely a convenience, useful for "housework and copulation" ; with the evolution of the courtesan she came to be considered a luxury ; and, finally, the medievalists, with their *domnei,* made her a goddess. But, we are assured, the new worship of woman always existed together with two other attitudes : that which looked upon her as a "lustful animal," and that which regarded her as the devil's snare.

Mr. Cabell, I need not add, has chosen to adopt the latter points of view and to mistake them for the real *domnei.* One of his characters puts the matter rather crisply, as a matter of fact, when he tells us that "King James is bold enough to voice it as a truism that women go to the devil in search of congeniality." [9]

Thus, the worship of the gentler sex becomes too much of a good thing because woman, it would appear, is, indeed, too much of a bad thing — an observation which finds both affirmation and example in Rudolph Musgrave's admiration for Anne Willoughby until the time when she, perhaps not unreasonably, wishes to marry him. But to *marry*, Musgrave argues, sounds too much like being sentenced to eat ice-cream every morning for breakfast ! On this question of marriage Mr. Cabell has, until recently, been needlessly

monoptic, assuring us that our better novelists of today con-
temn it as strongly as did St. Paul (!), and that it is bound
anyway always to end in disillusion.

Pragmatic marriages, he concedes, are all well enough :
they sometimes bring us money; they get our socks darned
regularly. But little can be said in favor of the real love-
match, which shatters the demiurge useful in permitting the
human race to perpetuate its misery; and which allows our
illusions to disappear at the wedding breakfast. (The
domnei idea is perhaps best illustrated in *Domnei* or in that
trilogy which the author calls *The Witch-Woman,* and which
consists of *The Music from Behind the Moon, The White
Robe,* and *The Way of Ecben.*)

Mr. Cabell's Humor. No critic can deny this novelist's
trenchant wit, suave humor, or positive genius in employing
the richest undertones of irony. When he lashes out, for
example, at the insipid romanticism prevailing two decades
ago and represented by the whole "pollyanesthetic" school
of Caine, Chambers, Wright, *et alii,* Mr. Cabell is diverting
and genuine. He is the same when he is talking about his
own struggles as an author : such scenes as those in *The
Cream of the Jest* wherein Kennaston offers us parodies of
rejection letters or talks over the problems of his craft with
his rather unsympathetic wife — such scenes are among the
best that Branch Cabell has written.

Let me give a few examples. Kathleen Kennaston never
could bring herself to read her husband's books; there was
always so much work to do and always also, of course, enough
gossip to keep her busy and permit her to defer the reading
to a summer which never came. Is it any wonder that
Kennaston planned, sadly, one morning at breakfast, to write
an essay on "The Lost Art of Conversing with One's Wife"?

If there was any magazine in America that had not rejected some of the tales in *The Certain Hour,* it was only

because he could not find that magazine's address, Mr. Cabell assures us! He habitually kept his records of rejections by placing a semicolon after the latest, taking it so much for granted that another would follow! He wrote a play once which the cast so revised that he could hardly recognize it as his own! Given a contract providing that he was to receive royalties after seven hundred and fifty copies had been sold, and then finding that only some six hundred had been printed, he suspected some "sarcasm" in the contract! And when he went to England to examine a copy of a family will, he there had as much difficulty in securing access to it as if he were a criminal!

Our novelist is at his best when he diverts us with such genuinely humorous comment on himself, instead of indulging in cheap and "clever" cynicism. Also, in justice to him it ought to be added that his more recent volumes indicate a marked improvement in the direction and tone of his humor.

Mr. Cabell's "Humor." I think it may be said that his wit is being sharpened with the years. But it needs, it must be emphasized, much cutting loose from the atmosphere that enshrouds the vaudevillist: from self-conscious posturing, flippancy, and pseudo-cleverness. He is still too fond of breaking the lance of his satire off with mere jibing. When his usually alert intelligence becomes clouded with the mists of egoism, he can mistake flippancy and even scurrility, for humor.

Thus he can include in one of his volumes an appendix of unfavorable reviews of his books; his egomania leads him to write, in *Special Delivery*, a letter to a young girl who is to be imagined as having generously offered to trade her virginity for some of Mr. Cabell's secrets about getting books published; his invectives against those who persist in writing him for autographs become increasingly bitter; he can in-

dulge in a vaudevillian spree which permits him to refer to
Heaven as a "conjectural" kingdom, paradise as "fugacious,"
the story of Christ as nothing more than Cinderella's story
told in "more impressive terms," and tag-days as a kind of
"brigandage and blackmail" which gives women the strum-
pet's privilege of accosting a man on the street.

Fact versus *truth*.   I have tried to show that Cabell is not,
in the true sense of the term, a romanticist at all.   Nor, it
can be argued, is he a realist, though he argues desperately
that his composite picture of human failings is a history of
humanity.

There is a difference between a fact and a truth, however,
which he has never fully realized — a difference which I
might suggest with the following anecdote : A mate on board
a sailing vessel was one night, for the first time in his life,
caught drunk by the captain who, in the interests of truth,
insisted upon recording the disgrace in the day's log.   On
the next night, however, it so chanced that the duty of filling
in the log devolved upon the mate.   He ended the record
with this simple statement: "The Captain was sober to-
night."

On pronouncing the word adultery in the presence of a lady.
Ellen Glasgow describes one of her characters by saying that
he would rather commit adultery than "pronounce the word
in the presence of a lady."   And Meredith says of the jokes
which Adrian tells in *The Ordeal of Richard Feverel* that
they were "delicately not decent, but so delicately so, that it
was not decent to perceive it." [10]

As a final charge which I wish to lay at Mr. Cabell's door,
I mention what seems to be his never-failing delight in in-
sisting that indecency is never to be deplored when it is
delicately expressed.   When we do deplore it in him, it is
really we who are indecent.   For we are to remember that

our author has already anticipated all objections to his work ; that we have failed signally in understanding that work if we think it often indecent ; that it is really only a character rather than the author who is doing the speaking ; and that, anyway, whoever does do the speaking manages always to do it like a gentleman !

The inadequacies and indecencies lie not with Cabell or the Cabellians : they lie with us, his readers.   No author, we are told to believe, no author is to be blamed for his characters — and especially when they maintain the aristocratic pretense of gentility and so capably illustrate the irony of life.

And so I take leave of Mr. Cabell, his style, alert intelligence, wit, irony, and the incomparable position which he has in most respects quite deservedly achieved as one of the most brilliant of present-day writers.

CHAPTER IV

FREUDISM AND THE STREAM-OF-CONSCIOUSNESS

"But what was the alternative they proposed? A microscopic analysis of the minute in man, as if the highest imaginative art consisted in decomposing him into his constituent atoms. . . The new technique might be right, but their application of it substituted pathology for invention. Man was man by virtue of the integration of his atoms, not of their dispersal. It was not when you had taken him apart that you could realize him, but when you had built him up. The fishers in the turbid stream-of-consciousness had reduced their fictitious characters to a bundle of loosely tied instincts and habits, borne along blindly on the current of existence. Why not reverse the process, reduce the universe to its component dust, and set man whole and dominant above the ruins? What landmarks were there in the wilderness of history but the great men rising here and there above the herd? And was not even the average man great, if you pictured him as pitted against a hostile universe, and surviving, and binding it to his uses?"— Vance Weston's reflections in Edith Wharton's *The Gods Arrive*, pp. 112-113.[1]

CHAPTER IV

FREUDISM AND THE STREAM-OF-CONSCIOUSNESS

THE tall, slender young man, with the steel-blue eyes and the ashplant cane, was being introduced to William Butler Yeats. "We have met too late," said James Joyce. "You are too old to be influenced by me." [2]

1

But of Joyce's influence upon the present literary generation there can be no doubt. A.E. once taunted him : "I'm afraid you have not enough chaos in you to make a world." [3] This was, however, before the publication of *Ulysses* (1922). That book did make a world — or at least it opened up a world for our novelists, that of man's subliminal life.

By which I do not mean to imply that James Joyce was the first novelist to concern himself with the subconscious. Even Sterne occasionally put one foot across its threshold ; and George Eliot, of course, was not unaware of what lies beyond the door of man's conscious thought. Still, it was Joyce who first opened that door wide enough to attract contemporary novelists with the possibilities of using the stream-of-consciousness as a valuable technique.

For it is a valuable technique. It has dug a good shaft and it has hit some rich deposits : some pay-dirt that should be mined. But, unfortunately, it has also hit a good deal of what is merely — dirt. A number of our novelists who have been mining it have tended to concentrate too much on the digging, on mere experimentation. They have brought up a good many tons of muck, at times, for the sake of a negligible quantity of the metal.

By way of examining the uses to which the technique has been put, I propose in this chapter, first, a brief consideration of *Ulysses;* secondly, a consideration of the special features of the stream-of-consciousness as they are reflected in *Ulysses* and in the work of our younger American writers; and, thirdly, a review of some of the by-products of the technique when it is united in literary wedlock with Freudian psychology.

Ulysses versus *the United States Circuit Court of Appeals.* "That's folk . . . for your book. . . Five lines of text and ten pages of notes about the folk and the fish-gods of Dundrum. Printed by the weird sisters in the year of the big wind." [4] Some few of the critics think that these words of Joyce's Buck Mulligan aptly describe *Ulysses:* that it is a *tour de force,* a collection of drivellings about strange folk and fish-gods, thrown out to stuff an auctorial ballot-box in the year of some publisher's big wind.

"As vulgar as a bed pan," says one such critic,[5] adding that the book is a "Demogorgon of literature," a novel which more than any other since the invention of printing has exercised a "baneful . . . malignant and perverting influence" upon our letters. With which point of view, I must add in passing, I am in full accord: *Ulysses* has a greater cloacal content, I think, than any other book written in English.

But the United States Circuit Court of Appeals does not think so. True it is that Judge Manton, when a test case was made of the matter in 1934, said: "Who can doubt the obscenity of this book after a reading of the pages referred to, which are too indecent to add as a footnote to this opinion? Its characterization as obscene should be quite unanimous by all who read it." [6]

Still, Judge Manton's opinion was the dissenting one. Judges L. and Augustus N. Hand, in the same appeal, concluded that *Ulysses* is a valid experiment in the "stream of consciousness method of presentation . . . it is fair to say that it is a sincere portrayal with skilful artistry of the 'stream of consciousness' of its characters. . . The net effect even of portions most open to attack, such as the closing monologue of the wife of Leopold Bloom, is pitiful and tragic rather than lustful. . . In the end one feels, more than anything else, pity and sorrow for the confusion, misery and degradation of mankind." [7]

Cerebral Huddle. As a result of this majority opinion, *Ulysses* is presumably here to stay. And whether its influence has been preponderantly bad or not, it cannot be denied that it is one of the most influential books of our century. Let me therefore suggest the nature of the interior monologue, which it employs, and the contents of the book itself.

The father of that literary device known as the *monologue intérieur* is said to be Edouard Dujardin, whose *Les Lauriers sont coupés* (1886) antedated *Ulysses* by some thirty years and to whom Joyce admits a great debt. The novelist who makes use of the interior monologue "attempts to portray life and character by setting down everything that goes on in his hero's mind; notably all those unimportant and chaotic thought-sequences which occupy our idle or somnolent moments, and to which, in real life, we pay, ourselves, little attention." [8]

The stream-of-consciousness technique employs, it will be noted, an intensively crowded canvas. Thus we are told that Joyce's Buck Mulligan remembers almost all "ideas and sensations." Thomas Wolfe's Eugene Gant tries to recall all of his experiences and sensations until they have become "a part of his whole memory." When Farrell's Studs Lonigan is dying he sees a phantasmagoria made up of every one of the friends he has ever known. Dos Passos' characters spend hours following out extremely detailed thought-sequences that most of us would ordinarily disregard; Faulkner uses the *monologue intérieur* to suggest the most chaotic mental processes of morons; in Rex Stout's *How Like a God* (1929) the whole book is used to depict the reflections of a man in but the short while it takes him to walk up several flights of stairs; in the anonymously written *A Man in Arms* (1935) the *monologue intérieur* is strategically employed to portray the entire flood of scattered impressions of the soldier, Aburdon, while he is going under ether before an operation; in Fritz Faulkner's *Windless Sky* (1937) the technique is utilized to intensify highly personal experiences; and in S. M. Steward's *Angels on the Bough* (1936) it is made to secure very detailed subjective effects.

Ulysses. The Joyce novel is, however, a better and a more famous example of the technique consistently used, than any of the books I have mentioned. It records everything that flows through the minds of its two central characters, Leopold Bloom and Stephen Dedalus, during but *one day* of their lives: June 16, 1904. Strictly speaking, the book has no plot. But I shall suggest its general nature.

As the story opens, about eight o'clock in the morning, in the Martello Tower near Dublin, Buck Mulligan finishes his shaving and then sits down to eat breakfast with his two friends: the Englishman, Haines; and the tutor, Stephen Dedalus. Stephen's conscience is bothering him because before his mother's recent death he had refused her request to pray for her soul. These reflections and his general religious apostasy torment his conscience throughout the entire day which the novel records. I think it important to mention this because his tortured conscience explains most of his conduct during the day and lends a kind of unifying *motif* to the entire book.

After breakfast Stephen goes to Mr. Deasy's school where he gives lessons to a group of school-boys. The "Bullock-be-

friending bard," Deasy, pays his instructor and asks him to
secure for him the publication of an essay he has written on
hoof-and-mouth disease. Further reflections occupy another
half hour of Stephen's morning while he walks by the sea;
and in the meantime we are introduced to the advertising
solicitor, Bloom, the time being flashed back to show him
getting breakfast for his wife and otherwise beginning his
day.

A complete summary of *Ulysses*[9] would be a lengthy affair. Suffice it to say that there are several general divisions
to the book: details of how Bloom spends his morning at
the market, at the public baths, and at the funeral of his
friend, Patrick Dignam; satires on journalese and the
methods of journalism; a picture of Dedalus at the Library,
meditating upon Shakespeare and other writers; scenes in
which Bloom and Dedalus meet during the day; trenchant
parodies of Malory, Bunyan, and others; a description of a
flirtation which Bloom is having with young Gerty Mac-
Dowell; a series of phantasmagoria in a red-light district;
a final meeting between Dedalus and Bloom, in which the
former is drunk and is taken home by the latter; and a long
closing monologue, of some forty pages, in which Mrs. Bloom,
before falling asleep, indulges in a series of reminiscences,
chiefly sexual and excremental. In the whole book the inner lives of the chief characters are revealed in full. Nothing is spared.

Ulysses and Ulysses. My husband is a great man in spite of
"his necessity to write those books no one can understand,"[10]
Mrs. Joyce tells us. Even those critics who profess a great
admiration for *Ulysses* frequently admit they do not understand the book. But in an attempt to interpret it, they
have, for one thing, drawn our attention to an intended
parallel which it bears with the *Ulysses* (Odysseus) of Homer.
In the Joyce book the characters wear, it will be observed,

certain psychological lineaments of the Homeric people: Bloom resembles — after a fashion! — Ulysses himself; Dedalus, Telemachus; Marion Bloom, Penelope; Gerty MacDowell, Nausicaa; Bella Cohen, Circe; the "Citizen," Polyphemus; Dan Dawson, Eolus, etc.

I suggest this comparison because it will nicely serve, I think, as a spring-board for the plunge into my more detailed discussion of the stream-of-consciousness. The older classical method, which prevailed in both our poetry and our fiction way up into our own century, was, in short, everything that the stream-of-consciousness is not. In mentioning this, of course, I intend no derogation of the newer technique when it is used judiciously: I only want, at this point in the discussion, a convenient basis of comparison.

In the first place, the older method employed a large canvas: thus, even *Tristram Shandy*, which attempts in the classical manner somewhat to suggest the inner life of its hero—even *Tristram Shandy* covers half a life-time. In the second place, the older technique related ideas which find a ready association in the average mind; depended chiefly upon easy and important thought-sequences; focused its attention upon action and what Arnold called "our sense of conduct"; dealt with men and women usually attuned to the norms of human experience; encouraged extrovert characters, who directed their attention to their environment, rather than themselves; and found expression in conventional and highly communicative language.

The stream-of-consciousness, on the other hand, tends to exploit the incoherent and to intensify individuality, to focus its attention upon psychopathological types, to emphasize feelings and sensations rather than action, to explore the subliminal, to encourage introspection, and to seek for overtones by employing a language that is frequently difficult or even unintelligible.

In brief, the classical manner considered man as a perfectly comprehensible and a complete organism : it was content merely to recognize man's component parts. But the stream-of-consciousness goes quite a bit further in showing us certain hitherto unsuspected springs in the human mechanism : springs that make that mechanism run as it does. It tries to demonstrate that the watch is running even when we cannot hear its tick. It emphasizes the importance of the springs we either ignore or take for granted ; and it attempts to show that many of the springs are worn or bent.

Sandymount shore and Sinbad the Sailor. To enter now into my explanation in a more detailed way, I might suggest as the first characteristic of the *monologue intérieur* its manner of *exploiting the incoherent.* Not all writers do this, of course : novelists like Virginia Woolf, Dorothy Richardson, and some few of the Americans — novelists who have learned to swim, rather than to splash with imitative strokes, in the stream-of-consciousness — such novelists have not forgotten the communicative purpose of writing. Even in *Ulysses* the reader will note an occasional passage that finds expression in rather intelligible and coherent language :

Woodshadows floated silently by through the morning peace from the stair-head seaward where he gazed. Inshore and further out the mirror of water whitened, spurned by lightshod hurrying feet. White breast of the dim sea. The twining stresses, two by two. A hand plucking the harpstrings merging their twining cords. Wavewhite wedded words shimmering on the dim tide.[11]

To come upon such an island of intelligibility in the welter of incoherence which the stream-of-consciousness often encourages, is a refreshing thing, indeed. It is pleasant, I say, to come upon nouns and predicates united in holy verbal wedlock — even though most of us realize, of course, that all minds including the normal, when uncontrolled by the will, *tend* toward the incoherent. "Our psyche is such an imperfectly integrated bundle of memories, sensations, and impulses, that unless sternly controlled by some dominating motive it is likely to be at the mercy of every stray wind of suggestion." [12]

But sometimes these winds of suggestion blow a bit too strongly, as in these three passages from *Ulysses*:

God becomes man becomes fish becomes barnacle goose becomes featherbed mountain. Dead breaths I living breathe, tread dead dust, devour a urinous offal from all dead. Hauled stark over the gunwale he breathes upward the stench of his green grave, his leprous nosehole snoring to the sun. [13]

. . .

What, reduced to their simplest reciprocal form, were Bloom's thoughts about Stephen's thoughts about Bloom and Bloom's thoughts about Stephen's thoughts about Bloom's thoughts about Stephen? [14]

. . .

He wished that a tale of a deed should be told of a deed not by him should by him not be told. [15]

And, again, the design of such novels can become so echometric as to permit the reverberations of this nonsense in the same book:

Sinbad the Sailor and Tinbad the Tailor and Jinbad the Jailer and Whinbad the Whaler and Ninbad the Nailer and Finbad the Failer and Binbad the Bailer and Pinbad the Pailer and Mindbad the Mailer and Henbad the Hailer and Rinbad the Railer and Dinbad the Kailer and Vinbad the Quailer and Linbad the Yailer and Xinbad the Phthailer. [16]

Or, it can encourage a species of echolalia like this selection from John Dos Passos' *1919*:

sunny afternoon   through the faint after-sick of mustard-gas I smell the box the white roses and the white phlox with a crimson eye   three brownandwhitestriped snails hang with infinite delicacy from a honeysucklebranch overhead   up in the blue a sausage-balloon grazes drowsily like a tethered cow

there are drunken wasps clinging to the tooripe pears that fall
and squash whenever the near guns spew their heavy shells that
go off rumbling through the sky [17]

Sandymount shore and soiled shirts. A highly *impressionistic language* is usually another feature of the *monologue
intérieur.* In his *The Twentieth Century Novel,* Joseph
Warren Beach comments upon a relationship between experimental verse and the intensely impressionistic concepts
of the stream-of-consciousness. To illustrate, for example,
how Amy Lowell got certain effects, he quotes these lines
from her "The Taxi" :

> Streets coming fast,
> One after the other,
> Wedge you away from me.[18]

and calls our attention to the way in which Amy Lowell has
reversed the usual conception of the streets as being sta-
tionary. In somewhat the same manner, Ernest Hemingway, though he does not employ the interior monologue as
a rule, thus impressionistically describes a cloud : "It came
very fast and the sun went a dull yellow and then everything
was gray and the sky was covered and the cloud came on
down the mountain and suddenly we were in it and it was
snow." [19]

The intense impressionism of the interior monologue is
likely, however, to make a writer lose sight of all objective
standards of beauty. At one moment Joyce can write of
the beautiful dark green of the sea, and in the next of nasal
excrement or green mould on a putrefying corpse ! He can
write beautifully of young men, clean of limb, swimming
in the sun-lighted sea ; and then indulge in the highly impressionistic picture of Bloom eating "with relish the inner
organs of beasts and fowls." (Mr. Bloom was merely fond
of fried kidneys!) He can abandon himself to the highly

expressionistic spree of telling us, for example, of finger-
nails "reddened by the blood of squashed lice from the chil-
drens' shirts" ; and give us this picture of a man ruminating
on the way he becomes nauseated at the sight of certain food :

> His eyes unhungrily saw shelves of tins, sardines, gaudy lobster's
> claws. All the odd things people pick up for food. Out of
> shells, periwinkles with a pin, off trees, snails out of the ground
> the French eat, out of the sea with bait on a hook. Silly fish
> learn nothing in a thousand years. If you didn't know risky
> putting anything into your mouth. Poisonous berries. Johnny
> Magories. Roundness you think good. Gaudy colour warns
> you. One fellow told another and so on. Try it on the dog
> first. Led on by the smell or the look. Tempting fruit. Ice
> cones. Cream. Instinct. Orangegroves for instance. Need
> artificial irrigation. Bleibtreustrasse. Yes but what about oys-
> ters. Unsightly like a clot of phlegm. Filthy shells. Devil to
> open them too. Who found out? Garbage, sewage they feed
> on. . .[20]

Kay Boyle, in her *Year Before Last* (1932), tells us that "The
mountains were as bare as bones knuckling the sky." [21] That
may possibly be an imaginative figure — a justifiably impressionistic touch. But the same cannot be said when she
so distorts images as to say that "Charlotte's limousine quiv-
ered under the portico, the nickel buttock of the spot-light
elongating the chauffeur's mirrored nose until it hung
reflected like a fresh sausage . . ." ; [22] or when she says that
"the milk of the clouds flowed steadily out of the strong
teats of the southern wind." [23]

Waldo Frank's *City Block* (1922) affords further illustrations of an effective kind of impressionism. "He saw the
snow swirl in blue skeins outside his window. All the day
was a pale peace." [24] But, again, frequently in Waldo Frank
the *monologue intérieur* encourages an egocentric point of
view — a failure of the will to dominate its impressions —
which can verge off into such an offensiveness as brings the
reader to a start in the concluding lines of the selection

which I now quote. A woman is reflecting upon her young
son :

He is strange, he is generous and slow. He says nothing. Often
his words tell nothing to my mind. He is not good in school.
He was left back in school. Through him I am chosen of
God.
God loves him above all us. Above bright children, gay children.
This son of my sad flesh is the son of Spirit. He is many
strengths, he is many souls. He is old not to know how to
take care of wiping his nose, how to keep from dirtying his
pants. Grace and Light he is. . .[25]

Sex in the cellar. Sensual feeling can, of course, be a good
thing. It "isn't bad in itself. It's in the world because
we have bodies as well as minds — it's like the root of a
plant," [26] says Mrs. Marshall in Dorothy Canfield's *The Bent
Twig.* But the stream-of-consciousness has a *tendency to
concern itself too much with sexual impulses.*

The psychological explanation of this becomes, of course,
simple enough when we remember Freud's doctrine of the
libido, which I shall later discuss ; or even when we recall
anything of normal human experience. It cannot be denied that sex plays a large part in man's subliminal life, as
well as in his conscious life.

Still, too many of the practitioners of the stream-of-consciousness have made the mistake of writing as if these impulses completely dominate man's life. They write as if
these impulses were not only the roots of the plant, but the
entire plant ; not something often at the basis of human
society, but the actual structure of human society. They
sometimes give the impression that life is little more than
one prolonged moment of sex consciousness. They write
novels in which children act like perverted old men ; they
would convert even a Huckleberry Finn into a Marquis de
Sade ; they surround boyhood's baseball field with high

fences scribbled full of obscene words. And even the normal sexual relationships of marriage they tend to distort into "complexes," "inhibitions," and "neuroses." What son is worth anything unless he has an Œdipus complex? And what is home without a frustrate mother?

The most conspicuous example of such an over-emphasis upon sex occurs in the concluding forty-odd pages, without a single punctuation mark, of *Ulysses*. Mrs. Bloom, in this section of the book, lies in bed at night and recalls the series of lovers she has had, together with a large number of other matters that I have already classified as excremental. But John O'Hara's *Appointment in Samarra* (1934), a story of a band of Corybantes whose sensuality is over-emphasized against a background of Gibbsville, Pennsylvania, offers a parallel with the Joyce illustration. Caroline English has had a quarrel with her husband and lies in bed, musing upon her life, until the maid comes into the room :

Oh, I guess I better get up. There's nothing to be gained by lying here in bed and feeling sorry for myself. It's nothing new or interesting or novel or rare or anything. I'm just a girl who feels like dying because the man I love has done me wrong. I'm not even suffering any more. I'm not even feeling anything. At least I don't think I am. No, I'm not. I'm not feeling anything. I'm just a girl named Caroline Walker, Caroline Walker English, Caroline W. English, Mrs. Walker English. That's all I am. Thirty-one years old. White. Born. Height. Weight. Born? Yes. I always think that's funny and I always will. I'm sorry, Julian, but I just happen to think it's funny and you used to think so too back in the old days when I knew you in an Eaton collar and a Windsor tie, and I loved you then, I loved you then, I love you now, I love you now. I'll always love you to the day I die and I guess this is what they call going to pieces. I guess I've gone to pieces, because there's nothing left of me. There's nothing left for me of days that used to be I live in mem-o-ree among my souvenirs. And so what you did, what you did was to take a knife and cut me open from my throat down to here, and then you opened the door and let in a blast of freezing cold air, right where you had cut me open, and till the day you die I hope you never, never know what it feels like to have someone cut you open all the way down the front of you and let the freezing blast of air inside you. I hope you never know what that means and I know you won't, my darling that I love, because nothing bad will happen to you. Oh, lovely Callie, your coat is so warm, the sheep's in the meadow, the cows in the corn. *"No, I don't think I'll get up for a while, Mrs. Grady."* [27]

In the same author's *Butterfield 8* (1936), Gloria Wandrous suffers from a traumatic childhood experience; and after riding high on the tides of promiscuity, and detailing her experiences with deep plunges into the stream-of-consciousness, she ends up by drowning in Long Island Sound. You can call it suicide, if you wish — Mr. O'Hara does not make the matter very clear. But the two novels which I have so very briefly referred to, do make clear the fact that he seems to have dedicated himself completely to the ambition of becoming one of our most successful literary pornographers.

The novelist who uses the *monologue intérieur* finds much of value in exploring the subliminal. But, while he is down in the cellar, he very frequently gets into a cerebral huddle with himself and thinks there is only one game to be played there !

Do fish ever get seasick? As the fourth feature of the stream-of-consciousness I mention the ease with which *it permits writers to become cumbersome, diffuse, and pointless.* Often, it must be conceded, the details which it finds it necessary to adduce really enrich our understanding of character. These apparent irrelevancies of Leopold Bloom will find, I think, a not too difficult association in a reader's mind ; and they do add something to our interpretation of Bloom's personality :

Did I forget to write address on that letter like the postcard I sent to Flynn. And the day I went to Drimmie's without necktie. Wrangle with Molly it was put me off. No, I remember. Richie Goulding. He's another. Weighs on his mind. Funny my watch stopped at half past four. Dust. Shark liver oil they use to clean could do it myself. Save. . .[28]

Again, the famous forty-sixth and forty-seventh chapters of Dreiser's *An American Tragedy* tell us much about Clyde Griffiths; the soliloquy of the young suicidal maniac, Septimus Warren Smith, in Virginia Woolf's *Mrs. Dalloway,* forms a revealing background for the rest of a novel so skilful that I mention it here, though it is by a British writer; the "impressions" of the inebriates in Nathan Asch's *Pay Day* (1930) secure at least their desired effect of revealing the way in which the central character, a man with an inferiority complex, is always at odds with himself; the long monologues employed in Waldo Frank's *Holiday* (1923) effect an ingenious contrast between the psychologies of the white and the black races; the reveries in Thomas Wolfe's novels very frequently offer us significant glimpses into Eugene Gant's complex personality; and the very detailed thought-sequences in Conrad Aiken's *King Coffin* (1935) are genuinely valuable for their revelation of the "strange" mind of Jasper Ammen. Indeed, many passages from stream-of-consciousness novels could be listed to show that a use of carefully selected details may often be a valid and an effective means of giving us a more true and a more complete insight into character.

On the other hand, in most stream-of-consciousness novels the total effect is blurred and diffused, or the story more than occasionally encumbered, by the introduction of *superfluous* detail. In *Ulysses* — to take but one example — Bloom even wonders whether fish ever get seasick! What did Bloom do at the kitchen stove? What was in the first drawer of his desk? What did he admire in water? Why should one shave at night? *Ulysses* includes seventy pages of such questions, together with answers which each run from a half to a full page!

Doing and Knowing. Another one of the features of the stream-of-consciousness is *its over-emphasis upon the passive nature of man and its tendency to minimize the significance of his more willful nature : to neglect his conduct and actions.* The character who is portrayed by means of the interior monologue often becomes a mere sort of Æolian harp set on the window sill of his author's mind to catch the whispering winds of strange fancy.

Though the world of the mind is an important one, it is not a complete one; and the author who is inclined to deal too exclusively with it — to neglect man's will as dominant over the chaos of his thought — misses, I believe, a source of arresting beauty; and, furthermore, disregards the common-sense experience of mankind: ". . . there is no endless stream of sensation and revery flowing through the consciousness of these gentlemen. They stop the stream. They put their foot down. . . They pass moral judgments. They live . . . in a rational and ordered universe. They mean to keep it so, even if they have to go on lynching-bees." [29] And they recognize the component parts of man's real nature :

> A soul of each and all the bodily parts,
> Seated therein, which works, and is what Does,
> And has the use of earth, and ends the man
> Downward ; but, tending upward for advice,
> Grows into, and again is grown into
> By the next soul, which seated in the brain,
> Useth the first with its collected use,
> And feeleth, thinketh, willeth — is what Knows. . .[30]

as Browning says in "A Death in the Desert."

Is not the immense popularity, during the past few years, of such books as Hervey Allen's *Anthony Adverse* (1933) and

Margaret Mitchell's *Gone With the Wind* (1936) due in part
at least to a natural human hunger for characters that lose
themselves in action as well as reverie, and due to our admiration for an author who has the ability

> . . . to scan
> Not his own course, but that of man,[31]

— an author who recreates something of the colorful texture
of life, with man playing a dominant part in that life?

Philological Fumbles. As a rule, the stream-of-consciousness *encourages a great deal of experimentation with language, form, and mood.* At times, as I have already pointed
out, this experimentation unites itself with a wild kind of
expressionism or impressionism and begets a kind of bastard
offspring: a strangely mixed language that is annoying and,
often, even unintelligible.

Mr. Dos Passos combines words in a series in the following manner: "I got a date animportantengagementtosee-
about those lots ought nevertohavestayedinbedsolate."[32]
He speaks of a man as being "leadentired," and of eyes as
"dollarproud." And to secure a rapid reflection of the consciousness of his characters he uses what might be thought of
as mirrors contrasting their inner with their outer lives:
such cinematic devices as headlines, Camera Eyes, and News
Reels — experiments which I discuss elsewhere in greater
detail.

In Robert Cantwell's *Land of Plenty* (1934) and William
Rollins' *The Shadow Before* (1934) the same experimental
artifices accompany their authors' use of the stream-of-consciousness. Ernest Hemingway uses the technique only occasionally; but his work has absorbed certain aspects of its
impressionism. Thus he describes the central character in
A Farewell to Arms as speaking "winefully." Mr. Saroyan
gives us such combinations as "mazdalight" and "mazda-

sleeplessness"; while Mr. Wolfe achieves a cumulative and impressionistic effect by amassing adjectives: "His thin face, beneath the jutting globular head, grinned constantly, glutting his features with wide, lapping, receding, returning, idiot smiles." [33]

As a result of their experiments, many of our younger writers have come to feel that punctuation marks impede the current of the stream-of-consciousness. Kay Boyle, for example, in some of her books omits all quotation marks. On the other hand, she illustrates what are genuinely interesting — and in a very few instances may even be purposeful — experiments in the newer techniques that accompany the interior monologue. She uses extra spacings to get the effect of nervous speech:

If you will sit down in the   I will call my wife who is
The servants for the moment are [34]

With weird effectiveness, she omits all quotation marks to blend dialogue and action, as in this sketch of a barber cutting the hair of a critically ill man:

He parted the hair and laid it back and ran his scissors through. There's a superstition about cutting a man's hair in bed, he said, still smiling. The blades nipped near the temples and cut short the black silk hair. Sometimes we're called upon to do it. The steel ran through and laid the soft thick locks aside. After a man, he said, and he parted the hair on the other side and drew the comb through the depths of it. After a man has already passed on, he said.[35]

Waldo Frank is a little more helpful: he carefully employs the dash to indicate a shift to the stream-of-consciousness. Here, for example, is a scene in which a woman is sitting in her husband's tailor shop, waiting for him to finish his work:

Above her shoulder on the wall, was a large sheet of fashions. Women with wasp waists, smirking, rolling: stiff men, all clothes, with little heads. Under the table, where Meyer sits with his big feet so much to look at, Flora played, a soiled bundle, with a ball of yarn and a huge gleaming scissors. — No one perhaps comes, and then I do not mind sitting and keeping the store. I saw a dead horse in the street. — A dead horse, two days dead, rotting and stiff. Against the grey of the living street, a livid dead horse. A hot stink was his cold death against the street's cleanness. There are two little boys, wrapped in blue coat, blue muffler, leather cap. They stand above the gaunt head of the horse and sneer at him. His flank rises red and huge. His legs are four strokes away from life. He is dead. . . The naughty boys pick up bricks. They stand, very close, above the head of the horse. They hurl down a brick. It strikes the horse's skull, falls sharp away. They hurl down a brick. It cuts the swollen nostril, falls soft away. The horse does not mind, the horse does not hurt. He is dead.[36]

Finally, among other interesting artifices which have been encouraged by the stream-of-consciousness, we should note a tendency to strive for sudden contrasts in mood : contrasts between the lofty and the low, the sublime and the undignified, the climactic and the bathetic. In this manner Joyce offers us the parodies I have earlier mentioned ; and Thomas Wolfe burlesques Tennyson :

By the waters of life, by time, by time, Lord Tennyson stood among the rocks, and stared. He had long hair, his eyes were deep and sombre, and he wore a cape ; he was a poet, and there was magic and mystery in his touch, for he had heard the horns of Elfland faintly blowing. And by the waters of life, by time, by time, as Lord Tennyson stood among the cold, gray rocks, and commanded the sea to break — break — break! And the sea broke, by the waters of life, by time, by time, as Lord Tennyson commanded it to do, and his heart was sad and lonely as he watched the stately ships (of the Hamburg-American Packet Company, fares forty-five dollars and up, first-class) go on to their haven under the hill, and Lord Tennyson would that his heart could utter the thoughts that arose in him.[37]

It is quite impossible for me to list all of the stylistic experiments which have been encouraged by the stream-of-

consciousness. Many of them, I repeat, are interesting; a
few, I again emphasize, may even be valuable. But, in our
own fiction at least, I do not think that any great *creative*
intelligence (if we except the promise of Thomas Wolfe) has
yet arisen to make use of these experiments. In the meantime, though this highly experimental phase of our national
letters may possibly be paving the way for such an intelligence, *it should not be thought of as a substitute for it.*
Intense experimentation may even indicate some small measure of misdirection, confused purposes, or essential sterility.

When you cannot climb over a wall, you may be tempted
to do a lot of playing on your side of it.

"Ideas and sensations."   It will be recalled that Joyce's Buck
Mulligan could remember "only ideas and sensations."   It
ought carefully to be noted, however, that *the interior monologue is a suitable vehicle for the transmission chiefly of
sensory impressions.*   But men do more than feel. They do
more than remember "only ideas and sensations."   They do
more than "play" with ideas in reverie. For example, they
often have very definitely conceived philosophies. The
stream-of-consciousness novel tends to ignore this. Does one
finish reading *Ulysses* with any clear conception of Bloom's
philosophy? Or Stephen's? Even in Mrs. Woolf's excellently written *To the Lighthouse* "one knows every fine
shade of the philosopher's personality without once having
had a satisfactory glimpse of his philosophy." [38] To be
highly satisfying, character should be presented as completely as possible. And no author makes the most of his
opportunity for enriching his characters when he employs
too exclusively a technique which becomes an instrument
delicately tuned for the measuring chiefly of sensations.
Man both *Does* and *Knows*. And when he knows, he is
cognizant of much besides his sensory impressions and
thought-sequences. He is cognizant of a will which at least

tends to dominate these sequences, and find some order in their chaos.

Let us say, then, that the stream-of-consciousness is seldom adequate as a technique for an entire book ; but that it becomes extremely effective when a genuinely creative mind uses it judiciously as a complement to the more traditionally valuable methods of literary analysis and expression. In my opinion, it has very rarely been so used by our American novelists.

2

In seeking a complement in Freudism, moreover, the stream-of-consciousness united itself in a kind of incestuous relationship which has not always been for the best interests of its literary offspring. Freud's experiments in psycho-analysis had been known on the Continent, of course, before the turn of the century; but it was not until he visited America in 1909 to deliver his "Concerning Psychoanalysis" lectures at Clark University that such terms as the *"libido,"* "psychoses," "repression," "sublimation," "complexes," and the "censor" became common topics of American conversation and a flood of Freudian books [39]— some two hundred of them in the next decade alone ! — was released upon us. Readers interested in some of Freudism's mass effects upon our civilization will find *Our Neurotic Age* (1932) an inform-ing symposium ; while those of us who may be inclined to think neuroses out of fashion can find reassurance in Dr. Louis Bisch's *Be Glad You're Neurotic* (1936) — a book highly advertised with the quotation that "to be normal is nothing to brag about."

By way of explaining the nature of Freudism, let me ask my readers to imagine that man is a kind of building. The well-constructed building has, of course, a good foundation : and this foundation is extremely important not only as a base, but for its enclosure of the dozens of pipes, switches, and wires which somewhat control the life in the building itself. But a cellar seldom extends down into the earth farther than the rest of a building extends above the ground. In the Freudian psychology the proportions of the structure are reversed : the cellar, or the subliminal life of each individual man, becomes the deepest part of the edifice; and is explored exhaustively to account for most of the ideas — even the dusty and apparently unserviceable ones — which somehow find their way into the cluttered attic of man's brain.

"Sigmund Freud turns psychology upside down. He studies not what the mind knows about itself, but what it does not know, or, at least, does not know that it knows."[40] By this process the subconscious becomes the key to the conscious : really to understand what is going on in the attic, we have only to call up a few interesting apparitions from the depths of the cellar : our *"libido,"* or sexual hunger ; our "complexes," or those "ideas" which are the result of strong emotions, have been repressed, and yet obviously influence our conduct ; and our "fixations," or arrested subconscious tendencies.

It all sounds simple enough. There is a commotion in the sub-conscious part of us. Our conscious life is having havoc played with it. Only let a few of those struggling fellows that are down there, out ; bring them upstairs, find out what the trouble is, and they will do no further damage.

Unfortunately, there is a locked door between the cellar and the upper part of the house ; and the key to that door is kept by a disagreeable chap whom the Freudians call our "censor" — a chap who stubbornly refuses to permit the emergence of many of those aforementioned desires, complexes, and fixations. His resistance is hard to break down ; often, indeed, it is only when he is napping that those occupants of our subconscious can manage to escape at all ; and then they do so largely in the form of our dreams.

Enter at this point the psychoanalyst. It is his job to help overcome the censor, to free the repressed prisoners, to interpret our dreams and find out what it is that the clamorous fellows really want. This he attempts to do by arranging a number of meetings with his patient, during which he encourages him in every way possible to allow his mind to wander and to give the freest expression to every association that occurs to him. As Freud says in his *The Interpretation of Dreams*, the patient is to relax, close his eyes, tell "everything that passes through his mind" and not "suppress one idea because it seems to him unimportant or irrelevant." [41] But for a more complete account let us go to Hitschmann, one of Freud's students:

. . . He has the patient recline comfortably on a couch while he sits on a chair behind and outside his line of vision. He does not insist upon the eyes being closed, and avoids any touch, as well as every other procedure which might lead to hypnotism. Such a séance goes along like a conversation between two similarly awake persons of whom one is relieved of every muscular tension and every distracting sense impression, which might disturb the concentration of the attention upon his own mental affairs. Before he proceeds to details, he urges them often, for several sessions, to sketch a general picture of their whole illness and most intimate family and life surroundings, to tell him everything which comes into their heads, whether they think it important, irrelevant, or nonsensical. With special emphasis, it is asked of them that no thought or association be omitted from the communication because this telling might be shameful or painful.[42]

Ultimately, the Freudian psychologist thus discovers his patients' neuroses — neuroses which can perhaps be best explained by this remark of Freud's: ". . . I maintain that neurotic anxiety has its origin in the sexual life, and corresponds to a libido which has been deflected from its object and has found no employment." [43] The psychoanalyst therefore finds that most dreams have some deep sexual significance. Let me emphasize this by adducing a few examples.[44]

Freud tells of a woman who dreamed she had gone out to buy vegetables. The vegetables become phallic symbols! A woman dreams that she loses a button from her coat; and does not want to remove the garment when her hostess invites her to. She has recalled an early dissatisfaction with her figure! A patient of Dr. Schrötter's is hypnotized into dreaming of homosexual relations with a friend. The friend appears in the patient's dream, carrying a traveling-bag labeled "For ladies only." Another woman dreams that she is arranging flowers for a birthday party. The violets suggest the French *violate ;* the lilies become symbols of her early chastity; the carnations suggest her later carnality!

But not quite all of the dreams which Freud analyzes are, it should be noted, of a sexual significance. Some of them, Freud admits himself, are even "witty." Thus, a person dreams that his uncle kisses him in an automobile. The interpretation? *Auto*-erotism! A man sees a girl, in his dream, dressed in a white blouse and bathed in a white light. The explanation? The patient remembers that he had had a love affair with a Miss White. A dreamer sees himself on a mountain from which he gets a very "extensive view." The reason for the dream? He is identifying himself with his brother who is editing a "review."

Also, according to the Freudian, we perform some subtle arithmetic in our dreams. We are told, for example, that one person dreamed of quarter past five in the morning: this was symbolic of five years and three months: at that time a younger brother of his had been born! Robbers, ghosts, and burglars — dreams of these originate in our childhood recollections of the attendants who awakened us at night.

When we dream of robbers, we recall our fathers; ghosts, however, suggest the white night-gowns of the women who aroused us!

But enough. I shall be accused of deprecating genuine advances in psychology. I do not : I speak only against some of the counterfeit coins which it has minted — coins which have been made to ring so enticingly upon the counters of modern thought and fiction that we are beginning, I fear, to mistake their exchange value.

"A man hardened with a secret should especially avoid the intimacy of his physician." However, if the physician possesses "native sagacity," if he has the "power . . . to bring his mind into affinity with his patient's . . . then at some inevitable moment, will the soul of the sufferer be dissolved, and flow forth in a dark but transparent stream, bringing all its mysteries into the daylight." A quotation from Freud? No, indeed. From Hawthorne's *The Scarlet Letter*. Genuine psychoanalysis has its place in our literature as this great novel proves.

But when Freudism turns into Fraudism — that is another matter. And when Freudian fiction becomes — as it has become in America — but an inviting wall on which to scribble Fescennine filth — that, too, is another matter. "In this country psychoanalysis has been widely accepted by critics and creators who were longing for a diagrammed excuse for their sensual admirations, and these people, of course, have plastered it with phallic exaggerations. . . Back of this farce [this is putting it mildly!] stands the psychoanalyst, with his enticing implication that nothing exists in human beings except sex. . . He has, indeed, become the god-father of most contemporary American prose and poetry, and he is, indeed, very much in need of a metaphysical spanking." [45]

The psychoanalyst has given us, in the words of Mr. Joseph Wood Krutch, who himself leans toward the psychoanalytical theories, what is "certainly the most far-reaching of any of the recent attempts to rob man of such shreds of dignity as had been left to him." In our fiction he has over-emphasized the introvert; he has capitalized upon these introversions; he has deflected the stream-of-consciousness until it has often become but a whirling eddy of erotic sensations; he has made the abnormal serve as a seriously misleading index to the normal.

"As a matter of fact, there is little to write about today except the abnormal,"[46] the Freudian Vridar Hunter goes so far as to observe in Vardis Fisher's *No Villain Need Be*. And one of Professor Hunter's very young friends upon another occasion asks him: ". . . what is wrong with me? Is it paranoia or is it dementia praecox? Paresis or anorexia? Algolagnia or claustrophobia? Or is it euphoria? . . . It's algolagnia."[47]

Here is at least one student of the psychoanalytic method who needs something more than a *metaphysical* spanking!

Sigmund Freud had scarcely ended his American lectures before our fiction began to catch some of the echoes of psychoanalysis. Novelists like James Oppenheim — the author of such early novels as *Wild Oats* (1910), *Idle Wives* (1914), and *The Beloved* (1915) — set a fashion which was to gain considerable momentum in the second decade of our century, and to become definitely established in our own decade.

Floyd Dell had himself psychoanalyzed; and wrote autobiographical novels dealing with the technique. His *Moon-Calf* (1920), a competent though not very engaging novel of Vital Forces and the younger generation, depicts what its author himself designates as the struggle "between the narcistic and sexual-social impulses." Felix Fay, the book's hero, spends a self-centered adolescence in the world of dreams; and later seeks out "kindred souls" that read Haeckel. He wears a carnation on Ingersoll's birthday; thinks of himself as a Superman after reading Nietzsche; tries to get his sweetheart to rebel against the idea of a conventional marriage and be true, above all else, to her "own soul"; and lets her kiss him "in the conscious knowledge that she was obeying the urge of the Life Force."

Fay and his friends "talked . . . of books, and ideas, and Nietzschean philosophy" and then at dawn "went out in search of an all-night restaurant where they could get a breakfast of ham and eggs." [48] And when he drank champagne, "The icy particles tingled with a splendid rebellion against God." [49] *The Briary Bush* (1921), the sequel to *Moon-Calf,* does not lean quite so noticeably toward the psychoanalytical method as does Mr. Dell's later *Runaway* (1925), a novel of "evasion."

Edwin Björkman's *The Soul of a Child* (1922) bears, however, strong technical resemblances to the earliest Dell novels; and narcism forms one of the themes of Evelyn Scott's *The Narrow House* (1921). A somewhat similar interest in the subjects of "evasion" and "repression" is united, in Joseph Hergesheimer's *Cytherea* (1922), with that of fetishism; and the question of "inhibitions" also engrosses the same author in *Linda Condon* (1919).

Waldo Frank is another of the stream-of-consciousness novelists who has resorted often to the Freudian technique. The demented dreamer who is the hero of *Chalk Face* (1924) has become insane as a result of a struggle between his censor and his complexes; and finally, becoming a kind of Freudian Ethan Brand, he commits suicide by jumping into a lime kiln. Frank's *Holiday* (1923) is curiously reminiscent of Anderson's *Dark Laughter* which was to be published two years later; and the collection of stories — "a single organism" their author calls them — entitled *City Block* (1922) deals, among other things, with alcoholics, *libidos* which emerge so powerfully in a stolid policeman's frame that he arranges assignations in a hall bedroom, parents who discover their child to be a pervert and a cretin, nymphomaniacs, hypochondriacs, and a woman with a maternity complex somewhat suggestive of that of the central character in a

much later novel, *Madonna Without Child* (1929), by Myron
Brinig. (*The Sisters,* the Brinig novel which appeared in
the spring of 1937, is marked, however, by a general departure from the more usual methods of the Freudian.)

One of the characters in *City Block* offers a pointed illustration of that Freudian point of view which colors most of
Frank's work. Paula Desstyn, we are told, *could not resist*
meeting her lover : "She was a crumpled creature dragged by
a long leash. She went : she had to go . . ." [50] And as an
illustration of the way in which the psychoanalyst in Frank
often turns psychology upside down by making the abnormal
the key to the normal, I quote a further passage. A natural
maternal instinct is made into a "complex" which causes a
childless woman to kill, with her embraces, a child she is
permitted to tend :

> Sophie had no sense of her self separate from this life upon
> her. She had no sense of its shriek above the shriek of her
> flesh. She folded her arms about the infant and crushed her
> close, feeling her breasts crush, bruise, feeling her breasts swell
> out and encase the child and the shriek. She drew her hands
> about her naked shoulders, she pressed with her hands and with
> her throat, with all her imprisoning self she pressed, that had so
> long pressed in, what now was sweetly escaping. She moved up
> and down in her chair, pressing, pressing. . . And the child's
> shriek was over. [51]

One of the Ben Hecht men is both a sexual monomaniac
and a megalomaniac, living only for "sensual swoons"—the
kind of debased love that Aldous Huxley termed a "sweating
of palm to palm." He is "continually and harmlessly cruci-
fying himself on billboards." Another of the same author's
puppets has a body that "felt a sudden almost unendurable
need of possession" and made her feel an irresistible desire
"to scream filthy words." "What remedies were there for
desire?" the author reflects, contemplating one of his sensualists. "He had tried them all and desire seemed only to

feed on them." [52] Paranoics, exhibitionists, sensualists, fanatics — the Hecht characters run through the entire gamut of abnormalities which the jargon of psychoanalysis has so far classified. Furthermore, in several instances, the specific methods of psychoanalysis are employed in the Hecht novels to interrogate characters regarding their past lives and intimate relationships.

"You may be able to get over it. Go to a psychoanalyst," [53] advises a character in John Dos Passos' *Manhattan Transfer*. And a little later in the same book another says: "Everything would be so much better if suddenly a bell rang and everybody told everybody else honestly what they did about it, how they lived, how they loved. It's hiding things makes them putrefy. By God it's horrible. As if life wasn't difficult enough without that." [54] Tallow-faced, bright-eyed pyromaniacs, neurasthenic women, melancholiacs, homosexualists — Mr. Dos Passos has dealt with almost every type of abnormality.

A growing preoccupation with abnormal types has likewise characterized the work of Eugene O'Neill, who by common consent today stands out as the greatest figure in modern world drama. Mr. O'Neill has more than deserved the three Pulitzer Awards which he has already won, and the Nobel Prize recently bestowed upon him. He has never stood unctuously in line to receive the splashes of literary log rollers: his rich imagination, his poetic insight, and his positive genius for the theatre are all pleasingly complemented by his complete dedication to the dramatic art. Also, in theory at least, he has had a high classical dream — he thinks the classical "the noblest ever" — as to the aims of that art: "to develop a tragic expression in terms of transfigured modern values and symbols in the theatre which may to some degree bring home to members of a modern audience their ennobling identity with the tragic figures on the stage." [55]

When Mr. O'Neill has followed this dream he has discovered rare moments of beauty and brought about a genuine enlargement of the values of life. Yank's gnawing fear that he will be buried at sea; the complete catharsis, in the closing scene of *Ile,* when old Captain Keeney rushes out of the cabin, leaving Mrs. Keeney insanely playing a hymn on the organ, wildly and discordantly, while she sways back and forth to its rhythm; the sure unfolding of Stephen Murray's love for Eileen Carmody and the hope born in his heart; Olson, in the grimly brutal forecastle, remembering his mother; Robert Mayo finding at last the horizon beyond the blue hills; Lazarus and the enthralling spell of his laughter "like a great bird song triumphant in depths of sky, proud and powerful, infectious with love" [56] — the transfiguring power of certain scenes and emotions in the O'Neill plays cannot be denied. Mr. O'Neill has had his dream; and, at times, that dream has indeed been "the noblest ever."

But not when he has called Freud in to interpret the dream for him! And, more and more, in the progress of his career as a dramatist, has Mr. O'Neill done exactly this. Surveyed in their proper order, his plays reveal a steadily increasing interest in the findings of psychopathology, and a growing preoccupation with such abnormal types as might have stepped directly out of a psychoanalyst's casebook. Luke Bentley's deranged old father ("God roast his soul"); Luke Bentley's sister ("as stinkin' mean as ever"); the insane Bartlett, with the neurotic daughter and the sadistic son; the Strindbergian neurasthenic who makes a fetish of giving herself to an ex-soldier; Curtis Jason, living amidst a century's accumulation of self-tortures and hates; the malicious and insane Ella — Sigmund Freud has been O'Neill's unacknowledged collaborator in painting a gallery of characters too extensive to describe here.

Desire Under the Elms (1925) is colored entirely by the Freudian point of view. There is Abbie, with a body that "squirms desirously," with eyes that are always "burning with desire," and with a voice that is "a horribly frank mixture of lust and mother love." There is the Freudian scene in which Eben "surrenders" himself to Abbie; there is the "complex" which prompts the seventy-five year old Ephraim Cabot to ride forth "t'learn God's message t'me in the spring, like the prophets done." There are the confined hates—no catharsis here!—between the father and sons; the relationships between Abbie and her doddering old husband; the Freudian *libido* which makes Eben's "censor" so powerless against Abbie's lusts. And there is the constant emphasis, also, upon that interesting Freudian idea that "Nature'll beat ye. . . Ye might's well own up t'it fust's last."

In *Strange Interlude* (1928) the "complex" which restrains Leeds from allowing his daughter to marry; the later fixation which Nina has on her son; and the way in which her "inhibitions" and battles with the censor finally lead her into promiscuity—all this is Freudian. So, also, is the depiction, in *Dynamo* (1929) of the megalomaniac with the fetishist's worship of electricity; and so, likewise, is the manner in which *Mourning Becomes Electra* (1931) treats of the old theme of the Æschylus trilogy. "The normal human horror at incest becomes an interestingly Freudian libido. The upstanding manhood of Orestes, his hard-fought battle for spiritual release, becomes a weak-kneed and neurotic pessimism ending in suicide. Electra herself is so tainted in mind that she wilfully renounces escape to the brighter world and closes all doors and shutters, the more deeply to enjoy the gloom of the House of Mannon. . . The Orestes, far from murdering his mother, is warmly Freudian toward her." [57]

Indeed, the "complex" which motivates Mr. O'Neill's whole interpretation of this classical theme is one thing, at least, for which the Greeks would not have had a name. The Greek idea of suffering, of catharsis, of fate, of wrong-doing

— none of these are to be found in *Mourning Becomes Electra*. What is to be found? A great Greek dream interpreted by Austrian psychology! Even the god of Æschylus (who "transcends them all"), in this play becomes *She*. Zeus gives way to Psyche.

The psyche of Sigmund Freud.

Elsewhere in my studies I discuss some of the Freudian conflicts in the novels of Thomas Wolfe and in certain of the Faulkner novels — especially in *As I Lay Dying*. With the exception of Sherwood Anderson, however, no present-day novelist has been so consistently Freudian as Vardis Fisher. When a student at Chicago, Fisher was advised by Robert Herrick, who was then one of his instructors, to give up the idea of becoming a novelist because he would "never write a novel worth opening."

In the beginning of Fisher's literary career, few people, apparently, did bother to open his books. *Toilers of the Hills* (1928) and *Dark Bridwell* (1931) passed, as a matter of fact, almost unnoticed; while one eastern publisher after another rejected *In Tragic Life* because, as one of them described the book, it was "too strong meat for our table." Finally brought out by the Caxton Printers, *In Tragic Life* was later reissued by Mr. Fisher's present publishers as the first volume of a gigantic tetralogy dealing with the "spiritual" conflicts of a man's life — a tetralogy that our critics were to hail as "extraordinary," "powerful," "profound," and "unique." Each of the volumes in the series derives its title from Meredith's "Modern Love"; and the last three are entitled *Passions Spin the Plot* (1934), *We Are Betrayed* (1935), and *No Villain Need Be* (1936).

With what the critics have called "unflinching courage" and "downright honesty," *The Vridar Hunter Tetralogy* — as Mr. Fisher has named the series — outlines the life of its central character from the time he is a small boy on an Idaho ranch, to the time when, after the War, he has married, his wife has committed suicide, he has remarried, become a college professor, and finally returned to his early home to write a monumental account of his inner struggles and his discovery of "moral freedom." As a boy Vridar had been held by the vice of adolescence, brought almost to the verge of insanity. Later on, when his first wife commits suicide, he blames himself for her death : "I was false to her by being what the world would call faithful." [58]   And both his childhood experiences and the memory of his wife are ever afterwards to remind him of what he considers his cowardice in letting the Freudian "censor" get the better of him !

"Make the sex-obsessed *think* sex, *act* sex, until he breaks that morbid fixation on it." [59]   This is the thing to do ! Accordingly, Hunter looks forward to the time, when, as he tells his second wife, "we can plot the destruction of ourselves as angels, and the understanding of ourselves as animals. . ." [60]   To free his *libido,* for example, he goes — and with the full "understanding" of the mistress whom he is to marry ! — back to his earlier haunts, to indulge in a few affairs intended to teach him that love — "good lusty physical love" — is "as natural as food and drink."   For "we men are like roosters," he insists.   And chastity "is the silliest vice among the virtues."   The thing to do is to become "animals so that we can be clean."

When he becomes a college instructor, Vridar Hunter is of course given unrivaled opportunities for practicing his Freudism.   Students flock to him for advice — students with every type of mental and moral quirk.   And then Professor Hunter "analyses" their cases for them.   He inquires into their dreams as wish-fulfillments ; he helps them see that a sense of sin serves only as an aphrodisiac that adds "zest to sexual adventure."   He interviews them, indeed, in long, revealing, intimate, and painful scenes which would, I think, somewhat embarrass Sigmund Freud himself.   But Mr. Fisher's most recent novel — *April: A Fable of Love* (1937)

—makes somewhat more pleasant reading. It is a sensitively written tale of an Idaho girl who dreams of a love denied her because of her ugliness—a tale only remotely Freudian.

Eleanor Carroll Chilton's *Shadows Waiting* (1927) applies a subjective, Freudian technique to a theme which Dreiser had attempted to deal with objectively in *The Genius*. In Winifred Van Etten's *I am the Fox* (1936), a neurotic girl identifies herself with the fox, which she sees as a symbol of the hunted. Gladys St. John Loe's *Smoking Altars* (1936) deals, among other things, with a suicidal maniac; James Gray's *Wake and Remember* (1936) has overtones which will easily be recognized as Freudian; T. S. Matthews' *The Moon's No Fool* (1936) is heavy with "obsessions" and "suppressed desires"; Cora Jarrett's *Strange Houses* (1936) makes use of the theme of dual personality and has a psychiatrist as one of its characters; John Evans' *Shadows Flying* (1936) introduces a study of sexual abnormalities; Murrell Edmunds' *Sojourn Among Shadows* (1936) makes use of certain of the themes of psychopathology; Julian Green's *The Dark Journey* (1929) was largely written from the point of view of the Freudian; and Joanna Cannan's *Frightened Angels* (1936) is a somewhat Freudian study of a man who becomes a murderer as the result of a "clutch of circumstances."

Making use of either the methods or the materials of the psychoanalyst are such further volumes as Mary Dunstan's *Snow Against the Sky* (1936), which is a Rousseau-like story of two men, half-brothers, cut off from the world in a mountain cabin; Claude Houghton's *Christina* (1936), which has been called an incursion into the theme of "retrospective sexual jealousy"; Harvey O'Higgins' *Clara Barron* (1926), which is an account of an extremely neurotic woman; Ludwig Lewisohn's *Trumpet of Jubilee* (1937), an attempt to apply Freudian psychology "to society at large"; Leonard O. Mosley's *So I Killed Her* (1937), a picture of distorted minds, sadists, and a nymphomaniac; Millen Brand's *The Outward Room* (1937), a story of a girl who has spent seven years in an insane asylum because she has come to identify her brother's death with her own; John Rathbone Oliver's *Victim and Victor* (1928), a portrait of a clergyman, strongly influenced by the findings of psychopathology; Djuna Barnes' *Nightwood* (1937), a tale of a freakish nobleman, a freakish doctor, and two perverted women; and Ramona Herdman's *Today Is Forever* (1937), a study of a young woman in the grip of neuroses. Some of the titles which I have mentioned are by British authors; but all of them have been published in this country. It will be noted that, for the most part, I have tried to suggest only recent volumes; but scores of others could be given to show how thoroughly Freudism has filtered into our present-day literature.

However, I have no desire to convert this chapter into a bibliography of Freudian fiction; and so I bring it to a close with a consideration of Conrad Aiken and Wilbur Daniel Steele. The former has been the most consistently successful, and the most frequently artistic, of all of our writers who have employed the techniques of Freud and the *monologue intérieur*.

Abnormal types have claimed a share of Aiken's attention, it is true. For example, *Blue Voyage* (1927), a book which owes much to *Ulysses*, depicts the half-crazed reflections of an erotomaniac, suffering from schizophrenia, and lying awake in his second-class ship's cabin, while he thinks upon the woman who has snubbed his love. And *King Coffin* (1935) — to offer another illustration — is a study of a megalomaniac who, because of his hatred for humanity, decides to show his supreme contempt for the race by planning a "perfect" murder. Suffering from a sort of "Jehovah complex," Jasper Ammen thinks a murder can be, for him, the "only natural purification." But it must be "simply an act of destruction": it must lack all personal motives:

The stranger must be some one to whom one could be completely indifferent. He must be neither attractive nor unattractive, not to be loved or pitied, nor hated nor feared, some one whose strangeness and anonymity (in the sense that one knew nothing about him and *felt* nothing) was pure. The face must be quite ordinary, just a face, the bearing and gait must be neither offensive nor enviable, the clothes of a sort of universal character-lessness. In short, it must be simply "a man." A mere lay figure, or drawing of a man, such as you saw in a newspaper advertisement of ready-made suits for sixteen dollars and fifty cents.[61]

What fun it would be, Jasper reflects, to invite a group of friends to a party, and then commit suicide, so that those friends would make the "charming discovery" of their host's corpse when they arrived!

There is no doubt but that Mr. Aiken has dealt often with abnormal types! But he does not, as a rule, make their abnormalities a key to normalities. He does not capitalize upon his own introversions; he *creates* characters. Nor does he often attempt to make sexual abnormalities palatable and fashionable.

He has both skill and humor. The former talent I can illustrate with the story entitled "Mr. Arcularis" from *Among the Lost People* (1934). Bierce would have been proud of this story and, indeed, it bears more than a curious resemblance to Bierce's "An Occurrence at Owl Creek Bridge." We see Mr. Arcularis in his hospital room after a critical operation; we watch him leave for Europe to recuperate, suffering, while on the boat, a series of nightmares and vague fears. And then, suddenly, a few final words disclose the horror of the whole story: "at this point in the void the surgeon's last effort to save Mr. Arcularis's life had failed. He stood back from the operating table and made a tired gesture with a rubber-gloved hand." [62] The whole story has taken place in the patient's mind before he has sunk into an unconsciousness from which he never recovers!

A rather grim story; but one which finds pleasant relief in the more pleasant humor in many of the other tales. I can give but one example of what I mean. In the first story in the collection, a woman exhibits one of her paintings which vividly portrays mounds of sand. Very realistic, she insists! And then she confesses that she has actually mixed sand with the paint! But her amused friend asks her what she intends doing with the painting: use it to strike matches on? There is a cosmic irony in this humor that my brief words must miss.

"If meat make my brother to offend, I will eat no flesh while the world standeth, lest I make my brother to offend." In *Meat* (1928) Wilbur Daniel Steele has done an extremely well-written novel that, despite a few very disagreeable scenes, competently illustrates what I think is one of the legitimate uses to which a certain kind of Freudism may be put in our fiction.

The wealthy young publisher, Sam India, and his wife, Anne, have two children who seem to possess dependably wholesome and strong wills. But the obviously weak will of the third child, Rex, alarms Anne. As a consequence, she wishes to shield him from all temptation; although the father thinks it wiser to expose him to a few minor perils, and teach him to face them and master them.

There is, for example, the temptation of the cellar, where five generations of the India family have kept their wines. One day Sam takes his sons into this wine-cellar, shows them where the key of it is kept, and tells them of their grandfather and great-grandfather:

"It never entered their heads to become drunkards. It never entered their heads even to be afraid they might. They respected their wine, too much for that. They weren't going to make pigs of themselves with liquor, because they knew that if they did they would be shabby and silly, just as they knew that if they swilled too much food at meals they would be pasty and fat.

Your great-grandfather had one funny thing about him; he couldn't eat honey. It gave him blotches and stomach-aches, so he didn't eat honey, though he was fond of it, and always kept bees." [63]

So Sam India wants to keep the door of the wine-cellar open; but Anne locks it and throws the key away. Who can deny that the children would have been stronger morally, and much happier, if Sam had had his way in this matter at least? The Freudian, likewise, thinks it is better to leave the cellar door open: he wants to face the disturbing complexes of man's subliminal life.

Unfortunately, he wants to do even more than this. He wants us not only to remember that these complexes are in the cellar, but to let them all come upstairs. He tells us that we should face them; but he adds that we should not try to fight them. We can't win anyway. Each of us is "but a crumpled creature dragged by a long leash," as Waldo Frank says of Paula Desstyn. The leash may extend back to our childhood, or even to our ancestors. But it is futile to tug at it! Or, again, each of us is entirely "rudderless," as Lawrence says of two of his women characters in *The Virgin and the Gypsy*.

Entirely rudderless. Especially when the stream-of-consciousness novelist resorts to the Freudian technique is he likely to take away our moral rudders — our wills. He refuses to let us seek out a direction; often he will not permit us even to keep afloat. He assures us that not only are there some very bad swimmers amongst us — some abnormal types; but he also enticingly implies that none of us can swim except by cultivating our weakest strokes. We are to close our eyes and relax; and while he helps us to get to the bottom of everything (in more than one sense), we are to sink quietly into the alluring waters of the stream.

CHAPTER V

SHERWOOD ANDERSON : CONGENITAL FREUDIAN

". . . I maintain that neurotic anxiety has its origin in the sexual life, and corresponds to a libido which has been deflected from its object and has found no employment."— Sigmund Freud, in *The Interpretation of Dreams*, p. 165.[1]

CHAPTER V

SHERWOOD ANDERSON : CONGENITAL FREUDIAN

SEX and symbols, evasions and epidermis, repressions and rivers, physiology and poplar trees, secret sins and standardization, mysticism and mush, nostalgias and sheer nonsense, the machine and marching men, the nervous dark laughter of the nymphomaniac and the full-throated song of the Negro, the shiftlessness of the poor white and dreams which drive men to invent coal dumpers that make a hundred thousand dollars — with a kind of Whitmanian sensuality Sherwood Anderson has woven all these subjects, and hundreds more, into what we must certainly recognize as the most influential Freudian novels America has yet produced.

Whereas Dreiser strove for the objectivity of the naturalist, and Cabell sought escape in the high places of the past, Anderson has entered into an exclusive kind of compotation with his own psyche; tippled orgiastically upon the delights of a world seen almost entirely in communion with himself; and gone off chanting bacchanalia about his being "pregnant," a "sacred vessel" familiar with "soft lips" and the "sweeter brotherhood," and "wading in a long river" until his "feet are wet." Inebriated with ecstasy, he sounds, more than occasionally, it must be conceded, as if he were addressing a lamp-post. Thus, in A New Testament (1927), a volume of verse, he rants about how he is, at times, an Alexander, a Napoleon, or a Cæsar; and he feverishly asks his friends to "surrender" themselves to him, offering to carry them about as would a woman who is pregnant!

At such times he seems slightly in his psychical cups: both muddled and maudlin. Nor does he seem to care whether we think him muddled or not — whether we understand him or not. As he says in *Tar*, all one has to do is to group words together : one may not know the meaning of them, but that makes no difference. And later, as one walks along, repeating to himself the words he has written, he will learn to like at least the sound of them, the way they get along together as certain people do.

. You do not always understand Sherwood Anderson any more than he at any time clearly understands himself. For, although his intensely sincere groping may win you for a time, you are always conscious of its mist rather than its "mysticism." His work annoyingly fails to exhibit order or design. His characters babble about symbols that only the devil could understand; and that, perhaps, only the devil is meant to understand. He crowds details into his work that are both irrelevant and monotonous. He thinks with his nerve cells; and he seems to live rapturously upon a kind of Swinburnian "spasm of erotic emotional exquisite error."

Withal, he has done some enduringly creative work: several fine short stories, for example; some penetrating comment upon our machine age; some few memorable portrait studies; and several unforgettable pictures. Scenes from his own boyhood; accurately revealing descriptions of our post-War America; the old widow of a railroad man getting up in the night to pick up coal which her dead husband's fellow-brakemen throw into her yard as their trains hurl by into the darkness; smoky Pete roaring down the street to reform his fellow-citizens; the live-stock dealer, Hawkins, mumbling his fervent prayers beside his wife's grave while the rain pours down upon him; an old woman frozen to death, and lying in the snow, with the white moonlight upon her body; the poor factory girl, Kit Brandon, going to her friends to return the shoes she has had to borrow, and leaving them on the porch, with a dollar bill to show her gratitude — vivid and memorable pictures of such things do manage, somehow, to arise out of the Anderson mist.

Also, directly or indirectly, he has influenced so many other writers that, even for this, he could not be ignored. Hemingway, who later repudiated his master, began writing under Anderson's inspiration; and Faulkner was launched upon his highly publicized career while Anderson's guest in New Orleans. Moreover, the influence of these two younger authors alone has been so incalculable that their mentor might be said to be, not only in his own right the father of our Freudian novel, but also, in a sense, the grandfather of a large part of our present literary generation.

About that generation there is something both interesting and paradoxical. It boasts of Naturalism but subscribes to Unnaturalism. There is very little, in truth, that is natural about it. Indeed, industrialism and the frenzy of an intensely competitive world have tended to conspire with the same forces which produced Naturalism, in order to bring about a nemesis in the form of a subversion of most natural activities.

The vaunted materialism which supposedly attests our human genius, frequently proves only our spiritual impotence. We think of ourselves as having become small bundles of neuroses that huddle in the fissures of a steel and concrete civilization. We boast that we cannot escape from our whole environment; and then unceasingly try to "escape" from ourselves. We become "repressed." We live amidst compromises and contradictions.

The world, we brag, is full of a number of things which affirm a high standard of living: but we contemplate suicide rather than life. We think of ourselves as *super*men: and then refuse to concede that we are even men.

Love, we say, has come into its own for the first time, since a certain queen died at Osborne: but at least in literature we tend to think of love as eroticism. We congratulate ourselves upon the death blow we dealt the Puritan doctrine that the *homo* is not sexual : and then we speak of homosexuality. We try to escape from a whole world by seeking out the darker corners of our own souls, and then pretend we are gazing at a portion of infinity.

Is it any wonder that, like the dragons' teeth which Jason sowed, Freudism has sprung up from this fertile ground? Everything in life that we cannot comprehend, will become at once intelligible if only we refer to the books which Freud has written, as Bruce Dudley says in Sherwood Anderson's *Dark Laughter*. An increasing number of our novelists have been consulting the work of Dr. Freud, but none have had so great an influence as has Sherwood Anderson.

1

A man who loves to spend most of his time telling yarns should live with his family in haunted houses where he will not be expected to pay much rent. In the winter, if his children do not have sufficient bedclothes, they can always keep warm by sleeping three in a bed ; while on Halloween his enterprising wife can egg prowling boys into throwing enough cabbages on the porch to serve as food for coming weeks. And when his family is forced to evacuate one home after another, he can at least take their straw mattresses along with them, in the belief that "Nothing is too good for my kids." Meanwhile, when farmers will let him, he can earn a little money by painting signs. He can always show some affection for his family : "Perhaps his way of getting drunk was a way of crying too." And he can always spin his yarns.

That great yarn spinner, "Major" Anderson, of *A Story Teller's Story* (1924), is supposed to be Irwin Anderson, the father of our novelist ; and, though the portrait I have drawn of him has no doubt been colored somewhat by his son's fancy, it does suggest something of that son's early poverty-stricken and nomadic life.

Sherwood Anderson was born on September 13, 1876, in Camden, Ohio. His early boyhood was spent in acquiring an irregular and elementary education until after the death of the mother, when the family became entirely a nomadic one. Then fourteen, the son spent much of his time at horse races where he learned much that he was later to put into some of his finest tales: especially those dealing with paddock and race track. For a while he was employed in a bicycle factory; he loaded kegs of nails in a warehouse; and he frequented bar-rooms and country stores, gathering a rich store of information and some understanding of character.

The boy read widely: Crane, Verne, Cooper, Twain, Whitman, Howells, Balzac, the Bible. In fact, he confesses that he saved his money chiefly that he might drink and read! From his father, a jaunty individual who loved good food and clothes though he seldom had money for either, and who loved also to tell his attentive friends of an ancestry that sometimes dated back to the Irish kings and at other times only to the Italian Barons, Sherwood Anderson acquired, I think, much of his own interest in yarns and his habit of coloring a tale. And from his mother I believe that he received many of his sensitivities, his love of poignant silences and the unspoken word.

The Spanish-American War broke out; Anderson enlisted and later returned to find himself a hero in his own town. "My natural shrewdness led me to take advantage of this situation and I enjoyed it thoroughly."[2] For a few months he attended Wittenberg College; then, after marrying, he became the head of a paint concern in Elyria, Ohio. He confesses that he was a bit too absent-minded to make a successful business man; nevertheless he remained at his job in this paint factory for about ten years. He wrote a great deal during this time; and he spent hours dreaming about all the luxuries he would like to buy — and would buy, when he became wealthy. In short, this whole period of his life might be described as one in which he was desperately trying to conform to American standards of material success.

He was unhappy at it, however, because all these years he had an "overwhelming feeling of uncleanliness." Gradually the conviction had come to him that he was really in his "whole nature a taleteller" and that by remaining a business man he was "prostituting" his life. So it was that one day he determined to leave his paint factory for good. At the moment he was dictating to his secretary:

It was a trying moment for me. There was the woman, my secretary, now looking at me. What did she represent? What did she not represent? Would I dare be honest with her? It was quite apparent to me that I would not. I had got to my feet and we stood looking at each other. "It is now or never," I said to myself, and I remember that I kept smiling. I had stopped dictating to her in the midst of a sentence. "The goods which you have inquired about are the best of their kind made in the —"

I stood and she sat and we were looking at each other intently. . .

Whether at that moment I merely became shrewd and crafty or whether I really became temporarily insane I shall never quite know. What I did was to step very close to the woman and looking directly into her eyes I laughed gaily. . . I looked at my feet. "I have been wading in a long river and my feet are wet," I said.

Again I laughed as I walked lightly toward the door and out of a long and tangled phase of my life. "They want me to be a nut, and why not? It may just be that's what I am," I thought gaily. . .[3]

On that impulse Sherwood Anderson left Elyria and went to Chicago where he secured a position with an advertising agency, worked hard at writing a novel, and met such other writers as Floyd Dell, Ben Hecht, and Theodore Dreiser. The last named author introduced him to the novels of

D. H. Lawrence; while Hecht and Dell championed his work before publishers and tried to get Mencken interested in it. Once more, Anderson began to feel "clean" and "unafraid."

Do you not see, O my beloved, that I am become strong to caress the woman! I caress all men and all women. I make myself naked. I am unafraid. I am a pure thing. I bind and heal. By the running of the pencil over the white paper I have made myself pure. I have made myself whole. I am unafraid. The song of the pencil has done it.[4]

He came to love clean sheets of white paper and all the tools of his craft. Also he learned, in succeeding years, how to write just as well along some highway, with his pad resting on a stump, as in his study; to spin off stories in a factory or a field. Once while he sat in a Mobile saloon writing parts of *Poor White,* three intoxicated sailors sat next to him in loud and ribald discussion, without disturbing him in the least! On another occasion he sat in a Detroit railroad station scribbling at *The Triumph of the Egg* until he had missed his train!

Though seldom an artist, Anderson is always, as will be seen from all of this, a craftsman who thrills honestly to his materials. The very sight of paper makes his fingers ache to get hold of a pen; and he confesses that he finds it difficult to refrain from stealing pens and paper while out visiting. Like one of his friends who brought a trunk half full of his favorite cigars to Havana, he carries "thousands of sheets of white paper" along with him when he travels, presuming "that all the stationers in the new place had died." And he even goes so far as to suggest that all manufacturers of paper be canonized:

Makers of paper, I exclude you from all the curses I have heaped upon manufacturers when I have walked in the street breathing coal dust and smoke. . . Last night I dreamed I had been made Pope and that I issued a bull, excommunicating all owners of factories . . . but ah, I left you out of my curses, you busy makers of paper. . . There was one man — I invented him — named Saint John P. Belger, who furnished paper to indigent writers of prose free of charge. For virtue I put him, in my dream, almost on a level with Saint Francis Assisi.[5]

2

It was Floyd Dell who was finally instrumental in getting a publisher for Anderson's first novel, *Windy McPherson's Son*. But the author refused to comply with the publisher's condition that it be revised; and it was not until 1916 that the volume was finally published. In the meantime Anderson had suffered from a nervous breakdown and had settled down in a cabin in the Ozarks to recuperate and start a second book — a novel which he himself was so displeased with that he hurled it out of the train window on his way back to Chicago!

Like all of his books, *Windy McPherson's Son* is highly autobiographical; for, despite its author's emphasis upon the necessity of "escape," he has seldom quite been able to transcend his own confused emotions or inadequately distilled impressions sufficiently to deal with material far from his own experience. As a result, the lineaments of Sam McPherson in this earliest novel are not only those of Anderson himself but of Bruce Dudley in *Dark Laughter*, John Webster in *Many Marriages*, Hugh McVey in *Poor White*, Tar in the "novel" by the same name, George Willard in *Winesburg, Ohio*, Beaut McGregor in *Marching Men*, and, of course, the speaker in *Kit Brandon*. Furthermore, other characters from the first Anderson book are to reappear again and again with but slight changes in the garb of their autobiographical identity; and a dozen scenes from Anderson's life are retold in the later volumes with but a slight variation in color. We might say, then, that this novelist cannot ever escape from the very theme of escape.

But to return to *Windy McPherson's Son*. Shell-shocked in the Civil War, Windy McPherson becomes a somewhat crazed braggart of the small town of Caxton, Iowa. His son, Sam, tries to escape from the stigma of hearing towns-folk laugh at his father's tales and shallow boasts; and so he decides to flee from his humiliation by acquiring the power and money which will win him respect. "Make money! Cheat! Lie! Be one of the big men of the world! Get your name up for a modern, high-class American. . ."⁶ Such was the Nietzschean advice tendered him by one of the local "philosophers."

About this time, also, Sam begins (like most of the following Anderson characters) to hear the "sex call." He begins to hunt for obscene words in the dictionary, to read obscenity into certain Biblical references. Finally, he goes to the city, where he becomes a successful manufacturer, marries the daughter of the man who owns his firm, and acquires railways, timber, shooting lodges, and oil wells. But he is not happy: "He did not dare think and in his heart he was sick of it, sick to the soul. . ."

And so Sam McPherson abandons his lucrative job and his wife, sets out once more in search of Truth and the "message his hand had written," and ultimately becomes a laborer "so that my muscles may become firm and sleep come to me at night." But the Socialism to which he turns fails to satisfy him; and after a series of mad indulgences in New York, Paris, and London, and a period of hunting in Africa, he goes back to his wife. The last paragraph of the novel then sums up Sam McPherson's final philosophy: " 'I cannot run away from life. I must face it. I must begin to try to understand these other lives, to love. . .' The buried inner thing in him thrust itself up."⁷ Most of the succeeding Anderson novels are to treat, as we shall see, of some complex thus buried and trying to thrust itself up.

The scene of *Marching Men* (1917) shifts to Coal Creek,

Pennsylvania; but the plot of this second Anderson book
has much in common with its predecessor. The escape of
Beaut McGregor to Chicago is the escape of Sam from
Caxton — or Anderson from Elyria — told over again. Men
have become mad with the curse of wealth upon them,
Anderson says. Whereas, in reality, they are children —
children who should never know such a curse. What would
happen, then, if they began to act like children? "Suppose they could just learn to march, nothing else." [8]

Seeing himself destined for that leadership which he believes can alone save the working classes and restore their
consciousness as a group, Beaut works hard at his restaurant
job and at his legal studies; and finally proclaims his intention of regimenting all labor into what he calls his Marching
Men: "You must march shoulder to shoulder. You must
march so that you yourselves shall come to know what a
giant you are. . ." [9] Only such a regimentation can give,
he feels, brain to the giant that is the laborer. This dream
for a Marching America colors somewhat even such a recent
Anderson book as *Kit Brandon,* in which the author thus
addresses all laborers: "It may be the time will come, in the
march of men, when your work will stand with that of other
unknown men who built cathedrals in the Middle Ages." [10]

Such volumes of verse as *Mid-American Chants* (1918) and
A New Testament (1927) space prevents me from discussing
here in detail. Nebulous and often extremely more prosaic
than much of his better prose, they reflect their author's
usual lush sentiment, rebellion against industrialism, and
general confusions; and yet they contain also some of their
author's most revealing passages. But the numerous short
stories brought together in the four volumes entitled *Winesburg, Ohio* (1919), *The Triumph of the Egg* (1921), *Horses
and Men* (1923), and *Death in the Woods* (1933) represent,
however, the most enduring work which Anderson has yet
done and I must speak of them briefly. For Anderson has

always believed that only the "rare moments" of life count; and in his better tales he has reflected this conviction in a sensitivity and in a penetration which the novels — covering dull and commonplace as well as "rare" moments — often lack. I do not say that all of these stories are good. Many are extremely repellent and offensively primitive. But many, on the other hand, are highly distinguished.

In *Winesburg, Ohio,* for example, there is some little humor — a quality unusual in this writer. I refer to such sketches as that in which Elmer Cowley chases the collar-button salesman from his store, or keeps his money hidden in a barrel because he is sure robbers would "never think of a place like that." There is also a successful communication of warm and genuine feeling in the portrait of George Willard's mother secreting her savings in the wall, that her son might rise above their drab, ugly, humdrum existence; and in the picture of the old grandmother finding the thirty dollars on the street and using it to give herself and her grandson a chance to flee from the hot city. "Most boys have seasons of wishing they could die gloriously instead of just being grocery clerks and going on with their humdrum lives."[11] When Anderson deals with themes such as this he often does work that has a lasting value.

The Triumph of the Egg and *Horses and Men* contain, indeed, a few stories that, in a way, promise to be minor classics. "I Want to Know Why" is the tale of a boy who leaves home to follow the races: "There isn't anything so lovely and clean and full of spunk and honest and everything as some race horses. . . I can pick them nearly every time. . . If my throat hurts and it's hard for me to swallow, that's him. He'll run like Sam Hill when you let him out."[12]

"The Egg" offers a mildly humorous account of a chicken farm and of a boy's feelings for his father. "I'm a Fool" returns to the subject of horse-racing, but blends with it a skilfully handled — if not always agreeable — adolescent romance. Sherwood Anderson has done his most memorable writing in his short stories.

Hugh McVey in *Poor White* (1920) was "born in a little hole of a town stuck on a mud bank on the western shore of the Mississippi River. . . It was a miserable place in which to be born." [13] He is "raised" by his father, who spends most of his time drinking and lying on the earth chasing flies away from his face. Later on Hugh goes to Bidwell, Ohio, where he invents a cabbage planting machine, and a coal dumper which brings him a hundred thousand dollars. Always he is the dreamer — inventions, money, power and sex become obsessions with him. He makes money and he is led into more than one ugly "love" affair; but the "buried thing" within him never quite succeeds in coming to the surface. Finally, however, Hugh marries into the family of old Butterworth, who had been one of Bidwell's most wealthy investors in his inventions. The town prospers for a time; and then begins to suffer from the very machine methods and the inventions which had once made it so prosperous.

Many Marriages (1923) introduces us to John Webster, one of the most autobiographical of the Anderson characters. A manufacturer of washing machines in a small mid-western town, Webster becomes deluded with certain ideas which lead him to believe that "grace and meaning" can be found in life only by those who do not wear any clothes! A kind of new way to acquire culture — by spending, let us say, fifteen minutes a day among the nudists!

At all events, after several painful and extremely obscene experiences, Webster deserts his wife in favor of his stenographer. Mrs. Webster is then left to commit suicide, and on this cheerful note the book comes to a close. *"Many Marriages* is a good example of what is often spoken of as Anderson's 'mysticism.' It is not real mysticism at all, but mystification." [14]   It is, also, I do not hesitate in saying, painfully repellent and obscene.

Sherwood Anderson's Notebook (1926) is a collection of essays for the most part garnered from earlier magazine articles.   Like *The Modern Writer,* which had appeared the year previously, the *Notebook* offers us interesting glimpses of Anderson's literary tastes and theories.   Alfred Stieglitz, Ring Lardner, Gertrude Stein, Sinclair Lewis, Paul Rosenfeld, George Bellows — most of the portraits in the book are vivid and colorful, but not very significant.   One of the essays deals with Mr. Anderson's native state ; one is devoted to a discussion of the profession of lecturing ; another concerns its author's favorite theme of standardization ; and several are made up of mere fragmentary jottings on a dozen unrelated subjects.   For the student genuinely interested in Anderson, perhaps the most revealing of the papers in this volume is that entitled "A Note on Realism."   Here our author draws a sharp distinction between realism and truly imaginative writing ; but insists, with sturdy common sense, that the intelligent writer must learn to let his imagination nourish itself upon realities, if he would not turn out work that is noticeable for its "holes" and for its "bad spots."

As far as it goes, all this is sound enough.   But many of the "holes and bad spots" in Anderson's own writing are the result of his feeding his imagination upon certain very special obsessions which he is inclined to mistake for universal experiences.   Are all boys like Tar ?   All wives like Aline Grey ?   Are many men like John Webster ?   Mr. Anderson's key to the abnormal will not unlock *so* many doors !

That orgiastic and primitive account of his own "midwest childhood" which Anderson entitled *Tar* (1926) I shall refer to later.   Let me now list Anderson's other books. *Hello Towns* (1929) is composed of items selected from the two newspapers which Anderson in 1928 bought in Marion, Virginia : the Marion *Democrat* (Democratic) and the

Smyth County *News* (Republican). In the editing of these two "rival" and small-town papers, he has found what he calls "a working compromise with the machine age" :

You will think that I have a quarrel with the machine age. I have, but not the quarrel you imagine . . . what we have to do is not to get rid of the machine, but to catch up with its beauty. The trouble lies in us. We have put all our energy into making these magnificent things — presses, harvesters, automobiles, engines, dynamos. . . But we have taken no time or effort to learn how to use them in a way worthy of their beauty. We build gorgeous great presses and feed them debased and lurid sensationalism. We construct beautiful swift automobiles and smash them on cheap parties. . . We let machines run our lives and rob us of our essential humanity.[15]

In *Perhaps Women* (1931) he continues his concern with this theme of our machine-made and material civilization. It is already too late, he concludes, for us to escape from these ugly forces which we have created; unless, perhaps, women show us a way. For the world of woman is the only world upon which the machine has not made serious encroachments. Only the spirit of woman has not been made "impotent" by our civilization. And only that spirit can light the way for the rest of us.

Since the publication of this book Anderson has brought out two volumes of essays entitled *No Swank* (1934) and *Puzzled America* (1935). He has also since published two novels : *Beyond Desire* (1932), whose central character, Red Oliver, is carried through the sexual experiences common to most of the Anderson types and finally becomes enmeshed in a series of labor troubles ; and *Kit Brandon* (1936) which is the story of a girl born, in Eastern Tennessee, of a moonshining father and a tobacco-stained, shiftless mother. Kit early learns "what a lot of men are like" from the farm stock and from her perverted father. She rather generally subscribes to a friend's advice to "Learn to use what you've got" ;

marries for money; and after becoming a driver for a powerful bootlegger, decides to settle down to a more genuine happiness that she sees promised by a simple life.

From one point of view, *Kit Brandon* is among Anderson's most significant books. It is more affirmative regarding his attitudes toward the poor, corrupting labor conditions, our natural resources, and the hollow promises of wealth. On the other hand, the plot has all the marks of a Hollywood script: a girl about to be killed in a bootlegger's cabin but enabled to escape by an opportune Federal raid; dashes through the night in sleek, powerful convoy cars, while the police are in pursuit, etc.

Kit is much impressed by Dreiser's *Sister Carrie;* and there are, indeed, many little melodramatic moments in her career which establish her kinship with the Caroline Meebers, so fashionable thirty years ago, rather than with the Kit Brandons of today. Kit uses some words that Caroline Meeber would not have liked to see in print; but had Caroline been escaping from a cabin of murderous bootleggers, she, too, would have remembered, as does Kit, to take along her little bag with its change of clothing!

Finally, *Kit Brandon* does not mark any appreciable advance in its author's ability to distinguish between a kind of cerebral emotionalism and hard thinking. Thus Anderson comments: "Wouldn't it be wonderful if all people should some day find out that there is, at bottom, no fun in being rich . . . rich in material possessions, money, land, things, while there is in the world one other human being who is in want?" [16] But have not people already found out that there *is* "fun" in being rich — even under such conditions?

Although *Dark Laughter* appeared in the year following *A Story Teller's Story*, I have deferred my summary of it to serve now as a convenient introduction to Anderson's Freudism. The novel makes use of a plot which has much in common with those in the other books by this author. After an unhappy journalistic career in Chicago, John Stockton decides to change his name to Bruce Dudley, desert his wife, and return to his birthplace, Old Harbor, Indiana. In Chicago, he had married one of his newspaper colleagues; but he had come to feel that Bernice and he possessed incompatible temperaments; and the conviction had grown on him that his life as a married reporter was keeping him out of "touch" with the laboring and artist classes that alone can teach one how rich life is. So it was that he had resolved to desert his wife and change jobs. He would move on, change his environment; and give himself a chance to discover the world of common things — that he might really discover the capacities of his own spirit. Thus he would really be taking a short trip into what he calls the "myself."

At Old Harbor Dudley secures a job at the Grey Wheel Works, where, at his factory bench, he watches the deft fingers of a fellow-workman, Sponge Martin, and thinks of the pleasures to be derived from all forms of creative work — even varnishing wagon wheels. It is interesting to note that, just before taking their final plunge into the Myself, most of the Anderson characters try to "sublimate" the Self entirely — in some work of the creator or craftsman. They fail, and sex proves the key to their failure. Enter here, then, the *libido*.

Aline Grey, the wife of Bruce's employer, determines that he shall become her lover; she advertises for a gardener, knowing that Bruce, with an irresistible "affinity" for her, will answer her advertisement! He does. Grey himself has a vague suspicion that his wife has a paramour; but he remains happily ignorant for a while of the fact that the child Aline expects is not his own. Ultimately, the adulterers inform him of their "love"; and Aline tells him that they are going off together. For she felt that to continue living with her husband would be to live a "lie." Not to follow

Dudley would be living a "lie." Then, just as the book closes, Grey hears the babbling voice of a young negress, a servant, who cries out shrilly that she has known of Aline's unfaithfulness right along. The girl's laughter floats in upon Grey's ears; and he is left alone.

3

By way of opening my comment on Anderson's Freudism, let me ask my readers to remember that Bruce Dudley advises people to go to Freud for an explanation of anything in life that is difficult to understand. Bruce adds, further, that Freud offers by far the most satisfying explanation of the entire conduct of men and women in love, and of such a "common" sight as a man passionately "aroused." In short, Freud is Bruce's Bible. And Freud is Anderson's Bible, too.

Sherwood Anderson's emphasis upon the introvert, his choice of characters, his use of the *libido* as an almost exclusive motivating force, his immersion in what Lewis Mumford calls the "Cloaca Maxima of the personality," [17] his use of symbols and association of incoherences — all of this in Anderson is directly suggestive of the Freudian method.

A little voyage into the myself. Like his Bruce Dudley, Anderson feels that very few of us know very much about the "myself." Most of his work he has therefore devoted to the Freudian procedure of taking "a little trip" into himself: in all of the novels, and in most of the sketches, there is, as I have already hinted, a startling kind of unoriginality of theme and a tedious use of his own personal experiences. His "midwest childhood" experiences, his "escape" plots, his groping attempts to solve the "problem" of "repressions," and his efforts at finding a way out of the complications of industrialism by "thinking" emotional reflexes rather than ideas : all of these suggest the way in which he has traveled — the way he has traveled around in a circle of obsessions.

His Myself is the Only Self. Or, at least it is the only self that he tends to use as a norm in interpreting other selves. He confesses [18] that he once set out in search of "the Truth." He searched for it, he says, under his desk, and beneath his bed. But Truth was not to be found in either of those places. Finally he scanned "the road" in the hope of finding it. Observe that he didn't get very far from home.

All of which is not to deny that Truth often lingers on one's own doorstep. Sometimes it even hides under one's nose. Jane Austen found it by squinting over the break-fast dishes. But Jane Austen's "squint" was really, as I think we are beginning to see, quite a bluff. Actually she saw beyond the dishes, far down the road, and far into the world through which that road ran. Her road was a real one : it went some place.

Anderson's road is only a path — a path circling around his own personality.

This world is full of a number of things. Eggs, for instance — eggs in crates, in baskets, in cartons, on the floor, on shelves, piled to the ceiling — millions of eggs. Or milk bottles — on the fire escape, the table, the window ledge, at tenement doors — row after row. Or dung — littering the ground, spread on the garden, covering the meadow, heaped at the stable door. Old maids and cripples — cowards and touts — children and sailors — clerks, stenographers, motormen. A futile world, sandy and monotonous.

It is all, of course, a matter of emphasis. It may be a globe-encircling world, signaling Mars — or just the world of Sherwood Anderson.[19]

The "shadow of the wall." In his study of neuroses Freud made a careful examination of over a thousand men and

women suffering from some kind of psychopathological dis-
turbance. Anderson has the psychoanalyst's interest in the
abnormal. That is the first thing to be noted in discussing
his methods as a Freudian. Morally healthy men and
women he seldom takes into account; instead he has focused
his attention upon only the shady side of the street and
upon the steady stream of day-dreamers, perverts, neurotics,
and morally atrophied people who slink along it.

This aspect of Anderson's work most of his critics have so
toned down that his deliberate choice of the abnormal is
made to seem like nothing more than a harmless whim — a
little crotchet to be tolerated as one would tolerate an old
man's fondness for recalling his youth. Actually, it is a
most vicious kind of monopticism. Let me give a few examples.

A demented physician; a neurotic and hysterical girl;
a monomaniac who ponders over the Bible until he thinks
he is called to sacrifice his own grandson; a wife who has,
not *one,* but *three* lovers; a Peeping Tom who hides in a
tower to spy upon a nude girl because "God has manifested himself to me in the body of a woman"; an exhibi-
tionist who takes off her clothes and runs down the street
in the rain; a school-teacher who tries to seduce one of her
young pupils; a girl who attempts to seduce a very young
boy merely to spite her fiancé; a woman who is narcistic in
the fullest psychopathological sense of the word; a father
who attempts, amidst a ceremony of perversion, to corrupt
his daughter; an erotomaniac who erects an altar in his
room and parades before it, naked, in search of "grace and
meaning"; a character of whom it is lushly said that he
might have loved his teacher had he "been able to creep
like the moonbeam" into her presence, but who flees from
his own wife on his wedding night — in listing such types I
scarcely begin to suggest the gallery of Anderson's distorted
pictures. "In an odd way he stood in the shadow of the

wall of life," [20] says this author of one of his characters.
In an odd way almost all of them stand in shadows.

A "Phallic Chekhov." ". . . I maintain that neurotic
anxiety has its origin in the sexual life, and corresponds
to a libido which has been deflected from its object and has
found no employment," [21] says Freud. Like the psychoanalyst, again, Sherwood Anderson attributes the neuroses
of his characters to some "repression" of their *libidos*: the
Anderson books, as a matter of fact, might be characterized
chiefly as studies in the employment of the *libido*. "Lust
and night and women." This phrase from one of the novels
aptly sets the tone of all of them. Of one woman it is said
that "in her whole attitude there was a suggestion of waiting." [22] Another, by way of keeping her *libido* from becoming deflected, finds it necessary to unburden herself of
all the obscenities she has witnessed at a Quat'z Arts Ball.
A third thus confesses her defections: "I've gone through
it with men I wouldn't spit on now. I thought I had to.
I guess it just happened so, it was the break I got." [23] Again,
a male character has the "conviction" that a certain girl "was
the woman his nature *demanded.*"

I have myself italicized that last word. It should be
illuminated, printed in colors. For even the Freudian
"censor"—never to be confused, we must remember, with
what you and I call the will—even the censor seldom stands
much of a chance with the Anderson men and women. And
when these characters do give the censor a little cooperation
it must be conceded that they do so in rather censorable
ways! One of them, for example, finds the "sex call" so
urgent that he runs out in the middle of a stormy night
and stands by a cold creek; another, whom I have already
mentioned, dashes down the street, naked, in the rain!

Is each woman, above all else, "a wanton"? So reflects
one of the Anderson women. And young Tar Moorhead

would seem to agree with her if one may judge by his affirmations regarding the number of "Madame Bovaries" in our smaller towns. I wish to add only that some of the Anderson Madame Bovaries make the Flaubert woman seem positively chaste by comparison. As Dr. Joseph Collins said of their creator:

When he had accomplished half the span of life allotted by the psalmist to man, he heard a voice saying: "It is hard for you to kick, but you are the chosen vessel to bear the message: Life is sex, death is sex-repression; living is sex-awareness; pleasure is sex-indulgence; beauty is sex realization; salvation is dependent upon the development of sex sensibilities." The scales fell from his eyes and he went to the typewriter. . .[24]

Paul Rosenfeld, who was one of Anderson's friends, once called him a "Phallic Chekhov." I do not, myself, perceive a great similarity with Chekhov.

Letting "the well empty itself." True Freudian that he is, Anderson next sees to it that his neurotics speak freely. In a preceding chapter, I have quoted Hitschmann's words describing the Freudian method: the patients must be urged "to sketch a general picture of their whole illness and most intimate family and life surroundings, to tell . . . everything . . . whether they think it important, irrelevant, or nonsensical. With special emphasis, it is asked of them that no thought or association be omitted . . . because the telling might be shameful or painful."

In *Many Marriages* Sherwood Anderson gives expression to the same Freudian point of view:

If one kept the lid off the well of thinking within oneself, let the well empty itself, let the mind consciously think any thoughts that came to it, accepted all thinking, all imaginings, as one accepted the flesh of people, animals, birds, trees, plants, one might live a hundred or a thousand lives in one life. Then each one of us could become "something more than just one individual

man and woman living one narrow circumscribed life." One
could tear down all walls and fences and walk in and out
many people. One might in oneself become a whole town full
of people, a city, a nation.[25]

And in *Kit Brandon* the central character observes: "We're
low and we're high. It's better to feel everything you can
feel—throw it away."

From even an aesthetic point of view, this doctrine does
not stand worthy of controversion. The artist is an artist,
for one thing, precisely because he does *not* accept "all thinking, all imaginings. . ." He is distinguished from his fellow men, among other things, by virtue of the fact that he
does *not* let the minds of his characters think just any
thoughts that come to them: he does not *let:* he *controls,
discriminates, selects, creates.* He does not "live a hundred
or a thousand lives in [his own] one life." He rather pro-
jects his own being, fully, richly, and creatively, into a hundred or a thousand other lives.

From another point of view, the same Freudian doctrine,
which Mr. Anderson has accepted, results in some extremely
distasteful material and even, be it noted, in much lushly
sentimental nonsense.

The "Dark hidden things, festering in the well" frequently
emerge hydra-headed rather than beautiful; and Sherwood
Anderson on his knees before them, perspiring with his
"pantheism," utters incantations that sound, let us be frank
about it, like the recorded cerebrations of a vegetable. "Men
should bathe me with prayers and with weeping . . ." he
sings in "Chicago." "In my breasts the sap of spring," he
chants in "Song to the Sap."[26] There are, indeed, many
times when it is better *not* "to feel everything you can feel."

Pigs is Pigs. This same "lifting the lid off the well of
thinking" has also resulted in Anderson's work in an orgiastic kind of primitivism that is often very repellent. I will

give but one illustration. In the autobiographical *Tar,* the central character, a young boy, goes out into the fields one day and watches a pig give birth to a litter of shoats. The whole scene is described most vividly. That night Tar lies awake in bed, listening, while his mother gives birth to a child.

Offered in repellent detail, his reflections are of the crudest kind, offensive and orgiastic. What is Mr. Anderson's point in offering them to us? They are merely the reflections of an abnormal boy; they fail entirely in having any of the purposeful or significant values which attend similar scenes of childbirth in, for example, *Gone With the Wind* or *Anna Karenina.* Bruce Dudley boasts that he is a primitive man. There are, indeed, times when this characterization fits Mr. Anderson himself. On such occasions, the coloring which he infuses into his work becomes what Elizabeth Drew calls "yokel color" and which she illustrates with this delightful parody:

WINSOME WESSEX or MR. BLASTER'S HOGS

In the road a small boy was torturing a frog; behind the hedge a tramp was raping a fainting girl; in the field an old woman was being gored by a bull, while the farmer enjoyed the joke hugely from the window of his house. . . In the Rectory the rector's wife was making jam and the rector appeared to be preparing his Sunday sermon. Though outwardly a bland, slow-witted but kindly man, inwardly he thought of nothing but money, food, and seducing young girls.

In the window of Mrs. Pansy's dingy house in the nearest seaport town there was a card, Lodgings: Special Terms for Seductions. Mrs. Pansy's chief joy in life was a young girl's ruin. Luckily the supply was enormous : they simply flocked to her lodgings to be ruined. One day the rector came down the street with his collar turned round, disguised as a seducer, and accompanied by the rectory housemaid. "This is the very place," he said, seeing the notice in the window. . .

Alice was going to drown herself in the pond. A kind lady
in a cottage took her in. She was one of the good characters,
so of course the village hated her, and said she had murdered
her brother and kept a brothel, and that made her have rather
a wistful look. She already had the idiot son of the rector living
with her and he and Alice fell in love with each other. But he
was a good character, too, so the night before they were to be
married, he met a tramp on the heath. "Who the bloody 'ell
are you?" said the tramp jovially, and then he kicked him to
death.

———

And Mr. Blaster just went on feeding his hogs. . .[27]

"Getting off" one's "base" with symbolism. The Freudian
neurotic is supposed, as we have noted, to tell everything—
even those matters which he may think "irrelevant, or nonsensical." For, often the "complex" can be arrived at only
by a careful study of symbols, chaotic thought-sequences, and
dreams. All of which play a large part in the Anderson
books.

Thus, in *Dark Laughter* Bruce Dudley thinks about one
of his wife's friends who is supposed to have fallen in love
with a store-window dummy! He is convinced that this
same friend has become the "hero" of a book Bernice happens to be writing; and he follows out a whole series of
tortuous thought-sequences in an attempt to discover the
meaning of the affair. Such a discovery, he feels, might even
afford him a clue to the entire "feminist movement."

Bruce likewise utters a number of ridiculously irrelevant
statements about the way in which, somehow or another, he
has confused the feeling he has for his mother with certain
notions that he has about rivers. And he admits that, with
all the symbolism in his head, he often feels "off" his "base."
In *Poor White*, Rose McCoy had "thoughts, or rather, sensations that had little to do with thoughts." Each one of this

author's books could be called upon copiously to furnish similar examples.

A "confused child in a confused world." Like his Rosalind Wescott in "Out of Nowhere into Nothing," Anderson feels that it is really impossible for people to "break through the walls of themselves." In the poem called "Chicago" he says: "I am a child, a confused child in a confused world. There are no clothes made that fit me." [28]

When his work has about it — as it so often has — the effective simplicity of a child's tale, Anderson is at his best. He is at his worst, however, when he obfuscates these moods with the confused gropings of a muddled adult. Young Tom Moorhead frequently reflects like a tired old man; the boy Sam McPherson faces many of the problems which belong to a later manhood; Hugh McVey, in his little "town stuck on a mud bank," is a kind of Huck Finn — but with mental sags that belong to senility.

Anderson's uncertainties and confusions are to be regretted, for they frequently render him inarticulate even when he has very much to say: when he is trying to break through to the "white wonder of life"; when he is speaking of adolescence; or when he is inveighing against standardization and our machine-made ugliness. At such times, he is like a man who, having an important speech to make, rises only to ponder a lot of questions; to propose a lot of jumbled answers; to "think," not thoughts, but "rather sensations that" have "little to do with thoughts."

"Are there no words that lead into life?" he asks in one of his tales. And in a letter to Upton Sinclair he once expressed the same sense of dismay: "To me there is no answer for the terrible confusion of life." [29] Here we have suggested what is, I think, one of Mr. Anderson's most basic weaknesses. Without quite realizing it, he is hunting, not for words that lead *into* life, but for words that lead *out of* it.

"There are no clothes made that fit me." This is not entirely true, for some of the Anderson techniques are almost instinctively perfect. But when Mr. Anderson does find the clothes, he is frequently all dressed up with no place to go.

Out of Nowhere into Nothing.

CHAPTER VI

ERNEST HEMINGWAY: SPOKESMAN FOR HIS GENERATION

"Life's a game."
"Play to win."
"Learn to use what you've got."
"If you don't put it over on them
they'll put it over on you." [1]
— *Kit Brandon*, by Sherwood Anderson. P. 155.

CHAPTER VI

ERNEST HEMINGWAY: SPOKESMAN FOR HIS GENERATION

"THE first thing that happened [sic] when we were back in Paris was Hemingway with a letter of introduction from Sherwood Anderson," [2] writes the author of *The Autobiography of Alice B. Toklas*. Twenty-three years old, "rather foreign looking, with passionately interested, rather than interesting eyes," Ernest Hemingway had arrived, with a letter from his literary godfather, to meet Gertrude Stein, who was destined to become his literary godmother. "Hemingway had been formed by the two of them and they were both a little proud and a little ashamed of the work of their minds." [3]

Later, in his parody, *The Torrents of Spring* (1926) Hemingway was to repudiate Anderson. Moreover, as a result of a rather uncomplimentary letter which Hemingway had taken it upon himself to write Anderson, "in the name of american literature," he was to be somewhat naturally frightened "When Sherwood came to Paris." But, in the meantime, Hemingway was twenty-three and determined to be a writer. So he cultivated the godmother to whom Anderson had introduced him; and in long walks and visits with Miss Stein he found encouragement and sound advice.

. . . One day she said to him, look here, you say you and your wife have a little money between you. Is it enough to live on if you live quietly. Yes, he said. Well, she said, then do it. If you keep on doing newspaper work you will never see things, you will only see words and that will not do, that is of course if you intend to be a writer. [4]

Hemingway was able to assure her that he did intend to become a writer. Shortly afterwards, he took his leave. On his next visit, it was apparent that he had something important on his mind which he wanted to talk about. Arriving at Miss Stein's home in the middle of the morning, he stayed until some time after dinner in the evening; and, then, finally blurted out the news that he was to become a father. Miss Stein says she "consoled him" and "sent him on his way."

When they came back Hemingway said that he had made up his mind. They would go back to America and he would work hard for a year and with what he would earn and what they had they would settle down and he would give up newspaper work and make himself a writer. They went away and well within the prescribed year they came back with a new born baby. Newspaper work was over.[5]

Hemingway had an instinctive genius for picking out apartments in neighborhoods where good food and good service were to be had; at his apartment, more often than at hers, then, he and Gertrude Stein spent hours while the latter read his work; while he copied out for her the whole first section of *The Making of Americans* which Ford Madox Ford wanted for the *Transatlantic;* or while he recounted for her the conversations which he was planning to use in his novels.

His health, at this time, was none too good: indeed, one of his friends remarked to Miss Stein that he seemed so worn out by the war and so "fragile" that whenever he tried any sport "something breaks, his arm, his leg, or his hand." There is even a story to the effect that upon one occasion while he was giving boxing lessons, his young pupil accidentally knocked him out! The story may be true — or it may be as legendary as those later ones about Hemingway and his friends recklessly entering a bull-fight and having to save themselves by running for their lives and leaping over the arena walls! Nevertheless, during these early years in Paris, Ernest Hemingway led that kind of active life which he was to deal with in his books: he boxed; played tennis; acquired an interest in bull-fighting from "Miss Toklas"; went on fishing trips; met such other young writers as Dos Passos, Fitzgerald, and Bromfield; and amidst the "lost generation" of the Paris Left Bank, he became the literary spokesman for the "lost generation" of our post-War America.

1

Ernest Hemingway was born on July 21, 1898, in Oak Park, Illinois. As a boy, he used to accompany his father, a physician, when the latter made professional calls; from such experiences, and from the Midwestern outdoor life which he lived, he gained a wealth of impressions which were to color many of his stories. After attending public schools in Michigan, he became for a brief time a reporter on the Kansas City *Star;* and then he saw service at the front with the Italian Arditi, where he was so badly wounded that he still has to wear a silver plate in one shoulder. After the War, Hemingway married; settled down in Europe as correspondent for the *Toronto Star;* and, finally, secured a job in Paris, reporting for the Hearst syndicates.

He began writing short stories. "The Undefeated," "My Old Man," "Fifty Grand," and a number of others were done at this time. But one editor after another returned them, saying that as "sketches" or "contes" they were all right, but not as short stories. As a result, there were times when Hemingway almost starved; on one occasion, his friend, Dos Passos, had to sell his typewriter to keep the two of them alive! [6] It was then that Hemingway got to work on *The Sun Also Rises,* finishing the novel in about eleven weeks. Its immediate success is indicated, among other things, by the fact that one of our monthly magazines at once offered him thirty-five thousand dollars for serial rights on his next book, and twenty-five hundred dollars for each of

his next ten tales.   Hemingway refused the offer, however —
as he was later to refuse a Hollywood offer of forty-five thousand dollars for his "advice" on the filming of *A Farewell to
Arms*.   Let it be said of him that he has always placed his
art above the money it could command.

His *Three Stories and Ten Poems* (1923), which Robert
McAlmon published in Paris, need not concern us here.   *In
Our Time* (1925), his first significant book, contains several
stories that are worse than inconsequential; but the volume
contains, also, two or three tales that its author has never
surpassed.   Moreover, it displays a characteristic later to become one of the strongest qualities of Hemingway's writing:
an ability to discover the satisfying goodness of elemental
things, to communicate a feeling for what is close to earth:
a Wagner apple found along the road, "shiny in the brown
grass from the rain"; ground that is "soft underfoot" as one
walks through the woods; the tightening of a fisherman's
heart as he sees a trout flash through clear, swift, silver water;
the sweet taste of apricot juice drunk after a plain meal by a
campfire.

"Indian Camp," the highly autobiographical first story in
the volume, introduces Nick, the young son of a physician,
who accompanies his father to the bedside of an Indian
woman in the labors of childbirth.   It has a simplicity that
is elemental in the best sense; and an understanding of the
Indian temperament that cannot be challenged.   "My Old
Man," the story of a jockey and his son, bears a resemblance
to Anderson's "I Want to Know Why"— a resemblance
that I can suggest by these remarks of the Hemingway lad:
"I went around to the paddock to see the horses with my
old man and you never saw such horses.   This Kzar is a
great big yellow horse that looks like just nothing but run.
He was being led around the paddocks with his head down
and when he went by me I felt all hollow inside he was so
beautiful.   There never was such a wonderful, lean, run-

ning built horse." ⁷ A true lover of horse-flesh wrote those words ! And a true fisherman wrote the following selection from "Big Two-Hearted River." A man has to throw one of his catch back into the water :

> He had wet his hand before he touched the trout, so he would not disturb the delicate mucus that covered him. If a trout was touched with a dry hand, a white fungus attacked the unprotected spot. Years before when he had fished crowded streams, with fly fishermen ahead of him and behind him, Nick had again and again come on dead trout, furry with white fungus, drifted against a rock, or floating belly up in some pool. Nick did not like to fish with other men on the river. Unless they were of your party, they spoiled it.⁸

With the publication of *The Sun Also Rises* (1926), as I have already pointed out, Ernest Hemingway's reputation was assured. Dealing with what Miss Stein called the "lost generation," the novel derives its title from these words of *Ecclesiastes:* "One generation passeth away, and another generation cometh ; but the earth abideth forever. . . The sun also ariseth, and the sun goeth down, and hasteth to the place where he arose. . ."

The Sun Also Rises pictures a group of expatriates in Europe who have been caught up in the vortex of postwar "emancipations" and disillusions ; and who attempt to anaesthetize themselves against thinking about their purposeless and bleak spinning, with innumerable drinking bouts, illicit love, trips to Spain to watch bull-fights, and fishing. Brett Ashley — the woman with whom the newspaper correspondent, Jake Barnes, is in love — has already married twice. Waiting for a divorce from her second husband, that she might marry a certain Michael Campbell, she still confesses her "love" for Jake ; and does not hesitate about attaching still other "lovers" : among them a young Jewish novelist, a wealthy American Greek, and a Spanish bull-fighter.

By the end of the novel, however, she has announced her

intention of returning to Michael because "He's so damned nice and he's so awful. He's my sort of thing."[9] Some of the dialogue in the book is as tedious and vapid as the characters themselves; but other pages of it are crisp and well sustained, and suggest that discipline which Gertrude Stein put her young follower through in those long hours when she had him recount over and over again the conversations which were to go into this novel. In the example which I give, two of the characters are talking about Lady Brett:

". . . She was a V.A.D. in a hospital I was in during the war."
"She must have been just a kid then."
"She's thirty-four now."
"When did she marry Ashley?"
"During the war. Her own true love had just kicked off with the dysentery."
"You talk sort of bitter."
"Sorry. I didn't mean to. I was just trying to give you the facts."
"I don't believe she would marry anybody she didn't love."
"Well," I said, "she's done it twice."
"I don't believe it."
"Well," I said, "don't ask me a lot of fool questions if you don't like the answers."
"I didn't ask you that."
"You asked me what I knew about Brett Ashley."
"I didn't ask you to insult her."
"Oh, go to hell."
He stood up from the table his face white, and stood there white and angry behind the little plates of hors d'œuvres.
"Sit down," I said. "Don't be a fool."
"You've got to take that back."
"Oh, cut out the prep-school stuff."
"Take it back."
"Sure. Anything. I never heard of Brett Ashley. How's that?"
"No. Not that. About me going to hell."
"Oh, don't go to hell," I said. "Stick around. We're just starting lunch."[10]

The second collection of stories, which Mr. Hemingway entitled *Men Without Women* (1927), is marked, I think we should note very carefully, by two especial characteristics. Like the earlier *In Our Time,* this volume displays an unusual skill in giving a name to legitimate human hungers, and in endowing images with a high evocative power. Take these lines, for example, from "In Another Country" :

It was cold in the Fall in Milan and the dark came very early. Then the electric lights came on, and it was pleasant along the streets looking in the windows. There was much game hanging outside the shops, and the snow powdered in the fur of the foxes and the wind blew their tails. The deer hung stiff and heavy and empty, and small birds blew in the wind and the wind turned their feathers. It was a cold Fall and the wind came down from the mountains.[11]

Unfortunately, *Men Without Women* also marks a growth in Ernest Hemingway toward a concern with the abnormal. One of the stories pictures an Army officer who is a pederast ; another deals with a dope addict ; another portrays a group of young Americans traveling through Italy and gaining most of their knowledge of the country from prostitutes ; and still another sketches a young man urging his mistress to have an abortion. "I wanted to try this new drink. That's all we do, isn't it — look at things and try new drinks,"[12] says a young woman in one of the tales — thereby uttering a remark which rather aptly characterizes most of the Hemingway men and women. It would be unfair, however, not to call attention in this collection to such a splendid and well-known story as "The Killers"—a skilful tale, in the determinist manner, which Crane himself might have written. Also, one must admit the effectiveness of two or three of the sketches which reflect their author's love of the outdoors.

A Farewell to Arms (1929) is commonly considered Hemingway's greatest book. Frederic Henry, an American enlisted in one of the Italian ambulance units, is introduced by one of his young Italian friends to Catherine Barkley, an English V.A.D., whose fiancé had been killed at the Somme. Objecting to his "nurse's evening off attitude," she at first rebuffs Henry. When he is wounded and sent back to a Milan hospital, however, she is stationed as his nurse, and not only falls in love with him but quickly becomes his mistress. Later, when she expects a child, Catherine refuses to marry Frederic Henry; and he leaves again for the front, where he finds himself in the midst of the Caporetto retreat. Then, when he is about to be shot by Italian military police, he escapes; joins Catherine at Stresa; and the two of them row across the lake into Switzerland where Catherine later dies in childbirth.

Certain adverse comment on this novel I reserve until later. But, in passing, I must note here briefly a few of the many high distinctions which it achieves. Those long passages telling of the Caporetto retreat constitute some of the most brilliant pieces of descriptive writing in our contemporary fiction. The two major characters are drawn with a searing vividness; and many of even the minor characters could not possibly be forgotten: old Count Greffi, for example, philosophizing over the billiard table at the age of ninety-four; or the young nurse who is Catherine's friend; or Rinaldi, the young man in the medical corps. Some of the episodes will long retain their animated freshness: Henry trying to have a seat saved for him on the train; the two lovers rowing across the still lake during the long night; the graphic horrors of the hospital scenes; and many others.

And, finally, *A Farwell to Arms* has, at least in its closing pages, a highly concentrated emotion that sets off pleasantly the truncated feelings of the characters in most of the other Hemingway books. The last paragraph of the novel is an artistic classic in the use of undertones, in the compression of tragic feelings. Henry has asked the nurses to leave the room, that he might be alone for a moment with Catherine's body.

But after I had got them out and shut the door and turned off the light it wasn't any good.   It was like saying good-by to a statue.   After a while I went out and left the hospital and walked back to the hotel in the rain.[13]

"An aficionado is one who is passionate about the bull-fights."[14]   Readers of Hemingway who are interested in following this author's love of that sport will do well to turn to his Death in the Afternoon (1932), a veritable "Baedeker of bulls" as it has been called.   But Death in the Afternoon is more than a handbook on bull-fighting.   It contains dialogues on Faulkner, Eliot, and a number of other writers, comment on the craft of writing, and much general philosophizing.   The later Green Hills of Africa (1935), a record of an African safari, is likewise not confined to its principal subject — that of hunting; but is interspersed with discussion of Thomas Wolfe, Melville, Emerson, Poe, Whittier, Hawthorne, revolutions, the Gulf Stream, some of the great books the author has read, and a number of other general matters.   As a discussion of neither of these two volumes is pertinent to the purposes of my study, however, I can immediately turn to the volume of stories entitled Winner Take Nothing (1933).

Mr. Hemingway's older concerns are here reflected again, though somewhat more tediously : "A Clean, Well-Lighted Place" suggests his concern with death ; "Wine of Wyoming," with his hunger for Europe ; "Fathers and Sons," with the moods of the adolescent.   But in addition to these older interests, there is also, it is to be regretted, on the part of the author, that growing preoccupation with the abnormal which, as I have already pointed out, had manifested itself earlier in Men Without Women.   "I turn my flame which is a small one down and down and then suddenly there is a big explosion," Ernest Hemingway once remarked to Gertrude Stein. "If there were nothing but explosions my work would be so exciting nobody could bear it." [15]

Winner Take Nothing comes dangerously close to being only a series of deliberate explosions. Thus, there is one sketch which pictures an adolescent who mutilates himself; one which portrays a homosexualist who allows his mother's bones to be cast out on a dump heap; and there are several which deal with erotomania and various other forms of perversion. "One wonders whether Mr. Hemingway can produce any more interesting volumes so long as he stops off as abruptly as this, turning to play the radio so loud that it can no longer be heard." [16]

2

Let it be said at least that Hemingway's Naturalism is more objective than that of any of our older Naturalists. For, despite all his disavowals of subjectivism, Dreiser has continually worn his grieving and dismayed heart upon his sleeve; Cabell — who, in a sense is a "Romantic Naturalist" — has created a kingdom composed entirely of personal states, and ruled from the capital of his own ego; Anderson has plumbed the depths of his own being until he has long ago hit bottom.

Like Anderson, Hemingway's immediate predecessors sought for the "white wonder" of life under their beds; Hemingway, and the generation which he represents, sought, instead, a kind of black Lethe; tried to forget about life by complete physical immersion in it; and went to sleep in their beds with pleasantly potent jags on.

For the older Naturalist credo which tended to minimize the individual, found crushing confirmation in a post-War society that inclined to anaesthetize him. And so it was that while Anderson was trying to get "the lid off the well of thinking," Hemingway and the "younger" generation were clamping it on again — telling us that to be saved we must abandon ourselves to physical sensations: in a word, that we must not think at all. "God saw that He had blundered and to help us endure His mistake He gave us gin." [17]

"One generation passeth away, and another generation cometh." Anderson made way for Hemingway. Introspection made way for a kind of intoxication.

The "period of being twenty-six." "It became the period of being twenty-six. During the next two or three years all the young men were twenty-six years old. It was the right age apparently for that time and place." [18]

The generation of which Mr. Hemingway became the principal spokesman was, in many ways a rather tired one and seemingly much older than it actually was; but its "emancipations" were those of twenty-six: ". . . rolled hose, midnight discussions, black coffee, and the discarding of wedding rings." [19] Such were its symbols of deliverance as Parrington saw them — somewhat inadequately expressed, however, unless we substitute gin for coffee, and think of the generation as one which, in the first place, did not bother to have any wedding rings to discard! But it did want to discard things; it did want freedom — though it did not always fully understand the kind of freedom it wanted. "Ask the romantic Younger Generation what it demanded," says Carl Van Doren, "and it answered: to be free. Ask it free for what, and it did not answer, but drove faster, drank more, made love oftener." [20]

In *A Farewell to Arms,* when Frederic Henry learns that Catherine is pregnant, he wants to marry her. But Catherine can't see the point of the ceremony at all: "We are married privately. You see, darling, it would mean everything to me if I had any religion. But I haven't any religion." [21]

"I'm damned bad for a religious atmosphere . . ." says
Brett Ashley in *The Sun Also Rises.* "I've the wrong type
of face." [22]

"World pessimism and personal cheeriness." For one thing,
the faces of the Hemingway characters are usually hidden
by the masks of a certain kind of hedonism which successfully covers up their true feelings toward the bitterness and
futility of life. Yet — though these people think life futile
and fail entirely in attempting to adjust themselves to it —
they still do not complain about it. Like the stolid Indian
in "Indian Camp" they may, in more ways than one, cut their
throats in the midst of the pain and disillusion which they
see about them; nevertheless, they do so always with an im-
passive kind of "courage" and even with a kind of grace.

Frederic Henry observes of one of his friends: "There
was a great contrast between his world pessimism and personal cheeriness." [23] I think this remark aptly characterizes
the men and women in the Hemingway books. It takes a
lot of gin, many bull-fights, and much facile dialogue to do
the trick; but the Hemingway "twenty-sixers" maintain, almost always, their personal cheeriness despite the world pessimism of which they are always conscious.

"Not made for thinking." Such personal cheeriness is possible to them only because they do not think. They refuse
to think; they dare not think. "You are better when you
don't think so deeply," [24] says Frederic. Again: "I lay down
on the bed and tried to keep from thinking." [25] And, again:
"I was not made for thinking. I was made to eat. . . Eat
and drink and sleep with Catherine." [26] In *Winner Take
Nothing,* we are told of Mr. Frazer: "He was thinking well,
a little too well." [27]

Coition, traveling, eating, drinking, fishing, bull-fighting:
all of these thus become anodynes — opiates against thinking,

means of satisfying appetites which are never very complex. For the Hemingway characters do not, as a rule, have very powerful hungers: their needs are simple ones satisfied by their going down to Spain to drink gourds of cheap wine, or by their taking a mistress off to red-plushed bedrooms in Milan hotels. From this point of view, they are not very satisfactorily human; they always fail signally in coming to any intellectual grips with life. Their emotions originate in the navel.

In emphasizing all of which, I mean to say, of course, that Ernest Hemingway has frequently failed to make the most of the material at his disposal. He rejects—and this is to be regretted—the cathartic value of action, in favor of the uses to which it may be put as an opiate. He has in his hands a bottle of explosives; he dilutes it into an anodyne. When, for example, Brett Ashley averages a lover a month, that is not (to use Mr. Hemingway's own idea) turning the flame down. It is turning it up so high that it begins to flicker out!

Let me give but one other example: the matter of eating. While his wife is in dangerous labor, Henry spends so much time running out of the hospital to eat, that he comes, in those pages, very close to being convincing as a *gourmet* rather than as a human lover. Again, in "An Alpine Idyll" the scene is set in a Swiss tavern. A macabre story has just been told about a peasant who, when his wife had died, had kept her body in a wood-shed for a whole winter:

". . . when she died I made the report to the commune and I put her in the shed across the top of the big wood. When I started to use the big wood she was stiff and I put her up against the wall. Her mouth was open and when I came into the shed at night to cut up the big wood, I hung the lantern from it." [28]

The young American has only this comment on the story: "How about eating?" And his friend, this reply: "All right."

Caught off base. These people may have rather belying appetites and they certainly do disguise their real feelings under a veneer of rapid and clever dialogue. Nevertheless, as I have already said, they think life predominantly cruel and deterministic. "You did not know what it was all about. You never had time to learn. They threw you in and told you the rules and the first time they caught you off base they killed you." [29] Another character says: "You always feel trapped biologically." [30]

In other words, you are bound to be caught off base even when you compromise by playing the game — not with principles and ideas — but with the soft-ball of impulses. You are trapped biologically. "I had seen nothing sacred, and the things that were glorious had no glory and the sacrifices were like the stockyards at Chicago if nothing was done with the meat except to bury it. . . Abstract words such as glory, honor, courage, or hallow were obscene beside the concrete names of villages, the number of roads, the names of rivers. . ." [31] Such was the trap.

Once in camp I put a log on top of the fire and it was full of ants. As it commenced to burn, the ants swarmed out and went first toward the centre where the fire was; then turned back and ran toward the end. When there were enough on the end they fell off into the fire. . . I remember thinking at the time that it was the end of the world and a splendid chance to be a messiah and lift the log off the fire and throw it out where the ants could get off onto the ground. But I did not do anything but throw a tin cup of water on the log, so that I would have the cup empty to put whiskey in before I added water to it. I think the cup of water on the burning log only steamed the ants. [32]

Cleaning conscience with a toothbrush. Rinaldi, the young physician in the war novel, upon one occasion refers to his friend as always trying to clean his "conscience with a toothbrush." In the Hemingway books the morality is a muscular one — not only in its extreme flexibility, but in the way in which it finds its sanction chiefly in physical aches or exhilarations.

When its fixtures seem to pain a little — only then is something wrong : you "contract" immorality the way you would rheumatism. "That was morality; things that made you disgusted afterward. No, that must be immorality." [33] "I know only that what is moral is what you feel good after and what is immoral is what you feel bad after." [34] And Jake Barnes muses : "Enjoying living was learning to get your money's worth. The world was a good place to buy in. It seemed like a fine philosophy." [35]

Speaking to her lover, Catherine wishes they "could do something really sinful. Everything we do seems so innocent and simple. I can't believe we do anything wrong." [36] In other words, as long as the red-plush furniture is comfortable and the waiter brings the food up regularly, let conscience be free ! Let the germs which men call scruples be eradicated by the antiseptics of physical comfort and exhilaration.

Love is a game of bridge. When Frederic Henry first meets Catherine, he frankly admits that he neither loves her nor has any intentions of loving her. It would simply be a game, in which he would play his hand well. "This was a game, like bridge, in which you said things instead of playing cards." [37] In the game of love you simply pretend that you are playing for stakes — though you don't quite know what they are !

To a lonely, homesick soldier, meeting a lovely girl who spoke his native language, this early attitude was perhaps natural. Later on, however, Frederic does fall in love with Catherine ; and the reader has a right to expect to find their love something more than a game. It is not. It is a game played more intensely, I grant. And it is a game with some interludes that are exciting, emotional, and sincere.

Still, it is a game. The hands are good ones. There are many aces in the pack. But neither of the two lovers is at all conscious of any stake that might make the playing worth while. Before falling in love with Catherine, Frederic had said : "Nobody had mentioned what the stakes were. It was all right with me." [38] Throughout the whole affair neither mentions any real stakes—and both are content merely to play the game—and only a game—of an irresponsible and passionate relationship with each other.

. . . The central theme of the book is the story of a Scotch nurse made irresponsible by heartbreak and an American soldier apparently irresponsible by nature going on an irresponsible honeymoon and getting away with it. That is the level at which the story was conceived and written, and that is its appeal : a daydream of extreme erotic indulgence divorced from the other normal human emotions and untouched by the normal difficulties and retributions. You will notice that the circumstances are carefully chosen to permit concentration on an exclusively erotic relation : the beautiful, passionate heroine, slightly hysterical and wholly devoted to being a perfect mistress ; the handsome, strong, brave hero, a gallant officer in the service of a foreign army, a popular he-man with men and promptly adored by women ; a foreign country, and a foreign country in the exceptional conditions of warfare ; a wound just sufficient to confine the hero without crippling him, while the heroine's occupation of nurse provides the circumstances ascribed by Shaw to marriage : "the maximum of temptation combined with the maximum of opportunity" ; the absence of responsibilities but the constant excitement of danger ; a relation outside the law and almost entirely divorced from any other human contacts, the few friendships being superficial and gradually eliminated until the couple is in complete isolation. . .[39]

All of which makes for some exciting moments, but not for what the publishers term a "love conceived in the muck of war which evolves into beauty." ". . . I had seen nothing sacred, and the things that were glorious had no glory and the sacrifices were like the stockyards at Chicago. . ."[40] Whatever merits *A Farewell to Arms* has, it at least does not

offer a convincing portrayal of a love that has any glory, of a
love that "evolves into beauty." The love of Catherine and
Frederic often becomes so dehumanized, as a matter of fact,
that it perilously verges off into only an "obscene joke."

Freedom has come, but with it a certain lessened sense of the
importance of the passions that are thus freely indulged; and,
if love has come to be less often a sin, it has come also to be less
often a supreme privilege. If one turns to the smarter of those
novelists who describe the doings of the more advanced set of
those who are experimenting with life — to, for example, Mr.
Aldous Huxley or Mr. Ernest Hemingway — one will discover in
their tragic farces the picture of a society which is at bottom in
despair because, though it is more completely absorbed in the
pursuit of love than in anything else, it has lost the sense of any
ultimate importance inherent in the experience which preoccu-
pies it . . . to take a perfectly concrete example, a conclusion
which does no more than bring a man and woman into complete
possession of one another is a mere bathos which does nothing
except legitimately provoke the comment, "Well, what of it?" [41]

". . . life isn't very hard to manage when you've nothing
to lose," [42] says one of the Hemingway men. Can anything —
including love — seem *worth* managing when you have nothing to lose? All of which is another way of saying that the
love affair in *A Farewell to Arms* fails to assume many of the
tragic proportions that are implicit in it.

"The earth abideth." With few exceptions — such as the
closing pages of the war novel — Ernest Hemingway's most
sterling qualities as a writer are to be found, I should say,
in what we might call his men-without-women work. In
his pages love and women may at times become only the
subject of an "obscene joke"; the more usual activities of
men, however, he describes with an unfailing fecundity of
inventive and convincing detail.

The tawdry bedroom scenes in a Milan hotel, Lady Ashley
dangling a succession of lovers, a young man trying to per-

suade his mistress to have an abortion — these things I do not believe we long remember as the stuff of literature. On the other hand, the Caporetto retreat; a matador desperately trying to regain his name in the arena; snatches of conversation at an Army mess — these things I do not think we can soon forget as the stuff of life.

In a sense, therefore, it might be said that this spokesman for his generation has done his best work when he has not spoken for his generation at all. While the generations pass, the earth abides; and Mr. Hemingway endures best when he abides with it. Flocks of dark, small grebes trailing through the water; the nostalgia that all men in foreign lands must feel when the electric lights come on; two-hearted rivers that flow by one's camp in the night; the inarticulate grief in which, overwhelmed by the death of one he loves, a man closes a strange door to walk back to his hotel in the rain; an attempt, in the midst of a "lost" generation, to "possess one's soul" as another angler — a great one! — did some three hundred years ago:

While I had him on, several trout had jumped at the falls. As soon as I baited up and dropped in again I hooked another and brought him in the same way. In a little while I had six. They were all about the same size. I laid them out, side by side, all their heads pointing the same way, and looked at them. They were beautifully colored and firm and hard from the cold water. It was a hot day, so I slit them all and shucked out the insides, gills and all, and tossed them over across the river. I took the trout ashore, washed them in the cold, smoothly heavy water above the dam, and then picked some ferns and packed them all in the bag, three trout on a layer of ferns, then another layer of ferns, then three more trout, and then covered them with ferns. They looked nice in the ferns, and now the bag was bulky, and I put it in the shade of the tree.[43]

— these things do not speak for any of the generations that pass. They remain; and what is built upon them will endure.

Hemingway's godmother once said that he looked like a modern, but smelled of a museum. This was, I think, a greater compliment to her disciple than Miss Stein intended.

Realism and paprika. When Ernest Hemingway serves up his realism in good plain dishes, I believe he can be surpassed by few other American writers. But his frequent attempts to fillip that realism with certain seasonings of profanity and obscenity are to be regretted. To show that ambulances are really stuck in the mud, let us say, he needs must have the soldiers trying to dig them out expend half of their energy in oaths. To show a love that was actually "conceived in the muck of war," he must leave no little muck clinging to the love.

For this fault Ernest Hemingway has never been adequately censured. Our critics, of course, will tell us that such language is the language really spoken by such characters: the fact remains, they will say, that an author's choice of certain themes gives him of necessity the fullest latitude in the choice of the language to be used in discussing those themes. But "the fact also remains that, in Isabel Paterson's words, such language isn't realism, it's paprika." [44]

It is not realism but "realism." It is the worst kind of Naturalism.

Style and Steinese. Highly individual, simple, and economical, Hemingway's style is, at its best, as pruned of superfluities as his characters are divorced of subtleties. A natural style, his is one which it is impossible to imitate successfully, and even difficult to parody effectively. He sees not words, but the people who speak those words. Or, to quote from his godmother, "like the motor going inside and the car moving, they are part of the same thing." [45]

It is true that from this same godmother he has absorbed a certain number of stylistic incoherencies and eccentricities.

His books have sometimes had an echometric design that has made them catch up too easily Miss Stein's repetitious phrases, drab monotones, sheer echolalic passages, four-letter words, and overly frequent pronouns.

Let me hasten to add, however, that this imitativeness has seldom long prevailed against Hemingway's originality and individuality.   Seen in their proper sequence, his volumes indicate a stylistic growth that is discernible despite even his imitations.   In *Green Hills of Africa,* for example, the sentences are longer than in any previous book; there is less monotony of style and a more widely variegated pattern in the thought.

Ernest Hemingway's genius is too individual and too original for him to content himself for very long with mere borrowing when he has so much capital of his own; in matters of style he need not depend upon his godmother any longer. One point of view, however, he might have borrowed from her with profit.   I dislike the abnormal, says Miss Stein, because "it is so obvious."

CHAPTER VII

JOHN DOS PASSOS AND THE MODERN DISTEMPER

"As one who regards himself neither as a pessimist nor altogether as a nincompoop, I have been successively abashed, ruffled, and bewildered by the cheerful chorus of despair until a little reading and a little meditation have convinced me that the singers swelling the chorus do not know the meaning of the words of the oratorio — as though the reiterated 'All we-e-e, like sheep,' were a hymn in praise of mutton. As I understand them . . . the 'healthy pessimist' is not a pessimist at all . . . but simply the type of Diogenes who thinks that he is willing to see what his lantern reveals, although he much prefers to see the things that hide in darkness and that are revealed only by artificial light."— *Some Contemporary Americans,* by Percy H. Boynton. P. 280.[1]

CHAPTER VII

JOHN DOS PASSOS AND THE MODERN DISTEMPER

THERE was a time when the majority of our writers looked upon America as a land of milk and honey. Today an alarming majority of them look upon America as a land of locusts, scorpions, wormwood, and gall.

Not, of course, that pessimism, defeatism, and the tendency to deprecate our national life were unknown in our literature before the present century. Under the Puritans, for example, thousands of children were privileged to know no literature except the heavy, deterministic, in-Adam's-fall-we-sinned-all variety; the "jigging octosyllabics" of Michael Wigglesworth were unnecessarily hopeless reminders of an inescapable day of doom; Jonathan Edwards, who proved so brilliantly that man's will is free, but that man does not possess free will, interminably droned to sleepy congregations about the flood-gates of God's wrath; and even Cotton Mather laid down his pen at last and died, refusing to admit that determinism can be damnably distressing even to him who believes in it.

One finds it increasingly hard to accept the point of view of the defeatist, however, when he stands on a mountain and sees trees fall and cities grow because of his own strength and will; and by the eighteenth century, determinism — and its consequences of despair and pessimism — were fast disappearing from American letters. The discovery of our frontier, together with the economic abundance which it offered and the initiative which it encouraged, brought our writers into grips with life at least sufficiently to doom Puritanism.

As a result, even before Jonathan Edwards had finished

175

his preaching, the curtain had rung down upon him; and the spotlight was turned upon Benjamin Franklin, symbol and apostle of a more hopeful literary and economic order. During the eighteenth century, then, America was reflected in our literature as a land of promise. In the words of Crèvecœur, men then found that "Everything tended to regenerate them; new laws, a new mode of living, a new social system; here they are become men."[2] And in the early nineteenth century, under the impact of the French Revolution, new agrarian ideas, and new democratic impulses, this same tradition of optimism received an impetus which sustained it for at least eight or nine decades.

Shortly after the *fin de siécle,* however, our literary complexion underwent a noticeable change. The pessimism of the Old World — reflected in the work of Ibsen, Sudermann, Strindberg, and Hauptmann — began to filter into our literary consciousness; the Russians — especially Gorki, Chekhov, and Tolstoy — soon began to lend a sombre color to our letters that is often indistinguishable from the darker shades of defeatism.

Nietzsche's theory of the superman, Freud's studies of neuroses, the work of the French Naturalists, the later frankly pessimistic philosophy of Spengler and the sombre writing of that great artist, Thomas Mann — such were but a few of the foreign influences which helped bring about a certain pessimism by causing us to focus our attention upon human failures, the misfits of society, the jagged and loose ends of life that are bound to dangle in a deterministic world.

As the decades passed there were also, of course, other influences at work. New economic problems, class struggles, an intensifying of racial prejudices, materialism and greed, our philosophy of "rugged individualism," the regimentation and exploitation of life under the new industrial order, the War with its debacle of demolished human values, the dismay of mankind at finding itself suddenly adrift without so many

of its older ideals, the callowness of the "younger generation" and all of its negations — all of these contributed,
obviously, to that spirit of defeatism which makes many of
our contemporary novels seem like nothing but vast dialogues
of discontent.

"For human life, after all, was a wearisome commonplace . . ." [3] reflects Vardis Fisher's Vridar Hunter. "Life
is a big joke. *Res est sacra miser*," [4] says the same author's
Becky Hammond. "God saw that He had blundered and
to help us endure His mistake He gave us gin," [5] observes
another one of the Fisher characters. Life is only an "evasion of death," [6] declares William Saroyan. It is but a
"tawdry pantomime . . . a pouring of blood, a grappling
with shadows, a digging of graves," [7] according to Ben Hecht's
Erik Dorn. ". . . the reason for living was to get ready to
stay dead a long time," [8] soliloquizes one of the Faulkner
women.

"Life is a damned muddle . . . a football game with
everyone offside and the referee gotten rid of . . ." [9] cries
Amory Blaine in F. Scott Fitzgerald's *This Side of Paradise*.
It is "just a long drawn out lie with a sniffling sigh at the
end," [10] insists Nina Leeds in *Strange Interlude*. Life "was
a pretty heavy thing that thinned one's face and fell like a
lump on one's shoulders," [11] says one of the characters in
James T. Farrell's *Guillotine Party;* while the same author's
Studs Lonigan early in life decided "that the world was
lousy. . ." [12]

"It is so easy to forget that there's any joy at all in life," [13]
decides Andrews in *Three Soldiers,* one of the earliest Dos
Passos novels. Of his Jasper Penny Joseph Hergesheimer
says: ". . . how hollow living seemed! He had missed
something; or else existence was an ugly deception, the false
lure of an incomprehensible jest." [14]

"The essential thing in life is hate" [15] — such is the opinion
of one of Conrad Aiken's men. And the same opinion is

echoed by such of Robinson Jeffers' characters as Fera, who in *Cawdor,* says: "This must be life, this hot pain."[16] (It will be recalled that Nietzsche thought life good only *because* it is so painful!)

In Sherwood Anderson's *Winesburg, Ohio* Hal Winters wonders if a man has "got to be harnessed up and driven through life like a horse."[17] Of two of the people in Louis Bromfield's *A Good Woman* it is said that "they had tried to escape from a life which circumstances or fate had made too cruel for them to bear."[18] And in Helen Hull's *Morning Shows the Day* one of the central figures offers us this observation on life: "Impossible to see the end, impossible to turn back, a long one-way street."[19]

To Margaret Bade, in Robert Nathan's *Autumn,* life seems to be just "so much spilt milk"; to a character in Glenway Wescott's *The Apple of the Eye* it appears that the only purpose in living is "to go on, just to go on." And finally: "It is one of Freud's quaint conceits that the child in its mother's womb is the happiest of living creatures."[20] So writes Joseph Wood Krutch in his *The Modern Temper* — an excellent study of what is not so much a modern temper, as a modern *dis*temper.

For, as reflected in at least an appallingly large number of our contemporary novels, it *is* a distemper — a bad state of mind; and it would be possible, of course, for any reader of present-day fiction to draw up an indefinitely long list of such quotations as I have given, to prove the point.

Questions confront our age today, as have confronted few ages before; and our novelists have preoccupied themselves with a large share of these questions. But one could count on the fingers of one hand those of them who have come to real grips with modern problems, who have not either entered the fight with a pretty ill-humor to begin with, or emerged from it in an even worse state of mind — that of the defeatist. One is almost inclined to include Mr. John Dos Passos in that small minority who have grappled with present-day problems with understanding and a real temper — with a really vigorous and unyielding spirit.   He has made a valiant beginning.   But, unfortunately, he, too, has succumbed to cynicism, determinism, and despair.   He, too, has found life nothing more than a "one-way street"; and to those of us who hope to find from him the way in which it leads, he gives no answer.

1

John Roderigo Dos Passos was born in Chicago on January 14, 1896.   After graduating from Harvard he soon enlisted with the Harjes Volunteer Ambulance Service in Italy; and then until July, 1919, he served in an American ambulance corps.   The War has profoundly influenced almost everything he has written — the War and his intense awareness of social problems.   During the Sacco-Vanzetti case, for example, he was arrested in a picket demonstration in Boston, and confined in the same cell with Michael Gold, the *New Masses* editor.   He has contributed frequently to this magazine; and, while not a Communist, has had broad sympathies with various world labor movements — especially the Russian.

Readers curious concerning the earliest development of his social attitudes will find little to reward them in most of the writing — stories, editorials, and free verse — which he did as an undergraduate for the *Harvard Monthly*.   But one of the articles he did for this same magazine is significant for its revelation of the social consciousness later so recognizable in the novelist.   Appearing in the issue of the *Harvard Monthly* which marked the month of his graduation, "A Humble Protest" is a sharp condemnation of an industrial order which has made all of us "like men crouching on a runaway engine" and "insensately" shoveling in fuel, while we remain "with no thought as to where we are being taken."

One Man's Initiation — 1917, the first Dos Passos novel, appeared in 1920. It is the story of the ambulance driver, Martin Howe, and his companions; and is, like the early *Harvard Monthly* article, an indictment of our age: of "all this cant of governments, and this reiteration of hatreds," of the way in which the "resiliency" of human life is rapidly being "crushed under organization, tabulation." The answer, Mr. Dos Passos says, lies in our seeking a disorganization, rather than an organization, of the present social order.

Three Soldiers (1921) is in many respects a classic that should be compared with Crane's *The Red Badge of Courage,* especially for the way in which, like the latter novel, it emphasizes the deterministic way in which war reduces men to mere automata and slaves. "They treat you like you was a steer being taken over for meat," [21] says one of the soldiers. And Fuselli, one of the other men, thinks of "the feeling he had of being lost in the machine, of being as helpless as a sheep in a flock." [22] There was the "endless succession of the days, all alike, all subject to orders, to the interminable monotony of drills and line-ups. . . He felt he couldn't go on, yet he knew that he must and would go on, that there was no stopping, that his feet would go on beating in time to the steps of the treadmill." [23]

Caught up on this treadmill, then, are three soldiers, each skilfully selected, because of his temperament, to reflect some different aspect of the horrors experienced by thousands of other soldiers. Fuselli, the young Italian from San Francisco, dreams of his girl back home; pathetically hopes for a corporal's rating for her sake; and is destined by his own temperament, to failure. Chrisfield, from Indiana, is more stolid, but also more uncompromisingly intense and more implacable in his hatred of the cruelty about him; he finally kills an officer who has insulted him, and becomes a deserter.

Andrews is the most sensitive of the three; and it is through him chiefly, I think, that the artist and the aesthete in Mr. Dos Passos, seek to become articulate. Formerly a musician, Andrews longs for the end of the War that he might return to New York to study music. He is wounded, sent back finally from the hospital to his detachment; and manages, after the Armistice, to get a traveling order enabling him to study at the Schola Cantorum in Rome.

But when the M.P.'s catch him at Chartres — to which he had gone on a day's outing with a girl from Paris — and find him without his permits, they knock him down, and haul him off to a labor battalion without giving him a chance to communicate with the officers of his School Detachment. Andrews escapes, and like Chrisfield, becomes a deserter.

I think no reader will blame him, after reading about the powerfully described and unmitigated brutalities he had been made to suffer. Always he had tried to keep his own individuality and a sense of the inviolability of his worth as a human being. "He must not let himself sink too deeply into the helpless mentality of the soldier. He must keep his will power." [24]

But the "system" had been against him. "It was the stagnation of the life about him that he felt sinking into every crevice of his spirit, so that he could never shake it off, the stagnation of dusty ruined automatons that had lost all life of their own, whose limbs had practised the drill manual so long that they had no movements of their own left." [25]

Men had been turned into dumb beasts: "You've got to turn men into beasts before ye can get 'em to act that way. Ever read Tolstoi?" [26] And, at the end of the novel, Andrews, too, has really admitted "inevitable defeat" — even before he is apprehended as a deserter, and carried away to the fate we know awaits him. There is an undeniable robustness of style in this book, a homely, natural quality of speech, a great deal of power, and even a kind of beauty, wistful, tender, and simple.

After the volume of verse entitled *A Pushcart at the Curb*

(1922), Mr. Dos Passos brought out a book of essays, *Rosi-
nante to the Road Again* (1922), and a second novel, *Streets
of Night* (1923), an "escapist" story of the "younger generation" which is so much in the nature of a pot-boiler as to
have no significance for the purposes of my discussion.

Manhattan Transfer (1925), however, is commonly considered one of his best books. Fulfilling somewhat Mr.
Saroyan's definition of a novel as "a thing of many fragments," it presents a composite picture of life in New
York City from 1898 to about the middle of the second
decade of our own century. The title of the book is derived
from the Manhattan Transfer where Ellen and her husband
have to change trains on their way to Atlantic City for their
honeymoon; and Ellen Thatcher and one of her husbands,
Jimmy Herf, might be considered the central characters in
the rapid series of portraits drawn for us. Furthermore, no
two "snaps" of the same characters are ever given in immediate succession; although it is possible to piece together the
general stories of their lives from the various facts that we
are able to gather from the frequently interrupted narratives.

There is Bud Korpenning who has come to New York
after running away from a father who had whipped him until
his back had become a welter of scars. Bud tries vainly to
get a job, frequents flop-houses, and finally jumps off Brooklyn Bridge. Ed Thatcher, a poor accountant in the first
part of the novel, later retires in fairly comfortable circumstances. His daughter Ellen grows up, and is married three
times: first to Oglethorpe, the actor; secondly, to the newspaper man, Jimmy Herf; and, finally, to the lawyer, George
Baldwin.

But there are many other characters. There is the milkman, Gus McNeil, who is hit by a trolley and who gets
Baldwin to collect large damages for him. There is Dutch
Robertson, who returns from the War and tries to get a job
that he might marry his girl; who turns hold-up man, at

last, and is sentenced to prison. There is the former Wall Street wizard, Harland, now starving on the streets; Congo Jake, the French sailor, who saves his money and becomes a prosperous bootlegger; Anna Cohen, who "scabs" at Madame Soubrine's fashionable dress shop and has her face and figure marred for life in a fire caused by poor fire regulations; Blackhead, the ruined financier, who dies swilling the whiskey forbidden him; and a score of other men and women, all set panoramically against the surging tides of humanity pumped through the great arteries of the City itself:

. . . soft-cheeked girls chewing gum, hatchet-faced girls with bangs, creamfaced boys . . . young toughs with their hats on one side, sweatyfaced messengers, crisscross glances, sauntering hips, red jowls masticating cigars, sallow concave faces, flat bodies of young men and women, paunched bodies of elderly men, all elbowing, shoving, shuffling, fed in two endless tapes through the revolving doors out into Broadway. . .[27]

Hundreds of images flash before the reader: the clatter of dray horses on the City's streets; the grinding wheels of produce wagons; spluttering "arclights"; cheap mechanical pianos; the Ritz; a milkman driving his wagon home under the "L" at dawn; the windows of Manhattan caught in the fire of the sun over Brooklyn; the haze-blurred hills of Staten Island; the sky, like "a vault of beaten lead" over the City's "cardboard buildings"; dark fog over the river, while the "ferryslip yawns . . . a black mouth with a throat of light"; all night restaurants where men spend a last dime for coffee while millionaires at clubs dip their forks into "the crispy white heart of lettuce"; Bonus Agitation Committees; "tall buildings . . . haloed with ruddy glare from street and electriclight sounds."

To show not only the high evocative power of the images, but also the skilful effects which Dos Passos gains by the use of contrast, let me quote a selection, the first part of which is not unreminiscent of Crane:

A fetor of mattresses and sleep seeped out from the blocks of narrow-windowed houses. Along the gutters garbagecans stank sourly. In the shadow of a doorway a man and girl swayed tightly clamped in each other's arms. Saying good night. Ellen smiled happily. Greatest hit on Broadway. The words were an elevator carrying her up dizzily, up into some stately height where electric light signs crackled scarlet and gold and green, where were bright roofgardens that smelled of orchids, and the slow throb of a tango danced in a goldgreen dress with Stan while handclapping of millions beat in gusts like a hailstorm about them. . .[28]

Suggestive of Crane, also, are such bits of impressionism as the following: "The newborn baby squirmed in the cotton-wool feebly like a knot of earthworms."[29] "The raindark houses heaved on either side. . ."[30] "He walked on fast splashing through puddles full of sky. . ."[31] "Dripping with a tango the roadhouse melted pink like a block of icecream."[32] "The telephone reached out shivering beady tentacles of sound."[33] And, finally: "Bright flakes of cloud were scaling off a sky of crushing indigo over the Battery."[34]

As a matter of fact, the whole groundwork for Dos Passos' later technical experiments is really laid in *Manhattan Transfer*. As in his succeeding novels, he here combines words to get certain "effects": "puttycolor," "sacredlooking," "supercil-superciliosity." He uses newspaper headlines to establish the time of certain of his episodes:

MORTON SIGNS THE GREATER NEW YORK BILL[35]

To achieve an atmosphere of contemporaneousness he employs newspaper clippings, songs played in night-clubs, merchandise lists, and telegrams; and to give acceleration and tenseness to the style, he makes use of such sharply clipped sentences as this: "Propped with five pillows in the middle of his wide colonial mahogany bed with pineapples on the posts Phineas P. Blackhead his face purple as his silk dressing gown sat up and cursed."[36] Finally, he introduces "prose poems" as a means of pointing the import of his various chapters. This one, for example, heads the chapter entitled "The Burthen of Nineveh":

Seeping in red twilight out of the Gulf Stream fog, throbbing brassthroat that howls through the stiff-fingered streets, prying open glazed eyes of skyscrapers, splashing red lead on the girdered thighs of the five bridges, teasing caterwauling tugboats into heat under the toppling smoketrees of the harbor.

Spring puckering our mouths, spring giving us gooseflesh grows gigantic out of the droning of sirens, crashes with enormous scaring din through the halted traffic, between attentive frozen tiptoe blocks.[37]

In the interests of my readers' time let me omit a discussion of the two plays entitled *The Garbage Man* (1926) and *Airways, Inc.* (1928); as well as of the two collections of essays called *Orient Express* (1927) and *In All Countries* (1934).

The 42nd Parallel (1930), *1919* (1932), and the recently published *The Big Money* (1936) constitute a trilogy which supposedly represents the best work John Dos Passos has yet given us. In general, these volumes are intended to cut through representative sections of American life, beginning at about the opening of our century, in much the same manner that certain storms "follow three paths or tracks from the Rocky Mountains to the Atlantic Ocean of which the central tracing roughly corresponds with the 42nd parallel of latitude. . ."[38]

Like *Manhattan Transfer* these three novels do not have what we commonly call plots. Instead, they offer a series of frequently interrupted narratives and a thousand character "flashes" which must be pieced together at the end of the books in order to get a composite picture of the many-sided and involved pattern of teeming life which they attempt to suggest, rather than depict.

The 42nd Parallel tells us of such people as Fainy

McCreary, whose early surroundings and life can be best suggested by this passage of Crane-like realism :

When the wind set from the silver factories across the river the air of the grey fourfamily frame house where Fainy McCreary was born was choking all day with the smell of whaleoil soap. Other days it smelt of cabbage and babies and Mrs. McCreary's washboilers. Fainy could never play at home because Pop, a lame cavechested man with a whispy blondegrey mustache, was nightwatchman at the Chadwick Mills and slept all day. It was only round five o'clock that a curling whiff of tobacco smoke would seep through from the front room into the kitchen. That was a sign that Pop was up and in good spirits and would soon be wanting his supper.

Then Fainy would be sent running out to one of two corners of the short muddy street of identical frame houses where they lived.

To the right it was half a block to Finley's where he would have to wait at the bar in a forest of mudsplattered trouserlegs until all the rank brawling mouths of grownups had been stopped with beers and whiskeys. Then he would walk home, making each step very carefully, with the handle of the pail of suds cutting into his hand.[39]

It chronicles the career of J. Ward Morehouse — whom we are later to meet as a famous Public Relations Counsel. It introduces us to Morehouse's wife, the wealthy Gertrude Staple, and his friend, Eleanor Stoddard. It traces in detail the affairs of Morehouse's secretary, the blond Janey Williams; tells of the various jobs she had had before coming to work for Morehouse; and gives much attention to her troubles in avoiding the men who are continually trying to seduce her. There are chapters, also, on one of Eleanor Stoddard's friends, Eveline Hutchins; and a concluding one on Charley Anderson, who works for a while for his brother in Minnesota, makes quite a business of seducing various not very reluctant women, and finally leaves for the War.

1919 continues these sharply etched portraits, and intro-

duces further characters. Joe Williams, the brother of
Janey Williams whom we have already met, spends most of
his time at sea and in various brothels — a feckless, will-less
character determined, in almost everything he does, by his
environment. Ann Elizabeth Trent, a Texas girl who had
been disappointed in love, goes to France to forget her
disillusions by drinking gin and being as promiscuous as
possible; contemplates suicide when she finds she is abandoned by one of her lovers; and is finally killed when she
persuades a drunken aviator to take her up in his plane.
The young literary dilettante, Richard Ellsworth Savage,
graduates from Harvard and lands with the American forces
in France, where he ultimately becomes a friend of Major
Morehouse, the character from the earlier novel. And Ben
Compton, the young labor agitator, is finally picked up as a
"slacker," is involved in labor troubles, and is sent to prison.

The Big Money, the final volume of the trilogy, is largely
concerned with the story of Charley Anderson, who, at the
beginning of the novel, has returned from the War with a
great reputation as an ace aviator, and with a new invention
for airplanes which soon makes him wealthy. After being
divorced by his wife, and after a sex life that is both indiscriminate and intense, Anderson loses most of his money and
is killed when he tries to beat a railroad train to a crossing.
One of his mistresses is Eveline Hutchins, by this time married, ready for a divorce, and so tired of life that she commits suicide.

The life of Marjorie Dowling is also offered us in detail.
She is, I think, the most promiscuous "heroine" in all modern fiction. Her "amours" would make Casanova blush —
and then vomit.

Raped by her stepfather, she marries an extremely offensive Cuban, tries her best to "catch" an extremely wealthy
young yachtsman, becomes Anderson's mistress, and finally
goes to Hollywood where, upon one occasion at least, within

the same fifteen minutes, she surrenders herself first, to her leading man, and then, to her director.

The only characters in the book, as a matter of fact, who seem to see anything worth fighting for except money and a widely distributed sex life, are Mary French, the social worker, and her "Comrade" companion; and even they are not nearly so effectively drawn as they might be because they are impelled chiefly by a confused emotionalism that spends itself in picket lines, distributing "Comrade" literature, and getting hit on the head by labor police.

It is Mary French, I think, who gives to the novel whatever contrast it is meant to achieve: that between the lives led by Big Money people, and the lives led by the poor. "The food they waste and the money they waste while our people starve in tarpaper barracks. . . I'm sick of this parasite life. . ." [40] But Mr. Dos Passos has made this "parasite life" so attractive, to tell the truth, that the balance between the systems of values he seems to be trying to set up is scarcely effective.

I find myself quite unable to go along with those who maintain that these later volumes are better books than either their author's *Three Soldiers* or *Manhattan Transfer;* but I shall reserve, for a moment, my reasons for this judgment. In the meantime, let me call attention to the technical experiments which have been used in the trilogy.

For one thing, Mr. Dos Passos employs a series of brief "Biographies" of people prominent during the period which each novel covers. Thus *The 42nd Parallel* has sketches of Minor C. Keith, Carnegie, Edison, Steinmetz, Debs, Burbank, Haywood, and La Follette. *1919* offers such portraits as those of Randolph Bourne, Jack Reed, Wilson, Roosevelt, Joe Hill, Morgan, Paxton Hibben, and Wesley Everest. And *The Big Money* includes, among others, sharply focused pictures of Ford, Veblen, Insull, Isadora Duncan, Valentino, and Hearst. Often, it should be added, these "Biographies" constitute by far the most interesting parts of the books; often they represent Mr. Dos Passos' rich irony and sharp satire at its best; and always they serve the purpose for which they were intended: "to plunge us even deeper into the current"[41] of the life he is depicting.

Secondly, he makes a more intense use of the "Newsreels" which he had only occasionally employed in *Manhattan Transfer*. These include slogans, fragments of songs, headlines, and quotations which help to establish both the time and atmosphere of his stories:

WALLSTREET EMPLOYERS BANISH CHRISTMAS WORRIES AS
BONUSES ROLL IN

Left my girl in the mountains
Left her standin' in the rain

OUR AIR SUPREMACY ACCLAIMED

LAND SO MOUNTAINOUS IT STANDS ON END

Got myself in trouble
An' shot a county sheriff down[42]

Thirdly, he inserts into the novels what he calls "Camera Eyes" — passages of highly subjective and extremely echometric prose:

Walk the streets and walk the streets inquiring of Coca Cola signs Lucky Strike ads pricetags in storewindows scraps of overheard conversations stray tatters of newsprint yesterday's headlines sticking out of ashcans
for a set of figures a formula of action an address you don't quite know you've forgotten the number the street may be in Brooklyn a train leaving for somewhere a steamboat whistle stabbing your ears a job chalked up in front of an agency
to do to make there are more lives than walking desperate the streets hurry underdog do   make[43]

And, finally, he employs again these experiments which we have already seen in *Manhattan Transfer*: words that are run together; long passages entirely free from punctuation; spacings that are intentionally irregular; ideas deliberately fragmentary; and sequences of thought which are purposely chaotic.

2

Arresting and original as these techniques may be, I am convinced that their effectiveness has been greatly exaggerated. But let us not quarrel about the bottles into which Mr. Dos Passos has, at times so skilfully, poured his wine. The point to be noticed, and the point which most of this novelist's critics have chosen to ignore, is that his wine, also, is often too new, too unaged.

Much of his thought smacks too suspiciously of the ferment of "modernism" to be enduringly satisfying. For, toward the universe, toward the definitely determined values of humanity, and even toward those social problems of whose urgency he is so sensitively and uncompromisingly aware, Mr. Dos Passos maintains an attitude that is born of the distemper of our whole modern life. These attitudes he shares, by and large, with most of the other writers whom I consider in this book; and these attitudes do much to fail in justifying Mr. Dos Passos' claim to being called a writer who has freshly or vigorously met the challenge of his age.

This "vast treadmill." His conception of the universe is that of the determinist. But it is more than that. It is a conception that takes on an increasingly deep coloring of despair and defeatism as one follows it through the novels in their chronological order. Martin Howe, Andrews, Jimmy Herf—most of the characters in the earlier books are occasionally "bound" to "this vast treadmill" of life. Fuselli felt a justifiable hatred of the "system" that made his feet "go on beating in time." And Andrews was sometimes tempted "to throw himself into inevitable defeat." And Jimmy Herf turned his back upon the City when he could bear it no more. But these early men did not take their whipping lying down. They tried to stand up to life, toe to toe. Like Andrews they are effective because each tries to "keep his will power." They put up a good fight.

The later men and women do not. As a matter of fact, they hardly think life worth putting up a fight for. "All we do," says George Baldwin in *Manhattan Transfer*, "is go round and round in a squirrel cage." [44] In the same novel Stan Emery wonders "why people have children. It's an admission of defeat. . . Procreation is an admission of defeat." [45] And Phineas Fletcher insists that life is "all a joke, a smutty joke."

In *1919* Ann Trent contemplates suicide and finally, I suppose, might be said to commit it. Eveline Hutchins crucifies herself with her own disillusions; Joe Williams finds himself ineffective against the conspiring impulses of his own temperament; Sardinaglia thinks it possible to remain sane only if one is "disgusted with nothing"; and "Ed" observes that this is a "rotten" world in which it is possible to do nothing without making other people miserable!

Then by the time we have reached *The Big Money* we are privileged to learn that Eveline Hutchins kills herself; to know that Marjorie Dowling so far loses her hold on life as to try to forget her disappointments by giving herself to two men within fifteen minutes; to see the earlier Dick Savage surrendering, and not only going the way of a good deal of flesh, but doing so in a particularly repulsive manner; and to see Charley Anderson "licked" by life long before he tries, unsuccessfully, to beat a railroad train to a crossing. I omit mention of the many other defeatists in the book.

Is there any indication, in all of this, of any attempt on the part of the author to come to real grips with life?

A "lousy cruel vicious dumb type of tailless ape." In the second novel of his trilogy John Dos Passos has one of his characters cry out that "It's a hell of a note when you have to be ashamed of belonging to your own race. But I swear I am, I swear I'm ashamed of being a man . . . it will take some huge wave of hope like a revolution to make me feel any selfrespect ever again. . . God, we're a lousy cruel vicious dumb type of tailless ape." [46]

Toward his characters as puppets caught up in a welter of their own biochemical impulses and cruel economic forces, Dos Passos maintains an attitude of honest sympathy. But he would seem to have little respect for his characters as men and women. This is proved, for one thing, by the fact that, with perhaps three or four exceptions, he makes none of his characters have any respect for themselves as men and women.

Now, in a manner which I have explained in my comment on Dreiser, even the most intensely honest sympathy is bound to lose much of its dramatic and literary significance when it is dissipated on an unworthy object. A real, broad, comprehensive humanitarianism — one of the distinguishing characteristics of enduring writing — seems to me almost impossible without, at the same time, some measure of humanism.

But the tragedies of Mr. Dos Passos' heroes and heroines, because of the defeatist's point of view of their creator, are hardly tragedies at all; and, upon certain occasions, indeed, (such as Marjorie Dowling's double surrender) they are almost farces. As one critic puts it, when Charley Anderson "made a drunken attempt to beat a train to a crossing it didn't make a great deal of difference when he lost." [47]

Reading these novels you come to feel that it doesn't make a great deal of difference when *any* of them lose. You know from the beginning, if you know Mr. Dos Passos, that they *will* lose anyway; and you can't be expected to have either that emotional or intellectual interest in their struggles that you usually do have when absorbed in the conflicts of really great novels.

As you watch a prize fight, for example, you will not have any too attentive an interest in the affair if you are certain, from the first gong, which of the two fighters is going to take the count — if you happen to have definitely learned, let us say, that the fight has been sold. And, above all, you won't put up any bets on the loser.

Mr. Dos Passos' fights are sold from the first gong; and you won't bet on his characters, though to be able to do so would certainly stimulate your interest! But, for one thing, you know that his people don't ever dare to bet on themselves! Mary French's father knows he is sold out long before he commits suicide; and so does Ann Trent, and Eveline Hutchins, and Charley Anderson. And so do most of the others. Like the prostitute in *1919* most of those who do not kill themselves, refrain from doing so, not because of their belief in God, or for any other rational reason, but for fear of how intolerably quiet it will be after death!

It is, to a large extent, this deepened and almost complete absorption in the spirit of despair that has made me rank the trilogy far below, let us say, the earlier *Three Soldiers* and *Manhattan Transfer*.

We are told[48] that John Dos Passos and Ernest Hemingway once went to a bull-fight together. Dos Passos leaped into the ring to try out his own skill in the sport; but when he saw the bull charging at him, simply stood there, waving the red sash back and forth until the animal caught him between its horns. The Dos Passos characters, however, seldom stand their ground.

Ideas like "contraptions of tissue paper." They see in life, as I have previously pointed out, little which is really worth standing ground for. Too many of them, from the outset, find their minds "permeated with dusty stagnation like the stagnation of old garrets and lumber rooms, where, among superannuated bits of machinery and cracked grimy crockery, lie heaps of broken toys." [49]

With the exception of a kind of forlorn and feverish sense of social justice, the ideals commonly recognized by humanity are by these men and women thought of as little more than broken toys cluttering up a futile, grimy, dusty civilization. Cracked crockery! Even one of the earliest protagonists wonders if they are not "all shams, too, these gigantic phrases that floated like gaudy kites high above mankind? Kites, that was it, contraptions of tissue paper held at the end of a string, ornaments not to be taken seriously." [50] And most of the later characters don't even bother to take an occasional look at the kites!

Let me give but two examples of the way in which ideals, in this author's work, are looked upon as "ornaments not to be taken seriously." There is, for example, the attitude toward woman. All the older respect which men have had for her, in these novels becomes only that "gaudy kite," made up of cheap tissue, and floating before the cynical eyes of men. "Women look in your pocket not in your heart." [51] "What leads up to it's [to matrimony] all right, but gettin' married is loike de mornin' after." [52] "I guess I don't love anybody for long unless they're dead." [53]

Chastity is another bit of Dos Passos crockery with a large crack in it. Also, the crack has widened with each succeeding novel. In *Three Soldiers* some of the affairs which the soldiers have—soldiers set against a background of passion and cruelty and bestiality—some of these affairs, I say, seem natural enough. But that atmosphere of "a huddled stuffiness of pigeonhole rooms where men and women's bodies writhed alone tortured by the night and the young summer" [54]—that atmosphere which is exploited in *Manhattan Transfer,* the next novel, finds less justification.

And as the reader progresses through the trilogy, he finds himself immersed in an entire sea of sensuality — sensuality that is deliberate, indiscriminate, and unnecessary. Indeed, the offensiveness which most readers will find in *The 42nd Parallel* and *1919* has, in *The Big Money,* become so pronounced as almost to shade off into the ridiculous. Charley Anderson, as a matter of fact, has so many mistresses that one is inclined to see in his defections about the same tragic proportions that one would find in the procreative activities of a good rooster. And what of Marjorie Dowling's mechanical promiscuities? And all that lush nonsense which our author offers us in the story of the "Comrade" who shared Mary French's bed, and at the same time remained so unwilling to share *himself* with anything but "the cause"?

There are times, surely, when any reader may be excused for wondering whether Mr. Dos Passos is really trying to understand our age, or merely attempting, rather ineffectively, to parody it.

"A man's morals aren't anybody's business." Against the vast impersonalized background of the "City of orgies walks and joys" with which this author has dealt in most of his novels, it is, of course, but natural and real to present people who, for the most part, think, as does Phil Sandbourne in *Manhattan Transfer,* that "A man's morals aren't anybody's business. It's his work that counts."[55]

In its thousands of shabby hall-bedrooms, on its countless streets, amidst the flow of its million lives, any great city necessarily breeds in its citizens a strong conviction that what they do is nobody else's business. It is easy to think, in such a city, that only a man's work counts. The morals-aren't-anybody's-business attitude, we might be inclined to say, must have therefore been necessitated by the realistic picture of metropolitanism which John Dos Passos has been trying to paint.

We should note carefully, however, that — even under the limitations of such a realism — morals are *somebody's* business: at least a man's morals are *his own* business; and even good realism demands that men be depicted as they really are — as creatures who pay *some* attention to this business.

With few exceptions, the Dos Passos characters fail to consider morals as one of the natural, human concerns which they happen to be. Like the majority of the Hemingway men and women, these people cut short their divorces, their promiscuities, their drinking, only for some extremely pragmatic reason — only when they have run through the unvarying formulae which their creator has bound them with. They stop getting divorces only when, seemingly, they realize the futility of being happy in *any* marriage (or when, like Eveline Hutchins, they kill themselves!). They refrain from being promiscuous, for a time, when they contract diseases (or when, like Charley Anderson, they are killed by railroad trains!). They curtail their drinking, for a short interval, when the morning-after headaches become too unbearable (or when, like Morehouse and Savage, they find that drinking interferes with business!).

"Round and round in a squirrel cage." In one respect, however, the people in the Dos Passos books are the very antitheses of those in the Hemingway novels. The latter, as we have seen, tend to avoid thinking: thought is for them too painfully disturbing to be frequently indulged in. The former, on the other hand, find it as necessary to spend their intellectual energies by thinking as they do to maintain their physical strength by eating. Thus it is said of Andrews that "He needed to lie awake and think at night this way, so that he might not lose entirely the thread of his own life. . ." [56]

To quote from Mr. Dos Passos' George Baldwin, many of us must feel, however, that too often these characters do nothing with their thinking except to "go round and round in a squirrel cage." Their thought processes, though always intense, are most frequently fevered and misdirected. When they are lying amidst a "fetor of mattresses" in a district in which "the gutters garbagecans" odors are unpleasantly discernible, they are as likely as not to be thinking of the World War, instead of such a practical thing as a way in which they can spend less money on prostitutes and move to a better neighborhood. And in the midst of the World War they spend unconscionably long and tortured hours wondering whether some one will arrive on time to take them to tea. Indeed, with all that they appear to be energetically concerned with the challenging problems of humanity, they actually spend a surprisingly small part of their energies on anything but their own personal affairs.

"I am an anarchist." Let me repeat again, however, that we must all of us admit Mr. Dos Passos' uncompromising awareness of the industrial and economic evils that confront our world today. With his graphic, searing, highly accelerated prose he has made these evils take on the urgency which they deserve to have.

He makes us realize that the problems are acute; but he fails, signally, in making us realize that they are answerable. Take the problem, for instance, of our modern tendency to regard promiscuity as something of no consequence. Mr. Dos Passos has his characters seek an answer here merely by acting, from the beginning, as if there were no answer. The way to organize one's moral life is so completely to disorganize it that there is no longer any need for organization!

In his social and economic theories he has his characters go around in the same kind of squirrel cage. Instead of admitting the imperious necessity for a carefully planned reorganization of our economic and class system, he would again seem to advocate complete disorganization. "It is disorganization, not organization, that is the aim of life." [57]

Obviously, I am not here concerned with any possible limitations of Mr. Dos Passos' personal social creed — whether or not he himself happens to be an anarchist, a communist, a socialist, or anything else. But I am concerned with the way in which his emphasis upon disorganization has affected both the importance and the validity of what he has to say in his novels. He thinks of himself, beyond a doubt, as a reformer, and as a reformer he must to some extent be judged.

But even more must he be judged as a novelist and I call attention to his anarchistic social creed because it has lent a color to his novels which no critic can disregard. It has made much of his writing conspicuously fevered, illogical, and unsatisfying. It has made many of his characters, upon occasions, seem, not pathetic, as such characters might very well be, but ridiculous, which such characters most certainly should not be.

The reader upon such occasions gets the impression that they are permitting themselves to be hit on the head by labor police, not so much because they are fighting for certain social principles, as because they gain pleasure from being hit on the head. He gets, as a result, the further impression that the convictions which their creator places in their mouths, are not nearly so cogently expressed as they deserve to be.

But not only does this author's petard thus often fail in hitting its mark. The mark itself is often a confused one. The conviction itself is often wrong. In *Manhattan Transfer* Marco says: "It's the same all over the world, the police beating us up, rich people cheating us out of their starvation wages, and whose fault. Dio cane! Your fault, my fault. . ." Then his friend protests: "We didn't make the world. . . They did or maybe God did."

Marco has the answer to this, however: "God's on their

side, like a policeman. . . When the day comes we'll kill God. . . I am an anarchist." [58]

Further disorganization can never, *in either the moral or the economic world,* be the answer to a crying need for further reorganization. Attempting to kill God — a pretty big job for even an anarchist — can never provide the answer. And killing even a policeman will not help very much. No amount of anarchism — either moral or social — can overcome anarchism. Defeatism cannot kill defeat. Distemper cannot serve where a real temper, a proper mixture of steellike courage and common sense, can alone bring one effectively into grips with life.

3

It is difficult, I have said, to succumb to the spirit of determinism and defeatism when one stands on a mountain and sees trees fall and cities rise by his own strength and will. When one stands on a skyscraper, the matter is different.

Metropolitanism is a very important part of American life; but not the most important part. "New York is not America," [59] as Mr. Ford Madox Ford has observed; and most surely many of the values which a whole school of modern writers have found in our whirling metropolitanism do not represent the highest values which America has to offer. It is so easy to get a shaded slant on certain modern problems, to view them without perspective and focus, to fail to face them to the end, when one sees them from the point of view of that bundle of neuroses, dwarfed in gigantic fissures of steel and concrete, that is the metropolitanite. It is so easy, from this point of view, to become a defeatist.

Our physical frontiers have long ago disappeared; but some of the courage that went with them is being rediscovered, I think, in our novelists' rediscovery of certain

regional patterns of life which they represented.   And in this
rediscovery lie, I am convinced, that example and challenge
which can do much toward giving our letters the invigorat-
ing color which they so sorely need.

There were problems — plenty of them ! — in the South
during and after the Civil War.   But Miss Mitchell's powerfully written *Gone With the Wind* (1936) must live, among
many reasons, because it is no record of despair.   There
were problems in the Middle West when its farms were being
developed.   But Miss Cather's Ántonia survived by lending
herself "to immemorial human attitudes which we recognize
by instinct as universal and true."   She "had only to stand
in the orchard, to put her hand on a little crab tree and look
up at the apples, to make you feel the goodness of planting
and tending and harvesting at last." [60]   This is no register of
defeat.

And those giants created by Rölvaag — with their eyes
wandering "from skyline to skyline, year in and year out,
without finding a resting place." [61]   They bend, but they do
not bow.   And Miss Glasgow, with such characters as Do-
rinda Oakley, who realized that she need not fear "the forces
without" just "as long as she could rule her own mind."

And Ruth Suckow's characters, and Zona Gale's, and Phil
Stong's, and Elizabeth Madox Roberts', and Edna Ferber's —
and the characters of a dozen of our other "regionalists."
". . . she had got that strength free at last, with pain and
blind struggle and outward necessity. . ." [62]   So says Miss
Suckow of Sarah Bonney.   "I will break through !   I *will !*
I WILL !   I WILL !" [63]   So cries Miss Gale's "Mister" Pitt.
"Life has no weapons against a woman like that." [64]   So
observes Miss Ferber of Selina Peake.

There is no sign of pessimism, defeatism, and despair in
all of this !   Does it not seem, then, that we must look to our
"regionalists" for that real temper which alone can counter-
act the literary distemper of our times?

CHAPTER VIII

WILLIAM FAULKNER: CRETINS, COFFIN-WORMS, AND CRUELTY

"I haven't written a real novel yet. I'm too young in experience. It hasn't crystallized enough for me to build a book upon one of the few fundamental truths which mankind has learned."
— William Faulkner. (Quoted by Marshall J. Smith, in "Faulkner of Mississippi." *The Bookman,* December, 1931.) [1]

CHAPTER VIII

WILLIAM FAULKNER: CRETINS, COFFIN-WORMS, AND CRUELTY

AGAINST the background of that gruesome galaxy of idiots, cretins, perverts, degenerates, and introverts which Mr. William Faulkner has evoked for us with such perverse skill — against this background the horrors of all our War fiction and of such "hair-raisers" as *Dracula* and *Frankenstein* seem like the quiet and chuckling reminiscences of a Charles Dickens and an A. A. Milne sitting down together to drink tea and eat English muffins.

Some twenty years ago Stuart Sherman ventured a hope that our post-War literature would logically reflect a new vindication of the "law for man" as opposed to the disillusion and cruelty of that "fiery ruin" that had been brought about "by those who made lust and law alike in their decree." Our post-War literature, he said, "should mirror a society more regardful of its ascertained values, more reverent of its fine traditions, more reluctant to take up with the notions of windy innovators." [2]

A deluge of War novels was loosed upon us, of course, some time before Sherman's death. In the very year (1917) in which Sherman had uttered his hopeful prophecy, there was published in this country, for example, one of the great novels of our times, Henri Barbusse's *Under Fire*, with its picture of "men squashed, cut in two, or divided from top to bottom, blown into showers by an ordinary shell, bellies turned inside out and scattered anyhow, skulls forced bodily into the chest as if by a blow with a club, and in place of the head a bit of neck, oozing currant jam of brains all over the chest and back. . ." [3]

A few years later saw the publication here of Remarque's

skilful *All Quiet on the Western Front;* Dos Passos' *Three Soldiers* (suggestive of Crane) appeared in 1921; Cummings' *The Enormous Room,* a vivid study of cruel tortures in a French prison camp, came out in 1922; Boyd's *Through the Wheat,* in 1923; Stallings' *Plumes,* in 1924. More recent novels indicting the barbaric cruelties of war — all of them have appeared since Sherman's death in 1927 — include Blake's *The Path to Glory* (1929), Scanlon's *God Have Mercy on Us!* (1929), Harrison's *Generals Die in Bed* (1930), March's *Company K* (1933), Cobb's *Paths of Glory* (1935), the anonymously written *A Man in Arms* (1935), and van der Meersch's *Invasion* (1937). A score of others could be added to the list.

Some few of these are admittedly great books; on the other hand, some of them have only what Kenneth Burke called "a charitable eye for excrement." Let that stand for the present. The point I wish to make is that Sherman's hope for a body of fiction that would more clearly reflect the "ascertained values" of humanity, has not, on the whole, been fulfilled. It is true that idealistic novels have been written indicting cruelty and all that war stands for. But from the War there has also emerged a school of writers who write not to impugn barbarism, but to set themselves up in a rather profitable literary business with unmitigated cruelties and abnormalities as their regular stock-in-trade. They see in cruelty (which my thesaurus says is a synonym of "inhumanity") only a merchandise which has a high value of exchange; they give it no transcending value by which we may rise above it with a vision truly human.

What is worse, the critics and the publishers have caught the fever. We are never without their assurance that, in the Meredith phrase, "there is a pleasure that is born of pain." Publishers' "blurbs" take particular care to hint at the horrors in the books they advertise; and critics, in the following manner, suggest the "exciting" nature of the "strong stuff" in the volumes they review:

. . . For those who like strong stuff this is an exciting piece of contemporary naturalism, in which blood, lust, torture, agony and violent death follow one another by turns. In Book One a graphic account of an appendicitis operation without the use of ether follows a series of vividly described vomitings. The invalid then has an affair with his nurse who, possessed of a weak heart, dies from the excitement. In Book Two a helpless man is beaten up in a police inspector's office. There is a seduction scene. And a suicide and a couple of shootings complete the carnage. Few details are spared the reader. In Book Three the description of a childbirth takes up much of the space. At the end, after elaborate physical details, there occurs the horrible death of a small baby. Throughout the book almost all imaginable states are described in language that is as frank as possible.[4]

In brief, we are not only being continually told that such-and-such a novel will "shake us to the very marrow of our bones," but we are given a tingling promise that our bones will be sawed in half and that the scalpel of cruelty will pull out a few of our nerves during the operation! The sad part of it is that many of our readers who once *had* nerves, or human sensibilities, are beginning to find it somewhat pleasant to do without them. As a cult, certain of our novelists are working definite harm upon readers' capacities for refined feeling: intellectual, moral, and aesthetic.

1

William Faulkner is today the most touted leader of this cult of cruelty. Born in 1897, in Ripley, Mississippi, of a family that included governors, generals, and statesmen, he spent his boyhood in the small town of Oxford and later attended the University there for two years. When the War broke out he joined up with the Canadian Flying Corps, was finally promoted to the rank of Lieutenant, and was wounded as the result of a plane crash. After the War he returned to this country for but a brief time; and then he set out on a tramping trip through Europe.

When Faulkner later settled down with Sherwood Anderson — at the latter's apartment in New Orleans — he was already the author of a slight volume of poetry entitled *The Marble Faun* (1924). Seeing that his young guest showed few inclinations to do any kind of ordinary work, Anderson at last suggested that he try writing a novel. Faulkner did, and *Soldiers' Pay* (1926) was finished in six weeks. Anderson apparently did not have time to read any of it, but that made no difference. He despatched the manuscript to his own publisher — and with it a letter of fervent recommendation. Upon this recommendation, the novel was accepted; and with some little difficulty Faulkner managed to place his next three books.

Let us inquire briefly into the themes of these early novels. *Soldiers' Pay* tells the story of Lieutenant Donald Mahon, who had been reported killed in the War, but who suddenly returns, shell-shocked and wounded, to his Georgia home, where he finds a sweetheart who has been unfaithful to him, and an entire civilization that seems to have collapsed and decayed. *Mosquitoes* (1927), the next novel, satirizes in a manner reminiscent of Aldous Huxley, a group of intellectuals who, through the generosity of a certain Mrs. Maurier, a dull devotee of the arts, are enabled to spend several days on a yachting party.

Sartoris (1929) repeats somewhat the theme of the author's first novel. Young Bayard Sartoris returns with his mind shattered by the War, to Jefferson, Missouri; he marries Narcissa Benbow; becomes obsessed with the idea of committing suicide; finds that he is a moral coward despite his brave assumption of recklessness; and is finally killed, leaving his wife with an unborn child. The narrative of *The*

Sound and the Fury (1929) — into which novel Mr. Faulkner assured us "I had just written my guts"[5] — is told largely from the point of view of the idiot boy Benjy. It describes the disintegration of a Southern family — a family which includes, besides the idiot already mentioned, a girl who is a prostitute, a suicidal maniac, and a sadist.

None of the above volumes sold very well but their author assures us that he was during all this time "hard-bellied" and "hard-gutted" and so did not mind their failure very much. Now, however, he found himself getting "a little soft." He had become tired of painting houses and carpentering. And so he decided to think up some deliberately "cheap idea" — something that would make him some real money! "I took a little time out, and speculated what a person in Mississippi would believe to be current trends, chose what I thought was the right answer and invented the most horrific tale I could imagine. . ."[6]

The tale that he invented, proved to be so horrific that it was deemed advisable not to publish it — for a while. "We'd both be in jail," his publisher wrote him. Perhaps they would have! *Sanctuary* deals, among other things, with a murder, a lynching, detailed scenes from a house of prostitution, and a disgusting "rape" of an innocent girl by an impotent degenerate — all the incidents deliberately timed and described to cause as much shock and offensiveness as possible. We can understand, I think, why Mr. Faulkner's publisher delayed bringing the book out!

That summer Mr. Faulkner therefore resigned himself to a life of manual labor. Securing a job on the night shift of a power-plant, he spent the early hours of the evening wheeling and dumping coal, still nursing, however, the dream of doing another novel. Then, while his fellow worker dozed, Faulkner rigged up a table out of a wheelbarrow; and, with the steady purring of dynamos to help him, in six weeks he wrote *As I Lay Dying* (1930) — the novel which he considers his best. Its success, despite its author's opinion of it, was not phenomenal; but it served at least to overcome its publisher's scruples sufficiently for him to release, in the following year, the book called *Sanctuary*, of which I have already spoken.

Because Mr. Faulkner considers *As I Lay Dying* his best book, I want to examine it somewhat more closely than space has permitted me to examine the other earlier novels. In general, it recounts the experiences of a Southern family — all of them cretins — who set out on a journey, that lasts for perhaps nine or ten days, with a putrefying corpse beside them in their wagon. But, more specifically, *As I Lay Dying* offers also a composite picture of the entire lives of the members of this family.

As the novel opens, the Mother, Addie, is dying. She has wrung a promise from her husband that he will bury her with her own "folks" in a cemetery some distance away. During the three or four days preceding her death, the oldest son is busy sawing up boards, fitting them together, and beveling them off, for her coffin. The screeching of the saw outside the window serves as a painful and horrible accompaniment to the macabre scene within the dirty house. From time to time, moreover, Cash, who is making the coffin, brings one of the boards up for his dying mother's careful inspection and approval! Two of the other sons, in the meantime, go off to earn three dollars by hauling produce; "hoping," however, that they will get back before their mother's death! One of the children, Darl, is an imbecile; the youngest son, Vardaman, continually identifies his dying mother with a bleeding fish he has seen; the daughter, Dewey Dell, is a demented creature who spends her time fanning the sick woman, and wondering how she can find some doctor who will consent to abort the child within her, for the ten dollars her lover has given her for this purpose.

But the coffin is finished at last, and Addie dies. The youngest son then bores holes through the top of the rough casket (to let his dead mother breathe!) and in so doing also bores holes through the corpse's face so that it has to be covered with mosquito netting during the funeral service. The clergyman arrives and we learn from his soliloquy that *he* is really the father of three of Addie's children! He says the prayers he has come to say, after this soliloquy; and the grim cortege sets out in a wagon with the box containing the now putrefying body.

Bridges have been washed out: for days the family is forced to carry along its loathsome burden. Buzzards begin to circle above the coffin. Once, while they are trying to ford a river, the whole wagon tips over; on another occasion, a barn, in which they had put the coffin for the night (because the wind had shifted), burns down and the body is rescued only with difficulty. One of the boys has his leg broken crossing the river: it is splinted by a veterinarian with ordinary cement; and, in the following days, this boy, too, lies in the wagon — on top of the casket. But they arrive — at last — at their destination; the father solemnly borrows spades to dig the grave; and then, after he has helped officers from an insane asylum pinion his idiot son, Darl, to take him away, he "borrows" the ten dollars which Dewey Dell had been saving for her abortion, and goes off to buy himself a set of false teeth! Such is the plot of Mr. Faulkner's "best" novel.

But we are told that the technique employed in *As I Lay Dying* is both new and interesting. It cannot be denied that it is intense in the way it makes use of a series of soliloquies, each designed to give us a different point of view toward the series of horrors — to light up, as it were, a different façade of this temple of pain and grotesquerie. By means of this method the reader is made to feel certain horrors over several times. Thus, even after the painful death scene, and even after the procession has started on its terrible journey, certain soliloquies bring us back and force us to witness that death and departure over again and again from different points of view. Other manifestations of this technique include a chapter which consists only of Cash's numerically listed reflections on carpentering; and another chapter which is made up of but one sentence, uttered by Vardaman: "My mother is a fish."

With the exception of *Absalom, Absalom!* — upon which I shall in a moment speak in some slight detail — I must content myself with but brief comment on the Faulkner books which succeeded *As I Lay Dying*. *These Thirteen* (1931) is a collection of painfully grim short stories containing characters that I shall refer to later; *Light In August* (1932) is a novel about a negro who murders his white mistress, and is tortured, castrated, and lynched; *A Green Bough* (1933) is a volume of "expressionistic" verse; *Doctor Martino* (1934), another collection of tales; and *Pylon* (1935) is another novel, dealing with an air-race pilot who has come to New Orleans to compete in a local race. He shares his wife with his parachute jumper, and does not, therefore, even know whether or not he is the father of his wife's child.

The characters in *Pylon* live in a typical Faulkner atmosphere of absinthe and execrable gin. They cannot speak without blaspheming, eat a sandwich without drooling, or get through a chapter without vomiting. One of them admits, indeed, that he has arrived at that unenviable stage where only the cigarette ends he picks off the floor have "any kick" to them. Nightmare. Neurotics. Nihilism.

We are assured by one of our most conservative literary reviewers that in *Absalom, Absalom!* (1936) there is "but a touch of incest and miscegenation, modestly and inoffensively added. . ."[7] Let us note this delicate "touch" as it manifests itself — "modestly and inoffensively" — in the plot of the most recent Faulkner novel.

After a colorful career in the West Indies, Thomas Sutpen abandons the wife he has there married, and comes to Mississippi, where, by some chicanery, he gains possession of a large tract of land and, with the help of twenty wild negroes he has brought with him, builds the largest home in the county. He marries Ellen Coldfield, the daughter of a deranged local merchant. Ellen bears Sutpen two children : Henry and Judith. In the meantime, however, he has had another daughter, Clytemnestra, by some negress ; and a son, whom he names Charles Bon, by a mulatto mistress. It is Sutpen's greatest delight, while his two white children are young, to take them into his barn and force them to watch him and one of his wild negroes — both of them almost naked — fighting each other and rolling upon the floor in a welter of blood and perspiration. The daughter is fascinated by the sight.

Later on, when Henry Sutpen grows up, he is sent to the University where he meets Charles Bon, whom, of course, he does not recognize as his brother. Bon has married an octoroon and has had a child ; but when he later meets Judith Sutpen, and even when he comes to know she is his own sister, he insists upon marrying her, and is prevented from so doing only when Henry murders him.

Years pass. Ellen Sutpen, old Sutpen's wife, has died. The Civil War is over ; and the old man wants a son to help him build up his estate. To his dead wife's sister he then proposes that she "breed" him a child, promising to marry her only if the child should be a boy. When Rosa Coldfield refuses this offer — made so "modestly and inoffensively" — Sutpen has the child by a negress on his estate. But it turns out to be a girl ; Sutpen insults the mother by telling her if she were only a mare, he might put her in his stables. To avenge this insult, the grandfather of the negress kills Sutpen by chopping him up with a scythe ; and then, after slitting the throats of his grand-daughter and her

new-born baby, surrenders himself to a sheriff's posse. The
novel then comes to an end when Clytie, the mulatto daughter of old Sutpen, sets the house on fire and, together with
Henry, perishes in the holocaust. Charles Bon's descendant,
the mulatto and idiot, Jim Bond, stands out in the yard,
howling and wailing, while the flames leap toward the red
sky.

". . . but a *touch* [8] of incest and miscegenation, modestly
and inoffensively added. . ."

The style of *Absalom, Absalom!* is easily the most involved that Faulkner has yet given us. Long lines of purely
parenthetical expression — in one instance almost a page of
them! — obtrude themselves between subjects and verbs.
The author continually finds it necessary to insert the name
of the speaker, or the antecedents of his pronouns, between
parentheses; and it is often difficult, even then, to tell who is
speaking. The time-focus of the narrative is hopelessly confused: in one sentence, for example, the author deals with
two events that actually happened fifty years apart, and fails
to distinguish between the two times!

Finally, *Absalom, Absalom!* is filled with such gibberish
as would make Father Divine's utterances conspicuous examples of lucidity. There are hundreds of phrases like these:
"that stultification of the burgeoning and incorrigible I," [9]
"polymath love's androgynous advocate," [10] "an anguished
emergence of the primary indomitable ossification." [11] And
the book is packed with such sheer nonsense as the following:
"In fact, perhaps this is the pure and perfect incest: the
brother realizing that the sister's virginity must be destroyed
in order to have existed at all, the man whom he would be if
he could become, metamorphose into, the lover, the husband; by whom he would be despoiled, choose for despoiler,
if he could become, metamorphose into the sister, the mistress, the bride." [12]

2

My preceding comment on the Faulkner books suggests two preoccupations which their author has: one with technique; and another with a world of pain, perversion, and violent cruelty. From this it will be seen that his work has a doubly sharp edge to it. The subject matter itself cuts deeply into the surface of our neurotic age; and the author's concern with a somewhat ingenious technique keeps his blade sharply honed for the horrors he then offers us.

Thus, he uses soliloquies to secure the effect of certain intense repetitions of his theme. He not only makes his readers peer through the door into the terrors of the temple; but he forces them to look, in turn, through each of several windows. What is more, Faulkner goes even further than this. He refuses to let his readers look through the windows with their own eyes; but instead, he has them see the violences within through the eyes of imbeciles, idiots, and morons.

What these cretins see is so much a part of their own perverted world that their very reporting of it seems mistakenly to be the grim reality of a world that is nothing *but* terror and cruelty. In *The Sound and the Fury* the idiot, Benjy, serves this purpose; in *As I Lay Dying* the same effect is achieved by the introduction of just a very few sane characters whose soliloquies lend violent contrast to the insanity of the moronic majority. And a similar plan is followed in most of the other Faulkner books.

That this technique secures its desired effects can hardly be denied. Its effect upon a reader is that not only of watching a succession of neurotics slinking along in a nightmare of horrors; but also of seeing those figures reflected back, as it were, in a whole series of mirrors which magnify their degeneracies. Mr. Faulkner also displays considerable skill in bringing about the cinematic association of ideas, in certain vivid and original word combinations, in an occasionally effective use of the stream-of-consciousness. And in a striking manner he employs italics to indicate rapid shifts from present time:

> But after Armstid gave pa a drink, he felt better, and when he went in to see about Cash *he hadn't come in with us. When I looked back he was leading the horse into the barn* he was already talking about getting another team, and by supper time he had good as bought it. *He is down there in the barn, sliding fluidly past the gaudy lunging swirl, into the stall with it. He climbs onto the manger and drags the hay down and leaves the stall and seeks and finds the curry-comb. Then he returns and slips quickly past the single crashing thump and up against the horse, where it cannot overreach. He applies the curry-comb, holding himself within the horse's striking radius with the agility of an acrobat, cursing the horse in a whisper of obscene caress. Its head flashes back, tooth-cropped; its eyes roll in the dusk like marbles on a gaudy velvet cloth as he strikes it upon the face with the back of the curry-comb.*[13]

Sharp as the Faulkner technique is, there are still a few nicks in its blade. His participles and his gerunds can dangle in desperation while Mr. Faulkner refuses to rescue a single one of them. Tortuous experiments often obfuscate his style; and what was in Crane an impressionistic method of art, most often becomes in Faulkner merely an obsession with the disagreeable. Not only does a road become an "eroded scar"; but band music resembles a "thin coating of tortured Tschaikovsky on a slice of stale bread"; [14] a man's eyes look like "two clots of phlegm"; and a waitress' hand seems to have "been conceived formed and baked in the kitchen." Again, words are run together in such a way as to make the expression annoyingly clumsy: "Yetdark," "August-tremulous," "garmentworried." Likewise, although Mr. Faulkner frequently employs the stream-of-consciousness effectively, he also frequently employs it merely as a sort of

tidal backwash to carry along such manifestations of logor-
rhea as these which I take from *Light In August* :

He was not thinking at all now ; thinking had not begun now ;
the voices had not begun now either.[15]

. . .

Memory lives before knowing remembers. Believes longer
than recollects, longer than knowing even wonders. Knows remembers believes a corridor in a big long garbled cold echoing
building of dark red brick sootbleakened by more chimneys than
its own, set in a grassless cinderstrewnpacked compound sur-
rounded by smoking factory purlieus and enclosed by a ten foot
steel-and-wire fence like a penitentiary or a zoo, where in random
erratic surges, with sparrowlike childtrebling, orphans in identical and uniform blue denim in and out of remembering but in
knowing constant as the bleak walls, the bleak windows where
in rain soot from the yearly adjacenting chimneys streaked like
black tears.[16]

. . .

Knowing not grieving remembers a thousand savage and lonely
streets.[17]

. . .

He thought for a while that he ran because of and toward some
destination that the running had suddenly remembered and
hence his mind did not need to bother to remember why he was
running, since the running was not difficult.[18]

And, finally, the stream-of-consciousness, as Mr. Faulkner
uses it, frequently becomes too clogged up with an association of mere fragmentary and irrelevant detail.   The stream
fails to flow.   To know what is going on in a character's
mind while he is planning to commit a murder may possibly
be significant.   But to be forced to follow the tortuous
thoughts of a man while he is wondering what he is eating,
is to note only a passage cluttered with incoherencies :

I'll know it in a minute.   I have eaten it before, somewhere.
In a minute I will memory clicking knowing *I see I see I more*

than see hear I hear I see my head bent I hear the monotonous
dogmatic voice which I believe will never cease going on and on
forever and peeping I see the indomitable bullet head the clear
blunt beard they too bent and I thinking How can he be so not-
hungry and I smelling my mouth and tongue weeping the hot salt
of waiting my eyes tasting the hot steam from the dish "It's
peas," he said, aloud.[19]

Mr. Arnold Bennett declared that Faulkner "writes like
an angel." If this be true, it is just as true, it seems to me,
that he troubles his waters somewhat much at times with a
technique which is, if anything, too experimental. His
stream-of-consciousness upon such occasions turns into a
seething whirl-pool of eccentricities; his phrases become
sharply impressionistic without being pleasantly impressive.

3

Mr. Faulkner's second preoccupation — namely, that with
a world of perversion and pain — seems at first sight to be but
a *deliberate exploitation* of what shocks and of what is abnormal. Mr. Faulkner has confessed an intentional and deliberate selection of such themes as are dealt with in *Sanctuary;* and he has illustrated it in the carefully considered
techniques of certain of his other books.

But, this preoccupation also derives from, and is inherent
in, Mr. Faulkner's point of view toward life — which he sees
as bitter, perverted, and cruel. "We are here to work. . ."
he says. "Where is there a law requiring we should be
happy?"[20] We are given our breath only "to want and fret
a span."[21] Were this preoccupation therefore less congeni-
tal, Faulkner might begin to outgrow it now that the necessity for its deliberate exploitation no longer exists — now that
his reputation is established.

Now that he is in the door, he might — were this obsession
not so inherent in his whole point of view toward life — be-

come willing to stop splashing blood all over the doorstep to attract our attention. But I do not think he will. He may do a book now and then that will be an exception; but on the whole I think his preoccupation too ingrained to permit his abandoning it. *Absalom, Absalom!*, his most recent novel, has a style so involved as to seem to conceal its author's concern with horror; actually, however, it marks no essentially new direction in Faulkner's interests.

By way of showing how deep-seated this interest in the abnormal has been, let me now introduce my readers to a few of the Faulkner characters:

Popeye : an impotent degenerate who manages, by a method too hideously vulgar to be mentioned, to rape an innocent school-girl. He can be remembered in one terrible scene, drooling saliva, and "making a high whinnying sound like a horse." At five he had been found, in the bathroom, cutting up two birds with a bloody scissors. Three months later he had done the same to a cat. As he grows older, however, in the pages of the novel in which he figures, Popeye turns to more elaborate cruelties.

An unnamed negro murderer in the same novel slashes his wife's throat with a razor. Her head tosses back "from the bloody regurgitation of her bubbling throat" as she runs up the lane in front of her cabin.

Snopes : a pervert, reminiscent of one of Anderson's Winesburg degenerates, who spends his nights on top of a porch, playing Peeping Tom.

Christmas : a negro who has an ugly affair with a white woman which ends with his murdering her, being caught, emasculated, and killed. He has no will of his own (except the will to do evil !). His creator tells us that it was impos-

sible for him to get outside this circle of his sensuality. And
Christmas himself echoes the same conviction.

Mr. McEachern : he whips young Joe Christmas at intervals
until, each time, the boy faints. Then he whips him again.
His punishment consists in making his victim study for
a while, whipping him, and then making him return to his
study.

Miss Burden : she has a repulsive affair with a negro. In the
midst of it she prays : "Dear God, let me be damned a little
longer, a little while."

Hightower : one of the cruelest of the Faulkner characters.
He deliberately tortures himself with the memory of the
wife who had left him. Another impotent degenerate.

Grimm : the head of a lynching party. To lynch his victim
he first cruelly tortures him and then deliberately fires a
whole succession of shots into the dying man. His specific
methods of torture are too offensive to be detailed.

Lena Grove : searching for the father of her child, she derives
an almost masochistic pleasure from babbling her whole story
to all the gawking and obscene men she meets along her
journey.

Emily : a perverted, morbid old maid, who, after being disappointed in love, lives out the rest of her life with only the
company of her negro man-servant. When she dies, they
find the body of the negro, decayed and sunk into the
mattress on his mistress' bed.

Minnie Cooper : an introvert and sadist who falsely accuses
a man of raping her and lets him be lynched just for the
vicarious pleasure of contemplating the man's dying agonies.

McLendon : a leader of one of the lynching parties : a gigantic symbol of every form of cruelty. After the lynching he goes home to wreak further cruelties upon his wife.

Susan Reed : in one of the stories we have traced for us the growth of a child into a mature woman of disreputable character. Her illicit loves are traced in detail; and we are told, in a reflection upon her, that in this world there is no such thing as *a* woman who is born bad, for the simple reason that *all* women are born bad : "born with the badness in them."

Such a list might, of course, be continued until it finally embraced at least nine-tenths of the Faulkner men and women. I have merely mentioned a few of the characters to give an idea of the general nightmare in which most of them walk. For to read these books is to cross a desert of terrifying nihilism; and in the midst of heavy silence to come at the most unexpected intervals upon crouching horrors, piles of what we would scarcely guess might once have been human bones, placed at almost mathematically calculated distances to afford us a maximum of shock.

We know that they have most often been deliberately piled there only to fascinate and frighten ; to keep us waiting in fearful expectancy ; and to draw us on, with our hair on end, to the next horrible scene. We cannot be expected to have any pity for the story their awful presence tells ; for that story fails to transfigure any human experience, to lift us above the image itself, or to suggest anything but the way in which cruelty can be used to curdle our blood.

All of this is not to say that Mr. Faulkner is without talent. On the contrary, I think he displays abilities that go far beyond even the technical ingenuities I have credited him with. He can create, when he really *wants* to, and despite his apparent belief in the prevailing harshness of life, characters that are human, full, and satisfying. Note, for example, the warm feeling and the humanity in the following portrait from *Sartoris*:

This was Dr. Lucius Quintus Peabody, eighty-seven years' old and weighing three hundred and ten pounds and possessing a digestive tract like a horse. He had practised medicine in the county when a doctor's equipment consisted of a saw and a satchel of calomel; he had been John Sartoris' regimental surgeon, and up to the day of the automobile he would start out at any hour of the twenty-four in any weather and for any distance, over practically impassable roads in a lopsided buckboard, to visit anyone, white or black, who sent for him, accepting for fee usually a meal of corn pone and coffee, or perhaps a small measure of corn or fruit, or a few flower bulbs or graftings.
When he was young and hasty he had kept a daybook, kept it meticulously until these hypothetical assets totaled $10,000. But that was forty years ago, and since then he hadn't bothered with a record at all; and now from time to time a countryman enters his shabby office and discharges an obligation, commemorating sometimes the payer's entry into the world, incurred by his father or grandfather, which Dr. Peabody himself had long since forgotten about. Every one in the county knew him and it was said that he could spend the balance of his days driving about the county in the buckboard he still used, with never a thought for board and lodging and without the expenditure of a penny for either. He filled the room with his bluff and homely humanity. . .[22]

Or, observe the undercurrent of humor in this picture of Miss Jenny from the same novel. A neighbor has enquired about her grand-nephew, who had been reported as hurt in an accident.

Miss Jenny thanked her tartly for her solicitude, and dared to say that Bayard was all right: still an active member of the so-called human race, that is, since they had received no official word from the coroner. No, she had heard nothing of him since Loosh Peabody 'phoned her at four o'clock that Bayard was on his way home with a broken head. The broken head she readily believed, but the other part of the message she had put no credence in whatever, having lived with those damn Sartorises eighty

years and knowing that home would be the last place in the
world a Sartoris with a broken head would ever consider going.
No, she was not even interested in his present whereabouts, and
she hoped he hadn't injured the horse. Horses were valuable
animals.[23]

Or, note the admirable quality of this description :

The moon had got up beyond the dark eastern wall of hills
and it lay without emphasis upon the valley, mounting like a
child's balloon behind the oaks and locusts along the drive.
Bayard sat with his feet on the veranda rail, in the moonlight.
His cigar glowed at spaced intervals, and a shrill monotone of
crickets rose from the immediate grass, and further away, from
among the trees, a fairy-like piping of young frogs like endless
silver small bubbles rising. A thin, sourceless odor of locust
drifted up, intangible as fading tobacco-wraiths, and from the
rear of the house, up the dark hall, Elnora's voice floated in
meaningless minor suspense.[24]

This is good writing — from Faulkner's best book. But it
is significant that when *Sartoris* proved unsuccessful, Faulkner
turned so deliberately to the exploitation of cruelty. And,
with one or two exceptions, he has since continued that
exploitation ; he has preferred to outrage sensibilities rather
than develop the special qualities of warmth and normal
human feeling displayed in *Sartoris*.

This, I say, is a significant thing. I say, also, that Mr.
Faulkner's preoccupations are bringing him face to face with
a dilemma which is an interesting one. For the more complete his exploitation with cruelty becomes, the less effective
it is. One might say that the more successful Faulkner is
in intensifying his horrors, the less successful he becomes as
a novelist.

"Those who play the game of exploiting the *frisson nou-
veau* find that its stakes are continually rising ; each must raise
his predecessor's ante. Mr. Faulkner has evidently determined not to be a piker." [25]   Mr. Faulkner has also, be it
added, just about arrived at that point where he cannot

raise the ante. What is he to do now? Already his horrors begin to give that effect we get from a parody — a fact
which I can illustrate by asking my readers to compare the
two following selections: the first from one of the Faulkner
novels; and the second from a parody done on the same
book:

He saw, facing him across the spring, a man of under size, his
hands in his coat pockets, a cigarette slanted from his chin. His
suit was black, with a tight, high-waisted coat. His trousers
were rolled once and caked with mud above mud-caked shoes.
His face had a queer, bloodless color, as though seen by electric
light; against the sunny silence, in his slanted straw hat and his
slightly akimbo arms, he had that vicious depthless quality of
stamped tin.[26]

·   ·   ·

They saw, facing them across the spring, a man of under size,
with two revolvers drawn and a slim dagger in his teeth. His
face had a queer bloodless color, like old rancid lard. Behind
him the bird sang again, in monotonous repetition; a sound
meaningless and profound, like the last drain in the kitchen sink.
Popeye reached around and wrung its neck, and commenced to
eat it slowly, without removing the dagger.[27]

Are Mr. Faulkner's novels eventually to become parodies
of themselves?

4

Whatever they become we ought in the meantime to remember that the most vicious aspect of such writing derives
from the fact that it is only part of a whole cult which
brutalizes human nature and blunts our emotional sensibilities. "There is a pleasure that is born of pain." Bounding against the sounding board of our neurotic age, this idea
of Meredith's is beginning to reverberate until its echoes
are being caught up in the work of enough of our writers

to make the tendency, when seen even as a tendency, an unpleasant one to contemplate.

It is not a new literary direction, but it is one which is gaining, I think, a dangerous acceleration. The publication in this country, some years ago, of Karl Huysmans' *A Rebours* (*Against the Grain*) was, indeed, but a symptom of our growing fondness for that kind of morbid microscopy which has since been filtering into our fiction with an ever increasing thoroughness.

Huysmans' Des Esseintess, it will be recalled, derived great enjoyment from the most morbid contemplations. A neurasthenic and a victim of dyspepsia, he found himself, for example, strangely fascinated by the decorations in his room: ". . . a collection of appalling plates representing all the tortures which the savagery of religious intolerance has invented, plates exhibiting all the horrors of human agony — men roasted over braziers, skulls laid open by sword cuts, pierced with nails, riven asunder with saws, bowels drawn out of the belly, and twisted round rollers, finger nails torn out one by one with pincers, eyes put out, eyelids turned back and transfixed with pins, limbs dislocated or carefully broken bones laid bare and scraped for hours with knives." [28] Much of our modern fiction is becoming merely a series of such plates of horror.

Robinson Jeffers, with whom Faulkner has often been compared, has also etched a share of such plates in our poetry. He has been called "the poet of tragic terror"; [29] but let it be added in his favor that his use of pain and violence often transcends mere terror to become tragedy and to make us see a vision of humanity transfigured above the cruelty itself. And yet, not always is this true. I do not agree with that large number of our critics who have insisted that Jeffers' high poetic sensitivity has always justified his material and his handling of that material. And

even when it does, his easy discovery of violence and perversion in the abundant neuroses of our times, is at least
symbolic of the whole tendency of which I have been
speaking.

In *The Women at Point Sur* (1927) a father, whom
Nietzsche would have loved for his religion of the superman, rapes his own daughter. *Cawdor* (1928) describes a
young girl who marries to assure herself and her aging father
a living; and then, after failing in an attempt to seduce her
husband's son, deliberately inflames the old man by telling
him the son has raped her. The girl tries to commit
suicide; and the old man "punishes" himself by piercing
out his own eyes! "This must be life, this hot pain," says
Fera. For pain is to pleasure what the sun is to the candle!

In one of the poems in *Dear Judas* (1929) we are introduced to a girl who murders her father when he discovers
one of her illicit relationships; who then turns masochist
herself; and who, finally, becomes obsessed with the idea of
atoning for her crime by freely surrendering her body to
make as many men as possible happy. For, it is her conviction that all human pain "comes from restraint of love."
All of which comes about as close to the Greek concept of
tragedy as Mr. O'Neill's *Mourning Becomes Electra*.

And yet, horrible as the Jeffers themes are, who of us can
deny his genius as a poet? Usually, let me repeat, he does
employ violence, not for its value as a crudely perceived
series of facts, but for its worth as a transfiguring symbol.
The same cannot be said, however, for many of the novels
done by the members of our cult of cruelty. In the brief,
though representative, list of those I am about to offer,
many are well conceived and beautifully written; but almost
all of them impinge likewise upon the unnecessary exploitation of certain abnormalities and violences.

Evelyn Scott's *The Narrow House* (1921) is a study of the
most confined hates and sadistic tendencies; the same im-

pounding pain and the same perverted cruelties are reported in her *Narcissus* (1922); and the whole tone of her *The Golden Door* (1925) is set by one of the characters of whom it is said that he had "no language for anything but pain." *Migrations* (1927) — as rich and as excellently written as the other Scott novels — portrays a negro lashed into a bloody welter until the "exquisiteness of pain left him slightly faint"; and a French lover "who was so brutal and so direct in his brutality" as to possess "a charm that was most engaging." [30]

Vardis Fisher's *The Vridar Hunter Tetralogy* is a veritable casebook of cruelties; and Morley Callaghan's novels, taken as a whole, are grimly lighted photographs of the most stark brutalities. One of them, for example, painfully records the derangement of a monomaniac obsessed with the idea of becoming a modern Aquinas. In a painfully detailed scene the insane man is even made to watch his wife in an illicit love with one of his friends. Another of the Callaghan characters first abducts a child; then brutally attacks the child's mother; and is finally captured in a scene as graphic as any of the Faulkner lynching episodes.

Certain of the novels of Kay Boyle reveal the same morbid microscopy, despite the beautifully limpid English in which they are written, and the delicate poignancy with which parts of them are conceived. *Death of a Man* (1936), her latest novel, is aptly described by one critic as "an immersion in neuroticism." [31] Dr. Prochaska, its central character, sees nothing to look forward to "because of the absolute cessation of living"; enmeshes himself in a love affair with a young and slightly insane woman who has, even during her honeymoon, discarded her husband as easily as one would discard an old hat; and then tries to find his way out of a morass of conflicting emotions by throwing himself as a sacrifice upon the altar of Hitlerism. *Gentlemen, I Address You Privately* (1933) not only borders upon the neurotic throughout, but verges off ultimately into the dark fringe of a perverted sex relationship. *Year Before Last* (1932) focuses its attention upon two lovers who travel about from one French hotel to another, while the man suffers a series of hemorrhages which are the result of his having been gassed in the War. All the while he derives a masochistic pleasure from a cruel "love" which one of his aunts bears for him.

And *Plagued by the Nightingale* (1931) — to go back to Miss Boyle's earliest novel — is the story of a young Frenchman who returns to his family in France with an American bride. The men of the family — including Nicolas, all suffer from an incurable bone disease; as a result, Nicolas does not want to have a child. When his father offers him a large sum of money providing he will consent to a child, Nicolas bitterly suggests to his wife that she deliberately find some other father for it. Hate for his family stifles him until his "mind is twisted and fixed in agony in his head":

Hate and hate and hate was in Nicolas' glance for each face at the table. Hate and hate for everyone except for Charlotte's face, but even for her he had some little irritation now because she had not protested and because she was willing to accept censure from Jean and Papa as if it were their right to dole out sense and reason to her. Hate and hate for Maman's face and her adroit toothpick spiking out great locks of shaggy artichoke at which she nibbled nervously. And hate for Luc's unfeeling cleanliness and charm. Like a man's face ill and turning on his pillow in pain, Nicolas' face turned from one to the other of them, eyeing them all. Hate for Marthe's hysteria and hate for Annick's unselfish heart that bade her not take the veil. Hate for Julie's sullenness that was a barrier to her womanhood, and hate for his own wife who should have somehow mastered circumstances and made the family bosom but a temporary resting-place. Hate it was that made him turn up Bridget and hold her captive in his bitter eye.[32]

William March's *Come in at the Door* (1934) features one character who, when abandoned by his prostitute-wife, finds pleasure in having his body tattooed as a symbol of his frustration; another who is a practitioner of the horrors of a certain voodoo cult; and a third whose whole life is shattered because, as a boy, he had watched one of his father's servants cruelly executed. Erskine Caldwell's *Tobacco Road* (1932) without a doubt owes much of its morbid appeal to the violences and cruelties which it reflects; and the same author's *God's Little Acre* (1933) sandwiches thick slices of sensuality between one brutality after another. "There was a mean trick played on us somewhere," observes one of the imbeciles in the book. "God put us in the bodies of animals and tried to make us act like people." [33]

Cinnamon Seed (1934), by Hamilton Basso, studies the violent effects which a father's suicide has on his son; the three volumes of Farrell's *Studs Lonigan* trilogy, and his somewhat recent *A World I Never Made*, run the entire gamut of brutality; and in Paul Green's excellent indictment of the chain-gang, *This Body the Earth* (1935), a whole series of cruelties culminate in a brutal flogging: "The prone body bounded from the ground like a rubber ball. . . And all the while the great Negro murderer who held Spike's head down in the dirt stared at the tattered pieces of bloody buttocks with a sickened hypnotic gaze." [34] Finally, the popularity of many of the stories in Ernest Hemingway's *Men Without Women* (1927) and in his *Winner Take Nothing* (1933) is in some small respect the result of this author's growing preoccupation with the abnormal. . . No purpose would be served by my listing further titles. I have already suggested the extent to which this cult of cruelty has grown among our present-day novelists.

Robert Gay once remarked [35] that he liked to think of every really great book as having at least one window open toward infinity. Classical literature, withal that it made use of every violence, still kept this window open. Hates were not confined; abnormalities were not used to titillate the jagged sensibilities of readers. Use the term so odious to modern critics, if you will, and say that classical literature had a "cathartic" value. Or say, simply, that it kept one window open toward infinity.

Our cult-of-cruelty writers close this window. The novelist who turns the majority of his puppets into degenerates looking with frustration only upon a cruel, bleak, and barren world—such a novelist closes this window. Like William Faulkner, and the rest of the cult, he may be an adept at showing us the *inside* of the house—a house of horrors. The intervenence of his cruelties may cause us, for a time, to rivet our gaze upon the nightmare within. But the distinctly human element in all of us makes us want to advance a bit; the divine element in all of us makes us want the window opened toward infinity. "A true classic," said Sainte-Beuve, "is an author who has enriched the human mind, increased its treasure and caused it to advance a step."

CHAPTER IX

THOMAS WOLFE EMBRACES LIFE

"It may be objected, it has been objected already by certain critics, that in such research as I have here attempted to describe there is a quality of intemperate excess, an almost insane hunger to devour the entire body of human experience, to attempt to include more, experience more, than the measure of one life can hold, or than the limits of a single work of art can well define. I readily admit the validity of this criticism."— Thomas Wolfe, in *The Story of a Novel*, p. 46.[1]

CHAPTER IX

THOMAS WOLFE EMBRACES LIFE

AND then when Gulliver awoke among the Lilliputians he was astonished to find himself tied to the ground with several slender ligatures across his body. And Gulliver, in astonishment and pain, roared to the skies. . .

Six and a half feet tall, and weighing two hundred pounds, Thomas Wolfe, our modern Gulliver among novelists, stood by while his editor, Maxwell Perkins, bound him with the slender ligatures of a criticism which had just cut some fifty thousand words from *Of Time and the River*. Wolfe banged his fist on the table; and then his gargantuan voice exploded: "This is the greatest crime since Judas betrayed Christ!" [2]

In pain, and with all the trials that author's flesh is heir to, Wolfe has written millions of words; he has banged his fist, I suppose, upon the Perkins desk a good many times while his work was being cut; he has even lopped away hundreds of passages of his own accord. Despite all this, he has still written two of the bulkiest books of our day. For example, when he delivered to his publishers the manuscript of "The October Fair"—later to go into *Of Time and the River*—it alone ran to over a million words: the length of twelve ordinary-sized novels! Again, as but an introductory *chapter* to the book the author found that he had written over a hundred thousand words of a description which told merely of a train hurling across a Virginia night!

On another occasion his fecund mind led him to fill in five minutes of actual time with a dialogue—of eighty thousand words!—a dialogue that would have taken up four hours! And so it was through both of his manuscripts: chapters of fifty thousand words always had to be cut down to about fifteen thousand. Some of us may wish he had pruned them even more; let us remember the artistic craftsmanship which prompted him to cut so ruthlessly what he did. There is no doubt about it. Thomas Wolfe is an artist of sincerity and integrity. That is the first thing to be said about him.

The second observation to be made is that out of his teeming mass of verbiage there has emerged, I think, not only the powerful individuality of a man who is one of our most promising younger novelists; but also some of the most eloquent writing, some of the most flashing figures, and most colorful transcripts of life that have yet woven themselves into the noticeably drab texture of our modern prose. Thomas Wolfe knows how to write; he knows how to tell a story, to give sweep and breadth to his canvas, and to infuse a gleaming vitality into his characters that is of the stuff of life itself.

Furthermore, he has inherited very few of the effete sterilities, and little of the egomania, of his age; and he is significant, among many other things, because he has proved that not only is the American novel not dead, but that it is even capable of growing strong again if it seek its greatness in the fullness of American life. Thomas Wolfe opposes our present-day mechanism with vitalism; in place of "escapist" novels filled with sophistication and ennui, he offers us books that are filled with all the hungers of the human heart. We need that kind of writing today; and we need it badly.

A "Gargantua bestriding the world," an "elephantine Proust," "the Whitman among novelists"—our critics have not been slow in acclaiming his genius. Sinclair Lewis has even gone so far as to say that "If Wolfe keeps up the promise of *Look Homeward, Angel,* he has a chance to be the greatest American writer of all time."

Extravagant? Perhaps so. But at least Thomas Wolfe is

the most *promising* of our younger writers. What is more
to the point, he is promising, among other things, because
he is growing and because he is so conscious of his inadequacies. There is none of that over-confidence in him — none
of the flippant disdain for critical tradition — that characterizes so many of our other younger writers. He admits that
he is not a skilled writer; he fervently insists that he is trying desperately only to find a language that will make his
articulateness more disciplined. He listens to the critics
patiently. He is tremendously sincere. And he is honestly
determined. "I'll learn 'em, yet," he once wrote jocularly
to a friend.[8] I, for one, think he has a good chance to do so!

1

Wolfe does not remember exactly when he first thought of
becoming a writer. As a boy peddling papers in Asheville's
Niggertown, he listened to the whistling trains that hurled
themselves into the immense mountains beyond his home.
He was filled with wonder about that remote world into
which those trains disappeared; and he was, even then,
seized by certain of those nameless hungers which were to be
so characteristic of his later work. But when he thought of
writers he thought of them always as resembling distantly
strange and formidable fellows like Tennyson, Longfellow,
or Byron. One thing did, however, inculcate in the boy a
genuine love of literature. In his home he heard poetry —
long tidal waves of it that rushed forth as his father, a stone-
cutter, gave rhetorical recitations from *Hamlet,* Gray, the
Mark Antony "Funeral Oration," *Macbeth.* And later on,
the memorable recitative quality of this verse was to find its
way into the author's own headlong rhetoric and apostrophes
and declamations and tropes, as he went about the world
still hungering at the symbol of a stone, a leaf, a door.

At Chapel Hill Wolfe edited the college paper; also, he

wrote three plays: *The Return of Buck Gavin, Deferred Payment,* and *The Third Night: A Ghost Play of the Carolina Mountains.* The first of these was his first published work (see *Carolina Folk Plays, Second Series,* 1924); the author himself acted in it so successfully that the nickname "Buck" stuck with him through his college days.

He went to Harvard where under Baker he wrote more plays in the famous Workshop. But all the while he was dissatisfied with the drama as a vehicle for his many ideas that clamored for utterance. He realized that he could no more find expression in the drama than a whale can be confined in a goldfish bowl; and so he left for London where, in a Chelsea sitting-room, he began to fill up large ledgers with the story of *Look Homeward, Angel.* Later he returned to New York to instruct in one of the universities there, and to finish his book.

But a publisher turned it down; and so Wolfe left for Europe again. While there, Scribners sent for him. They gave him a contract when he returned; and the young author one morning walked out into the Fifth Avenue crowds at the Scribner office to think about the five hundred dollar check in his hand and find himself, at last, up at 110th Street without ever knowing how he had got there![4]

Look Homeward, Angel sold steadily, but, nevertheless, its author worried. Returning at night to the unwashed breakfast cup, the scattered books, and the cast off shirt in his apartment, he wondered if he could do another novel, or if he was "just a flash in the pan." He was filled with conscientious misgivings. He learned, in bitter moments, when publicity was seeking him out, that an honest author really wants to forget his books as soon as the travail of giving them birth is over. He became fearfully aware of the fact that the "naked intensity" of his first novel would have to be disciplined when he came to write another book.

Also, there was the hostile reception of the novel in his

native town. That worried him. One man wrote that he would kill Wolfe if the author ever came home; an old friend took unfeigned pleasure in telling him she would like to see his "big over-groan karkus" hauled across the public square of Asheville; he was even preached against in pulpits. For the town thought it had been exposed; it felt naked in the presence of his genius.

Actually, Wolfe did not intend that first novel as autobiography: though he had admittedly drawn upon familiar characters and scenes — and what novelist does not? — he had tried to give those characters and scenes the transfiguring and imperishable qualities of art. It was, Mr. Wolfe tells us, as if some farmer should tell him he knew the farm from which his clay had been taken. But the shaping was his own.

In February, 1930, he resigned from New York University and in that spring went to Europe on a Guggenheim fellowship. There he found that for a while he could not write. But finally his old hungers came back to him; and out of his need for the America he had left he discovered an America that he could write about again. He found new materials. A galvanized iron railing around the Atlantic City boardwalk, the jinking of bottles in a milk-wagon on an American street in the early morning, scenes of his boyhood — all this he remembered; and out of this raw beauty he saw that he must fashion his next novel. Moreover, he resolved to find a new language to give articulation to his new hunger.

Like the Ancient Mariner, therefore, he had to tell his tale. And so he began to shape in his mind the pattern, not of one, but of three books he wanted to do. For he had a central idea that would unite them all: "And this central idea was this: the deepest search in life, it seemed to me, the thing that in one way or another was central to all living was man's search to find a father, not merely the father of his flesh, not merely the lost father of his youth, but the image of a strength and wisdom external to his need and superior to his hunger, to which the belief and power of his own life could be united." [5]

More ledgers were filled up; and, finally, in the spring of 1931 Thomas Wolfe returned to America with about four hundred thousand words written. Then it was that two difficult problems presented themselves to his conscientious and creative mind — that of the time element; and that of getting all his wealth of material into one book.

The former problem Wolfe solved when he realized the imperious necessity of actually using *three* time elements: present time to advance the narrative; past time to trace the backgrounds of his characters; and the immutable time of rivers, of oceans, and of mountains, to secure a rhythmic effect by contrasting those immutabilities with the brevity of man's life upon the earth. The latter problem Wolfe solved by deciding that he would write *several* new novels — novels that would deal with a century and a half of history, employ over two thousand characters, and be a vast panoramic study of American races!

Having determined upon this objective, he at once set to work with a kind of savage intensity. Here is the plan of the series he contemplated, with the books in the order of their probable appearance, and with the time plan of each:

Look Homeward, Angel	1884-1920	(published 1929)
Of Time and the River	1920-1925	(published 1935)
The October Fair	1925-1928	
The Hills Beyond Pentland	1838-1926	
The Death of the Enemy	1928-1933	
Pacific End	1791-1884	

By day he slaved, and at night he dreamed of slaving. Hours and hours he spent at his typewriter; but still when he lay down after the day's work he found he could not sleep. Then he would rise again, turn on the light, read what he had written, and go back to bed, only to dream of mountains of unmarked student themes and of classes still waiting for him after all the months he had been in Europe!

But *Of Time and the River* was published at last, and two more of the novels were written in rough draft. There came the day finally when Maxwell Perkins informed him that his second novel was finished. With relief Wolfe turned the manuscript over to his publishers before fleeing to Europe to await its release, in painful anxiety as he wondered what the critics would say about it. For three days like a mad monster he paced the streets of Paris waiting for news of his novel's reception. But Scribners cabled him at last. The news they had for him I do not have to repeat.

2

As the reveries which Mr. Wolfe brought together under the title *From Death to Morning* (1935) do little more than illustrate the many merits and the few deficiencies which the two previous novels had displayed, it will be sufficient if I refer to them later on when I come to amplify my remarks on the novels themselves. The contents of the novels, however, will first have to be understood clearly as a basis for this later discussion.

Look Homeward, Angel (the title is derived from Milton's *Lycidas*) is a panoramic first novel which chronicles, at least in large part, the life in Wolfe's own family up through the second decade of our century, when Eugene, its autobiographical and central character, leaves his home in North Carolina to go to Harvard. Wolfe's own father, William Oliver Wolfe, in the novel becomes Oliver Gant; and the author's mother, Julia Elizabeth Westall, becomes Mrs. Gant. Oliver Gant, the stone-cutter, powerful, lecherous, and querulous, marries Eliza Pentland to found the large family with which *Look Homeward, Angel* and its sequel, *Of Time and the River*, both deal.

While a boy Oliver Gant had seen companies of begrimed Rebels filing past his mother's farm; after the War he had landed in Baltimore; there he had become fascinated as he watched a passive stone-cutter carving out cherubim and lambs on granite tombstones. As a result, he had apprenticed himself to this stone cutter; and had finally set up his own shop. Eliza Gant, his wife, has a passion for wealth: while her husband carves "the smooth joined marble hands of death" on cold slabs of marble, she buys Dixieland, a great boarding house, and works night and day to keep boarders, that she might invest in more property. Eliza has little time for tenderness toward any of her many children; and Oliver Gant, the father, pauses seldom in his orgies of drinking and cursing, and then only long enough to revile his wife and family.

Look Homeward, Angel thus becomes, from one point of view, a study of the way in which the Gant children are drawn into the net spun out of their mother's calculating parsimony and their father's bitterness and lust. Two of the children escape only by death; and Eugene, the youngest son, a dreaming youth who cannot find his way out of the querulous atmosphere of his home, goes to Harvard in the end; but he still carries with him a feeling of bitter futility and hunger born of those early days.

In the sequel he neither escapes from his earlier futilities nor satisfies his hunger. *Of Time and the River* covers the time which Eugene spent in Professor Hatcher's [Baker's] play-writing class at Harvard, his career as an instructor in a large New York university, and his travels in Europe. Nostalgia and nameless hungers and frustrations remain with Eugene Gant even there: he becomes a prototype of the exile and the wanderer, destined ravenously to feed himself upon human experience and, finding no experience that satiates him, to drive himself on across the earth for ever.

There are some gloriously vital and unforgettable scenes in these books; their author's intense passion for eloquence has flowed into countless declamatory passages and whole pages of apostrophe; and his retentive memory, apparently a gigantic repository of all that his senses have ever apprehended, unloads itself of sights and sounds and tastes and smells, in his attempt to reconstruct, as fully as possible, every moment of his hero's past. There are dozens of biting parodies, hundreds of rhapsodic paragraphs of sensitive writing, a score of swift and sure satires, and a whole riot of colorful and gleaming characters to fill up the rich panorama.

The scene, for example, in which Ben dies; that describing Horse Hines the undertaker; that in the hospital in which old Gant is dying of cancer; those which burlesque Eugene's play-writing class or his teaching experiences — such scenes it is impossible to forget. You may like them; you may possibly be repulsed by them; but you cannot, in any circumstance, be indifferent to them.

They are some of the most powerful scenes that have yet been created in our American prose.

3

I have had some good things to say about Thomas Wolfe; and it is, indeed, only right that I should have said them. But it is now my intention to show just how certain limitations and points of view which this novelist possesses, justify my including.him in these inquiries into our new literary order. This literary order I see as one which has inherited certain late nineteenth century, and even more recent, dehumanizing attitudes toward the universe and toward the "insignificant and discordant" part which man plays in that universe. With all his freshness and force, Thomas Wolfe

has fallen heir to more of these tendencies than we are likely
to suspect.

The grappling-hooks of art. There is one of Mr. Wolfe's
characters [6] who claims that he will not only have the whole
cake of the world, but that he will eat it, too. Like this
character, Thomas Wolfe seems to be content with nothing
less than *all* of life taken at one great gulp. Not only this
— not only does he seem to think it the writer's duty to
"embrace" and "devour" *life* — but it becomes also the duty
of the artist to "fix" *eternity,* as he says, with "the grappling-
hooks of his own art." [7] In *Of Time and the River* it is
said of one of Eugene Gant's experiences that it became part
of the memory of his whole life — a life in which he could
forget no single part.

Wolfe, too, seems unable to *forget* anything: his technique
demands the inclusion of every fact and detail. As a result,
his canvas becomes too crowded with incidents and names and
ideas simply because he has disregarded the first principle of
enduring art — that of artistic selection. He forgets, in other
words, that genius must be disciplined. And long passages
of his novels show this lack of discipline, resembling as they
do, the diary kept by Eugene Gant himself: ". . . picked
out at random from the ferment of ten thousand pages,
and a million words — put down just as they were written,
in fragments, jots, or splintered flashes. . ." [8]

The Wolfe method of writing — that of crowding huge
ledgers full of fragmentary descriptions which have no design
— somehow feeds our author's ravenous hunger with too indiscriminate a diet. In his eagerness to "devour" the whole
of life he attempts to satiate his gargantuan appetite by
pouring into the monstrous maw of his literary method as
much raw experience as possible, grinding it all down into
an undigested mass of epithets and as many adjectives as
he can find.

Thus, his characters all seem to breathe "stertorously"; Eugene not only grins, but grins "in his entrails"; people not only curse, but they do so "in a tone of mincing and ironic refinement"; a lover must speak with "kissy, wettie talkie"; the hysteria of the Gant family is not only "welled" but "agglutinated"; laughter is not only "confused" but a "twiddle-giggle"; crowds are always the "man-swarm"; people cannot yawn unless they do so "cavernously"; men never smile except "lewdly"; an odor is not simply an odor, but "one huge gigantic Stink, a symphonic Smell, a vast organ-note of stupefying odor, cunningly contrived, compacted, and composed of eighty-seven separate several putrefactions." 9

As a consequence of this technique, pages of his novels read like a railroad time-table; and whole chapters of them sound like a lesson in geography. He loves to pile up boring catalogues of details and meaningless autobiographical reminiscences. He not only uses too much of the clay of experience for his modeling, but too often he fails to give any model whatsoever to the clay. Moreover, he affirms too little beyond his own hungers and a "thirst that gulps down rivers and remains insatiate." 10

So it is that, paradoxically enough, Thomas Wolfe frequently offers, with all his negations, not only a picture of a man who would both have and eat his cake, but the autobiographical portrait of a man who, in despair and futility, insists that there is not even any cake! There is only the hunger for cake.

A "phantom flare of grieved desire." Those unconscionably long catalogues of details are not worthy of Thomas Wolfe's fresh power. Further, many of them are just as tedious as the tired accents and stale repetitions of the Dreiserian school. Reminiscent of this school, also, are certain of Mr. Wolfe's attitudes toward the insignificance of man, in other words, toward man as a puppet: "We are a phantom flare of grieved desire, the ghostling and phosphoric flicker of immortal time. . ." [11]

One of the Wolfe characters is described as a "grain of human dust, an atom thrust by chance into the great roar of a distant city. . ." [12] Others are referred to as "atoms on the huge breast of the indifferent earth. . ." [13] And all of the Gants, though creatures of demoniac energy, are nevertheless so *ineffectual as human beings* that "with an insane fatalism they had surrendered to the savage chaos of life." [14]

Thomas Wolfe has learned how to give space to life; but that space often becomes a great chasm in which his characters fall, a cosmic vortex into which they are sucked, as creatures who are dwarfed, in everything except energy and hunger, by the magnitude of desolation encompassing them. They become, in the words of the author himself, merely people who thrive upon the "inexorable tides of Necessity . . . fanning with their prayers the useless altar flames, suppliant with their hopes to an unwitting spirit, casting the tiny rockets of their belief against remote eternity, and hoping for grace, guidance, and delivery upon the spinning and forgotten cinder of this earth." [15]

In literature of great and enduring proportions the author is justified in making man fall to any depth. But to get this proportion the author must first place man up high enough so that he CAN fall to some great depth.

The "groping accident of life." The Wolfe characters all confront life blindly: they are caught up in its "variety" and "strangeness"; but they present the contradictory spectacle of men without spiritual eyesight telling us over and over again of the wonder and the beauty they see. As Ben says in *Look Homeward, Angel:* "What's it all about? . . . Is it really so, or is somebody playing a joke on us?" [16] Again,

he asks: "Where do we come from? Where do we go to?
What are we here for? What the hell is it all about?" [17]
What the hell is it all about? In all the millions of words
which Mr. Wolfe has so far written this question has come,
I think, hardly any nearer to finding some intellectually
satisfying answer.

Loved with a monkey wrench. Again, in these novels, the
characters live continually not only in the "insane fatalism"
of life, but in an atmosphere so surcharged with sweltering
fury and hate that it is hard to *distinguish them as in-
dividuals.* Every one of them is seen through Eugene's —
or their author's — own fury and temperament: as they all
have the same ravenous appetites and bellow in the same
way, the reader, losing all the effect that Mr. Wolfe might
have gained by contrast, comes to feel that none of them
have very unusual zests, and that none of them is, after all,
speaking as loudly as he might. All emotions are given the
same significance: Gant lusts with only the same enthusiasm
with which he eats his breakfast.

Mr. Wolfe himself admits that the Gants "were so used
to the curse, the clamor, and the roughness, that any variation into tenderness came as a cruel affectation." [18] And one
of the Gant sisters "loves" her young brother so much that
her very love goads her into a fury which prompts her to
throw him down on the floor and stamp on him! As a
final neat little picture of family affection among the Gants,
let me remind readers of the incident in which Big Brother
— only in "an agony of petulance," however! — strikes at his
young brother's shin with a monkey wrench, knocks him to
the ground, and cripples him! [19]

"Ten million hours of cruelty or indifference." In *Of
Time and the River* Thomas Wolfe suggests another one of
his outmoded adherences when he observes that "The man

who suggests the strangeness and variety of this life most is Sherwood Anderson." [20]   The characters which Mr. Wolfe has created, however, at times outdo Anderson's in savagery, bitterness, and futility to such an extent that Anderson's Winesburg seems, by comparison, a cheerful little Dutch village sketched by Washington Irving!

All members of the Gant family seem to hate one another. Old Gant himself is almost always in some drunken orgy: the night that Eugene is born, Mrs. Gant has to lock herself in her room to protect herself from her husband; and the father does not know of the birth of his son until he becomes sober at dawn. The children all seem to despise their parents. They explode into anger even in moments when their creator is trying to show their tenderness.

In the second of the novels this ambivalent emotionalism is neatly illustrated by an incident in which Eugene falls in love with Ann and says to her (by way of showing his affection): ". . . You lovely bitch . . . You big, dark, dumb, lovely, sullen Boston bitch! . . . I love you! . . . Oh, you bitch. You Boston bitch." [21]   And, in the earlier novel, when the mother once pleads that they all ought to try to get along together, and be thankful, for their blessings, Eugene suggests the whole mood of "agglutinated hysteria" in the Wolfe novels by cursing:

"Yes, I have a great deal to give thanks for. . . I give thanks for every dirty lust and hunger that crawled through the polluted blood of my noble ancestors.   I give thanks for every scrofulous token that may ever come upon me.   I give thanks for the love and mercy that kneaded me over the washtub the day before my birth.   I give thanks for the country slut who nursed me and let my dirty bandage fester across my navel.   I give thanks for every blow and curse I had from any of you during my childhood, for every dirty cell you ever gave me to sleep in, for the ten million hours of cruelty or indifference, and the thirty minutes of cheap advice." [22]

Bull-laughter bellowing in the beanery. All of these men and women represent types whose entire nervous systems are highly disorganized. As a result, the novels themselves frequently suffer from a mere welter of emotions. Neuroses are confusedly presented as if they were intense passions; maladjustments are colored with tragic implications that actually do not exist at all. There are times when Mr. Wolfe attempts to build mountains of passions out of molehills of mere irritability or neuroticism.

Much of the possible effectiveness of the novels is also lost because of the exasperating lack of all intellectual sympathy between the characters. Not one of them lives in any kind of harmony with the universe, the other characters, or even with himself. The undertaker, Horse Hines, reeks continually of alcohol. Doctor Coker, the physician called in at Ben's death, puts his hat back on his head and lights his cigar before his patient is even dead. And in the Winesburgs of Wolfe's fancy not only can no one live in peace, but no one can die in peace.

Thus, in the scene, from *Look Homeward, Angel,* in which Ben dies, the whole family hysterically leaves the dying boy alone with Eugene and Eliza. Eliza holds her dying son's hands and sobs. Eugene tries to pray — not, we are told, because he believes in God or immortality, but because he is afraid *not* to believe in God or immortality. Just before Ben dies, the family is called back in. Immediately afterwards Luke and Eugene go down to a restaurant to enjoy a nice steak and get rid of their hysteria by screeching out ballads. There, we are told, in a choice Wolfian sentence, that "Their bull-laughter bellowed in the beanery." [23]

In *Of Time and the River,* when their father dies, the boys send one of the lodgers out after a gallon of whisky and "everyone drank a great deal, became, in fact, some-

what intoxicated; when the undertakers came to take Gant
away, none of the family was present. No one saw it. They
were all in the kitchen seated around Eliza's battered old
kitchen table, with the jug of whisky on the table before
them. They drank and talked together all night long until
dawn came." [24]

Suggesting the same exasperating and unconvincing abnormality of character is the story in *From Death to Morning* in which, when the dying father is taken off to the
hospital, one of the sons seriously complains that he had
been looking forward to enjoying a trip, but that now he
knows he will be disappointed! Is it any wonder that our
author says of the Gant family that "None of them was uncomfortable in the presence of madness"? [25]

Enter James Joyce. One of Mr. Wolfe's great admirations
is for the work of James Joyce — especially the Joyce known
for his skill in handling sense impressions. It must be
observed that Joyce's influence upon him has not been
wholly a good one. For most of what is commendable
in the American novelist is the result of his skill in making
things *happen,* in giving a sense of movement and power to
time, in portraying men *as creatures of action* rather than
passivity. On the other hand, when he tries to make time
stand still he sometimes becomes tedious. He interpolates
dozens of rhapsodic passages about rivers flowing and people
eating and cursing. His characters' thoughts are borne
along on the stream-of-consciousness until they come to a
dizzied stop in its seething whirl.

The scene (in the latter part of *Look Homeward, Angel*)
in which Eugene visits the spirit of Ben and sees the phantasmagoria of the townspeople; the quoted lines of poetry
intended as satiric commentary on Eugene's reading; the
introduction (in *Of Time and the River*) of a meaningless
diary recording a trip through France and reading like a

Baedeker; the way in which *Of Time and the River,* like *Ulysses,* is ambitiously made to follow a Greek plan — all this is reminiscent of Joyce; and all this, by retarding the movement of the novels, subtracts seriously from their vitality in a way that finds entire compensation not even from the more eloquent passages.

Why, for example, was that long diary introduced, unless, perchance, our author wanted merely to fill pages by transferring to them strictly autobiographic, but pointless, details? And what effect is achieved by such Joycian mannerisms as the following: "In Louisiana bayous the broken moonlight shivers the broken moonlight quivers the light of many rivers lay dreaming in the moonlight beaming in the moonlight dreaming in the moonlight moonlight moonlight seeming in the moonlight moonlight moonlight to be gleaming to the streaming in the moonlight moonlight moonlight moonlight moonlight moonlight moonlight moonlight"? [26]

The "man is naturally a philosopher." I have already remarked upon the fact that Thomas Wolfe is, despite his fresh and intense appetite for experience, a philosopher of negations rather than affirmations. As an illustration of this negative philosophy I might cite the following reflection from "Dark in the Forest," one of the stories in *From Death to Morning:*

Might it not be that in this great dream of time in which we live and are the moving figures, there is no greater certitude than this : that, having met, spoken, known each other for a moment, as somewhere on this earth we were hurled onward through the darkness between two points of time, it is well to be content with this, to leave each other as we met, letting each one go alone to his appointed destination, sure of this only, needing only this — that there will be silence for us all and silence only, nothing but silence, at the end? [27]

Such negations might possibly not be so worthy of notice if our author did not take himself so seriously as a philosopher as often to lend confusing purposes to his work. But he informs us that all the people from his section of the country are philosophers by nature — every man of them "is naturally a philosopher." [28]

And it is clear that Wolfe thinks of himself as a philosopher also. He pauses in the midst of the most interesting narrative to become a metaphysician while Eugene Gant indulges for pages in such reflections as this: "I am . . . a part of all that I have touched and that has touched me, which, having for me no existence save that which I gave to it, became other than itself by being mixed with what I then was, and is now still otherwise, having fused with what I now am, which is itself a culmination of what I have been becoming. Why here? Why now? When then?" [29]

He becomes the psychologist — limping, it is true, somewhat lamely after Freud — by reflecting upon Helen Gant's life: "She did not know what she wanted to do with her life; it was probable that she would never control even partially her destiny. . ." [30] And, still in the shadow of Freud, the author, in a manner very reminiscent of Anderson's *Dark Laughter,* tells us of Eliza Gant: ". . . her life was somehow beyond these accidents of time, training, and occasion, and the woman was as guiltless as a child, a river, an avalanche, or any force of nature whatsoever." [31]

With his comments upon determinism, environment, and heredity, Wolfe becomes the social philosopher in such scenes as that from *Look Homeward, Angel* in which Steve Gant, having become a drunkard, is made to blame his mother and Margaret for all his troubles: "He called them foul names and said they had poisoned his system." [32]

For almost none of the Wolfe characters seem to feel any personal responsibility for anything; they blame everything upon environment and heredity. Partly as a consequence of this, the conflict in the novels is often the result, not of a clash of wills, but of words. The characters bellow not because of some fury or frustration that involves their deeper nature, but because, let us say, they have got in one another's way in the kitchen. And when their creator comments on them, often he is merely rhapsodizing, instead of philosophizing.

There is a difference!

The capacity to shock. Ben had died; and Luke and Eugene had gone to pick out his coffin. The undertaker, Horse Hines, takes them into the embalming room to see the body of their brother. When one of the boys suggests that Ben looks pale, Hines briskly takes some rouge from his pockets and "touches up" Ben's cheeks. Seeing him do this, "Eugene staggered across the floor and collapsed upon a chair, roaring with laughter, while his long arms flapped helplessly at his sides." [33]—Old Gant is dying; he falls down upon the sidewalk and before Eliza can reach him, "her flesh turned rotten at the sight." "He was bleeding to death through the genital organs." [34]

— Eugene Gant, pauses for a moment at a subway station, while he looks at "a brawny lusty girl . . . breast, belly, arm, and thigh, and all her brawny lustihood. . ." [35]— A character meets a prostitute: "A swart-eyed fellow, oiled and amorous, sweetly licks with nozzly tongue his whore's rouge-varnished face. . ." [36]— A jeweler is repairing a watch: he pries into its "entrails."— A group of students gather around their instructor: "thick with their hot and swarthy body smells, their strong female odors of rut and crotch and arm-pit and cheap perfume. . ." [37]— One of the tales in *From Death to Morning,* describes the physical details of a death in a subway so graphically that, were a coroner called upon to read the description publicly, I am sure he would beg to be excused. — An Italian vendor, in the same volume, is hit by a truck:

his wagon of spaghetti, parts of his skull, and his brain all
mix together in one "horrible bloody welter" upon the street.

Too often Mr. Wolfe is merely repellent when we mis-
takingly think he is powerfully realistic.

But *a capacity to shock is not one of the distinguishing
characteristics of literary genius.*

Of Time, the River — and Bergson.   I have already com-
mented upon Thomas Wolfe's attempt to achieve in his second novel a sense of the rhythm of rivers and oceans, in
order that he might project against their immutable time
his feeling of the contrasting brevity of man's days upon the
earth.   To suggest the duration and flood-tide of the movement which went into his second novel he has therefore
employed as a sort of *motif,* throughout the entire book, the
figure of a river — a figure which he fortifies with a score of
pæans on the actual rivers of America, and with which he
merges the flow of experiences which his hero has : ". . . the
dark and secret river, full of strange time, is forever flowing
by us to the sea." [38]

This whole concept of experience is reminiscent of the
philosophy of Bergson, as I can demonstrate with a few quotations from the Frenchman's *Creative Evolution.*   Bergson's
idea of the "flux" of life made him define duration as "the
continuous progress of the past which gnaws into the future
and which swells as it advances." [39]   For, the real function of
memory, Bergson goes on to say, is not to file our recollections away — but to reproduce the whole flow or flux of
them : ". . . the piling up of the past upon the past goes on
without relaxation. . . All that we have felt, thought, and
willed from our earliest infancy is there, leaning over the
present which is about to join it, pressing against the portals
of consciousness. . ." [40]

Wolfe's Eugene Gant wanted to read the million volumes
in a certain library.   He wanted to know all about the lives

of fifty million people, to "possess" ten thousand beautiful
women, to learn a hundred languages.   In short, he wanted
to crowd into one life the sum total of all human experience.
He could forget nothing.   Wolfe will *let* him forget nothing.
Eugene's past must be piled up upon his past; it must progress continuously, swelling, like a great river, as it advances
into the future.   All that Eugene Gant has "felt, thought,
and willed" from his "earliest infancy" must — and I quote
Bergson's words once more — be permitted to press "against
the portals of consciousness."

But, in the same manner, the Wolfe novels pile up the past
upon the past "without relaxation": there is almost no possi-
bility in them of that serenity which would be valuable from
an artistic point of view, for the purpose of contrast with
passion.   The flux of time — the river — flows too fast to
enable us to see its depth, or its clearer and calmer recesses.
Also, it drags too much wreckage along with it.   So it is
that the whole technique tends at times, indeed, to defeat
its own purpose.

Upon such occasions it suggests *time* without leaving us
with any feeling of *timelessness*.

And so it is, also, that Mr. Wolfe must still overcome the
one great defect which his very method entails.   He must
give not only flow and flux, but some kind of framework, to
his ideas.   He himself realizes, I believe, the validity of this
criticism.   At all events, in *The Story of a Novel* he admits
that it is far better really to know the lives of a compara-
tively few people than to attempt to encompass the lives of
seven million; and he concedes that "naked intensity," the
result of his fiery ardor, must be kept within the bounds of
artistic discrimination.[41]

The ideas must be not only fecund and fresh, but disciplined and controlled.   The river must not only flow; some
of its power must be dammed and held in careful reserve.
The ravenous appetite for experience must be not only fed,

but satiated with at least some regard for literary dietetics; the author must not only embrace life and devour it; he must try, in his groping, to understand and really affirm life as an affair at least ordered enough to satisfy a few of the vague yearnings of his own heart.

In commenting upon the futile work done by members of Eugene Gant's play-writing class, Wolfe tells us that the plays there written were bad chiefly because their authors did not have that ability which every truly great artist must have: ". . . the ability to get out of his own life the power to live and work by, to derive from his own experience — as a fruit of all his seeing, feeling, living, joy and bitter anguish — the palpable and living substance of his art." [42]

This would seem to offer a challenge to Thomas Wolfe himself. Whether or not he will meet that challenge, it is perhaps too soon to say. At present he is at work on a long novel (tentatively titled *The Life and Times of Joseph Doaks*) which, I presume, is to be somehow fitted into the projected plan of novels I have previously mentioned in this chapter. Since *Of Time and the River* was published, however, he has brought out a brief serial — *I Have a Thing to Tell You (Nun Will Ich Ihnen 'Was Sagen)*.[43] This is made up of several thoughtful impressions of a young man who, together with his companions in the compartment of a train, watches the Nazis arrest a Jew trying to leave Germany with considerable money. The very brevity of this piece would seem to have forced upon its author a discipline in which much of his earlier work was lacking. For without losing either its flexibility or surging strength, without being cluttered up with repetitious details, the prose in this sketch is some of the finest Thomas Wolfe has yet given us. What he has to tell us has become more than a powerful cry: ". . . men find a land more kind than home, more large than earth." [44]

One thing is certain: if Thomas Wolfe does meet the challenge of his own accepted credo, he will have to do so alone.

He cannot, for example, continue to depend upon his publisher (as he did in the case of his second novel) to tell him when his books are completed. He must feel the growth of his novels as unified and complete organisms, within himself. He must rid himself of much of his mere "placental material." He must avoid the reporting of such contradictory scenes as are to be found in his second novel; and he must not fail, as he did in the same book, to translate the "I" (in which, apparently, he had written the first draft) to the "he" of Eugene.[45]

He must not only swim "in tidal surges of rhetoric," but he must learn to put some kind of "corset on his prose." He must remember that the "palpable and living substance" of art cannot be got at with "grappling-hooks." Only then will he be making the most of the splendid talents he possesses; only then will he begin to fulfill the real promise of his undeniable genius.

CHAPTER X

THAT DARING YOUNG MAN, MR. SAROYAN

"I never read such a crazy story in my life, even if I did write it. Who [sic] is it about? What's the meaning of all the noise?"— William Saroyan, in *Inhale & Exhale*, p. 66.[1]

CHAPTER X

THAT DARING YOUNG MAN, MR. SAROYAN

MR. WILLIAM SAROYAN has not only evoked perdition upon all the short-story professors by telling them they can go take "a jump in the river," but he has also hurled all their baggage-load of techniques into the river after them. As a matter of fact, long before Mr. Saroyan ever thought of becoming a writer he had decided that the only thing for him to do, would be to make his own rules. For one thing, his own rules might be easier to follow.

Some day, perchance, the literary historian might find it interesting to remember that William Saroyan's first break with the professors took place one afternoon when our future author was at the somewhat unpromising age of eleven. He had been sent home from school that day because he had talked out of turn; he had become "pretty sore" about the whole affair; and, then and there, he had formulated the first of his own rules. And what was it? Avoid all rules! For he found that people make laws for their own protection anyway: and, so, "to hell with them."

This is definite enough at least. But still more definite was the way in which Saroyan — after swearing to avoid all literary theory — then set about the business of elaborating more theory. "Several months" of mature deliberation elapsed, however, before he had arrived at the second of his canons: Forget all about Poe and O. Henry and all other writers and just "sit down and write." (He admits that he himself has even been able to "stand and write.") But it was not until he had formed his third guiding literary principle that his genius was given its fullest scope: the writer, he said, should learn to handle a typewriter so that he can "turn out" stories as fast as can Zane Grey.

This third principle was particularly effective. For example, when the editors of one of our better-known story magazines encouraged the young writer by accepting his "The Daring Young Man on the Flying Trapeze," they received for several months afterwards at least one story, and sometimes two, a day from their unknown contributor! Standing and sitting, typing and typing, Mr. Saroyan was at work.

He had arrived at authorship. What is more, and although he was only in his twenties, he found himself at that particular stage of authorship where he could offer advice to his young contemporaries. Learn to breathe as deeply as possible, he told them. Learn to get the real taste of food, to sleep soundly, to be fully alive, to "laugh like hell," to get *really* angry. For "You will be dead soon enough." [2]

In the meantime William Saroyan himself was very much alive. We began to hear a good deal about him. His father, we learned, had been born in Armenia, had been a teacher, and an unpublished writer in New York City; and had finally gone West to try his hand at grape-farming in the rich Fresno vineyards of California, where the son was born in 1908. The young man's grandmother — Saroyan has pictured her in one of his tales — was a born story-teller; with her countless legends of a curiously interesting past she furnished an inspiration and a source for much of the work our author was later to do.

Saroyan began to write, at first in Armenian, and later in English. He began to be published; he found himself famous; and his publishers found him prolific. But still he refused, despite his carefully formed rules and gratuitous advice, really to consider himself as a writer. ". . . I am not a writer at all," he says in "Myself Upon the Earth." ". . . I write because there is nothing more civilized or decent for me to do." [3]

Mr. Saroyan's publishers, however, disagree with their

young author. Not only is he a writer, and a great one,
they say, but he "can well afford to disdain the sure-fire
tricks of an old trade." [4] Now and then, it is true, one of
"the professors" has raised his voice in mild remonstrance
against this total abandonment of tradition. Thus, some
time ago Dr. Ernest Brennecke, of Columbia University,
pointed out that many of Saroyan's tales are not short-stories
at all. But such criticism does not disconcert Saroyan, as
witness his reply to Dr. Brennecke: "What the hell difference does it make what you call it just so it breathes?" And
to that incontrovertibly logical interrogation, there can, of
course, be no answer.

1

It doesn't make the least difference what we call Saroyan's
work. But it does make a difference whether or not we
understand it, whether we join the hallelujah chorus of his
admirers because we are honestly convinced of the literary
value of his work, or merely because everyone else is praising
him. Certainly Saroyan's work does breathe, though at
times a bit stertorously. It is compellingly vigorous; some
of it has captured at least a certain grace. Also we must
grant that its author handles subjective states of feeling with
a penetrating sympathy; and that his sardonic undertones
are often effective. But to say all this is not, I repeat, really
to understand Mr. Saroyan's work or his position.

An understanding of that position must at the outset take
into account a two-fold surrender which Saroyan has made.
For one thing, he has abandoned himself to the idea that to
be different is to be original. For another, he has subscribed
to the mistaken belief that intensity is to be identified with
vitality, that it is a valid substitute for artistry, and that
it can be secured by inventing startlingly new techniques and
loudly proclaiming one's independence from tradition and

freedom from self-conscious craftsmanship. As a result of these convictions, William Saroyan has thrown most of the traditional rules of literary art into the river. What is more, he has then completed the job by jumping into the river himself. And that river, as I shall show in a moment, is the river of the Bergsonian flux.

In all of this I do not mean, of course, to say that Saroyan is a conscious pupil of Bergson's — as a matter of fact, were Saroyan to see that learned Frenchman splashing about in the vortex of his flux philosophy, he would probably think of him as only another one of the plaguy professors. (And, so, "to hell with" him!) Nor do I mean to lay the blame for all our present-day flux philosophy at Bergson's inviting door. Aldous Huxley's "stream of life" theory, William James' conception of the "stream of thought," the whole school of our stream-of-consciousness novelists — all these must share the responsibility. But I do mean to say that William Saroyan has immersed himself in at least the overflow of all these philosophies; and though Bergson is not, I think, the principal villain in the piece, an interesting parallel can be drawn between his philosophy and the technique of the young American — a parallel which may reveal many of the latter's shortcomings as a thinker and as an artist.

That he is prolific cannot be denied. The "one-story-a-day author," he has been called; Harold Matson, his literary agent, lost his breath trying to keep up with his client! And out in his uncle's vineyards in the San Joaquin Valley, where Saroyan now lives when not in Hollywood, he is still doing as many as four stories a week; while more than a hundred of his tales have already been published. I mention this to show how obviously impossible it is for me here to inquire into the subject matter of all these stories. But I do deem it advisable to discuss a few of them very briefly by way of establishing a basis for my later discussion.

"The Daring Young Man on the Flying Trapeze" — which

is the title story of his first volume — tells of an impoverished young writer who haunts the employment agencies and libraries, tries desperately to get a story written, and dies of starvation before he can finish it. "Then, swiftly, neatly, with the grace of the young man on the trapeze, he was gone from his body. For an eternal moment he was all things at once : the bird, the fish, the rodent, the reptile, the man. An ocean of print undulated endlessly and darkly before him. The city burned. The herded crowd rioted. The earth circled away, and knowing that he did so, he turned his lost face to the empty sky and became dreamless, unalive, perfect." [5]

"War" describes a group of children, of foreign descent, fighting on the streets and reminding the narrator of the way in which nations fight because "the little boys seemed so very innocent and likeable, and whole nations seemed so much like little boys. . ." [6] "1,2,3,4,5,6,7,8 " describes a romance which a young telegraph operator has with a girl, another operator, hundreds of miles away ; and derives its curious title from a pattern of rhythm which the central character recognizes in some phonograph tunes he hears. "Aspirin Is a Member of the N.R.A." is a bitterly ironic tale of a young man who lived for months in a Manhattan hall-bedroom ; and during that time took dozens of aspirins to quiet the pain in his head, while he listened to the radio announcement that "Aspirin is a member of the N.R.A." "It made me laugh," he reflects, "to hear that. But it is the truth. . . Aspirin *is* helping to bring back prosperity. . . It isn't preventing anything, but it is deadening pain." [7]

A few of the stories — and especially the title one — from *The Daring Young Man on the Flying Trapeze* represent curiously imaginative, dexterous, and swiftly sure studies in interesting subjective states. And yet, and despite the critical blurb which attended the appearance of this volume, that is about all that can be said for it. It was a rocket, but it has burned out. I even think that most of us felt it growing cold while reading it.

Of *Inhale & Exhale* (1936) the same cannot be said. The flame is at least appreciably brighter here; there is a little heat as well as light. There is not only the appearance of virtuosity; there is, as well, more range and some little humor, a quality in which the first volume is almost entirely lacking. And humor may help! One thinks of the Scotchman's advice to the surgeon who was tending his wife: "Try her wi' a joke ance, Doctor."

In *Inhale & Exhale* an occasional frugal joke works wonders — and is much more effective than Mr. Saroyan's sardonic scalpel. It relieves the monotony of its author's megalomania; and proves a welcome leaven to a bread that is otherwise often bitter. One can, for example, laugh at the tale of the boxer who, in "Our Little Brown Brothers the Filipinos," refused to leave the prize ring until he had been declared winner — and who could not, until then, be budged by a hundred policemen! In "Solemn Advice to a Young Man About to Accept Undertaking as a Profession" there are amusing reminiscences of a mortician trying to sell an overly economical widow an expensive coffin for her husband who had just died and left her a comfortably large insurance. "My Picture in the Paper" humorously records the bewilderment of the author when, after the appearance of his first volume, publicity began to seek him out. And others of the stories offer interesting and whimsical accounts of Saroyan's brother, his sister, other members of his family, and his life in various California vineyards.

So far so good. The book has its merits — and of these the critics have told us in sycophantic unison. I need not repeat them here. But I do think it time that we now note some of Saroyan's defects, of which the critics have *not* told us — at least with any amount of clarity or confidence.

2

The melancholy flux. The general tone of *Inhale & Exhale* is suggested by the opening paragraph of the first story: "Everything begins with inhale and exhale, and never ends, moment after moment, yourself inhaling and exhaling, seeing, hearing, smelling, touching, tasting, moving, sleeping, waking . . . until it is now, this moment, the moment of *your* being . . . and I remember having lived among dead moments, now deathless because of my remembrance, among people now dead, having been a part of the flux which is now only a remembrance. . ."[8]

This same curiously strange philosophy permeates the entire volume, though more characteristically perhaps is it to be noted in the story which is entitled "The Gay and Melancholy Flux"— from which I take this revealing passage: "One day you were born, O God Almighty, you were lucky that day, and I don't care how miserable you've been ever since. . . Therefore, *while* is the world. I mean, *word,* not world, though either will do. *While* is the holy word. The word of God and man and earth and universe. While one thing, another. While sun and warmth, darkness and cold. . . While everything, nothing. While nothing, everything. While now, never. Forever and forever."[9]

"What's the meaning of all the noise?"[10] Referring to "The Gay and Melancholy Flux," the author is led to observe that it is the craziest story he has ever read, and to wonder what all the noise it makes is really about! Those who are familiar with Henri Bergson's *Creative Evolution* will find, however, a parallel which may throw some light on the matter.

Compare, for example, the two Saroyan passages which I have quoted above, with this selection from the brilliant Frenchman who is one of the sponsors of our school of "flux"

writers : Life is a "current passing from germ to germ through
the medium of a developed organism. It is as if the organism itself were only an excrescence, a bud caused to
sprout by the former germ endeavoring to continue itself
in a new germ. The essential thing is the *continuous progress* indefinitely pursued, an invisible progress, on which each
visible organism rides during the short interval of time given
it to live." [11] Having noted the similarity between the two
authors, let us now inquire somewhat more carefully into
the work of the Frenchman that we might pursue our comparison further.

The "beneficent fluid." According to Bergson, the real
function of man's intelligence is to touch reality and to live
reality ; but to do both only to the extent that they concern
ourselves and our own work — the furrow that *we* happen
to be plowing, as he puts it. Let happen what will to the
furrows in all neighboring fields.

For this job he tells us that we gain strength from a
certain "beneficent fluid" — an ocean in which we find ourselves — that is life's wonder itself. But whenever we im-
merse ourselves in reality, we note, of course, thousands of
incidents which seem absolutely unrelated to our past and
to our future, until we come to realize that all of this dis-
continuity finds some design in a background which is really
continuous. At first, therefore, each psychic experience
seems to be but a swell of water : it is up to us to see each
of these swells as part of the ocean.

Thus all individual experience merges into a flow or a
flux ; you cannot always tell, as a matter of fact, just what
part of the ocean is yours : which of your experiences are
distinct and valid, and which are not. That makes no difference. For the individual's mental state swells anyway
while he tries to swim. In much the same way as a snowball
does by *rolling upon itself!* — Such is Bergson's figure.

In this process the most that the individual can do is to reunite all these scattered and flowing elements by imagining itself a "formless ego." Individuality must become, I might suggest, a sort of very necessary spool, on which "it threads the psychic states which it has set up as independent entities." [12] For our intellects can form clear ideas of only one thing: immobility. And when we think, we "think matter"—ideas play a very small part in our existence: our whole past we see chiefly as a series of impulses and tendencies. These discontinuous impulses and tendencies become, then, the only parts of the swelling ocean of flux that we can really distinguish.

"Waves coming and going." By these tokens it will be noted that the author whose work finds a parallel with all the flux theories, thinks of life as being significant chiefly because it changes its colors with a chameleon-like swiftness. He does not try to name or understand the interesting animal, though he is fascinated by its swiftly changing spots. He sees in the flux of living nothing but a vast movement, unimpeded by any certainty, and carrying him along on the crest of its waters as they flow forever into some unfathomable darkness.

The writer who has absorbed the overflow of this philosophy can, I repeat, only look upon himself as a sort of forlorn figure — can only imagine himself the "formless ego" of which Bergson speaks — seated in a very shaky boat upon a current. He is carried along the stream with breathless rapidity; he sees no buoys or light-houses of tradition to guide him; and he recognizes only the necessity of keeping, somehow or another, in the flux itself. To use the words which Mr. Saroyan's publishers employ in speaking of their young author: "He takes a headlong plunge into the vivid life about him. . ." He does not have to learn to swim in his medium at all: "It cannot be said of William Saroyan that he has forged steadily and cautiously ahead by dint of a long apprenticeship in his medium." [13]

So it is, that Saroyan has so willingly disregarded all rules: they do not help with the swimming, with the comprehending of life, anyway!

To carry my comparison further, let me quote again from Bergson: "We are at ease only in the discontinuous, in the immobile, in the dead. *The intellect is characterized by a natural inability to comprehend life.*" [14] And Mr. Saroyan expresses the same idea in these words: "All that I have learned is that we breathe, and remember . . . and it begins nowhere and it ends nowhere, and all that I know is that we are somehow alive, all of us in the light, making shadows, the sun overhead, space all around us . . . and the sea sullen with movement like my breathing, waves coming and going. . ." [15]

Life is one grand toothache. Mr. Saroyan speaks, we will observe, of the sea being *sullen* with movement. And, indeed, the life portrayed in his tales is, for the most part, an unpropitious expanse of unbearable and dismal pain. A very few of his stories are, it is true, divertingly humorous. But an unpleasant majority of them reflect life, to use Masefield's figure, as "a long headache in a noisy street."

In "Laura, Immortal," for example, we have a typical illustration of this. A man returns to his old home only to find, as he describes it, "the desolation of my life from the first moment of its reality, on backward to the first moment of reality in the life of man." [16] Confronted by the sum of all human desolation, he stands before the house, praying and weeping and cursing until his heart makes "a violence in the earth." Again, in "The World & the Theatre," a boy suffering from toothache, says: ". . . a man doesn't begin to live before he begins to die, and I wasn't bawling about the pain of the tooth, I was bawling because I knew." [17]

Our author continually admits the varied wonder of life. But of what use is this wonder when it becomes only a sweet confection, leaving him, when he nibbles at it, with a great toothache, a feeling of desolation that causes him to gnash his teeth, curse, and — to quote from the above mentioned character — make with his own heart a violence in the earth?

Life is an "evasion of death." The current of life reflected in the short stories of this young American is not only sullen and painful. It is also without direction; it is meaningless and purposeless; it completely engulfs the pitiable figure in his little bark upon it — or trying to swim in it, if you prefer the Bergsonian figure. When there is "loud laughter, and dancing" we are immediately made to feel that both serve but to make us forget how purposeless our progress is — to cover up the Nihilism in which we drift continually. "There is no beginning and no end. You get yourself born somehow or other, but that's no beginning, that's more like an end, but it isn't even an end. Nothing is, nothing ever could be. . ."[18] Thus speaks the central character in "The Gay and Melancholy Flux."

And Bergson? We can have, he tells us, only a feeling of our own evolution and "of the evolution of all things in pure duration" — a feeling which forms but "an indistinct fringe that fades off into darkness." We can keep swimming, but it will do us no good. As one of the other Saroyan characters observes, it is impossible to win with "Dice or anything else. You lose. . . You only get to try. . ."[19] Life is just an "evasion of death." "We are just killing time now, waiting to get back into the emptiness."[20] In other words, we keep swimming though we realize we are only swimming toward some maelstrom up the river.

A "weak woeful clod of clay." Man will be sucked into this maelstrom, though in the meantime he is permitted to make a brief "shadow" in the sun upon the water. He is not, as William Saroyan sees him, much more than a "weak woeful clod of clay" who finds this business of trying to be a Christian a damnably distressing affair. His church is "so purely ornamental" and so annoyingly "statistical about the soul." [21] As an individual, man resembles "a lie for the next generation." He is "a document, the subject of bad poems." And, finally, "There is no dignity anywhere, not even among peasants. . ."

On thumbing one's nose at the universe. It should be remembered that the most important shadow which the stream-of-life author can cast before him, would seem to be his own. To exist we must change, and "to change is to mature, to mature is to go on creating oneself endlessly," [22] says the author of *Creative Evolution.* Man wishes, of course, to observe, but "he wishes above all things to observe himself," echoes the author of *The Daring Young Man on the Flying Trapeze.* Each one of us "is interested in himself, as an experiment. . ."

We might think of this point of view with the help of the following figure. While the author is being whirled along in his currents, he is not likely to be tempted into an understanding, into a true understanding, of the problems of the other people in the flux: "He lives, and he lives within himself, which is the universe." [23] As a consequence he has little time for quiet moments of beauty, or for the most significant problems which confront the human race.

It will be noted that Saroyan illustrates this attitude by refusing almost entirely to grapple with any of the deeper problems of humanity. He touches upon them, I admit. But he does not clarify them; and he refuses, above all, to hope for any solution to them: when a life-preserver, in the form of common human experience, is thrown out to him he persists in stubbornly pushing it away, though it might often be a helpful thing to cling to. It does not always pay to reject human tradition altogether.

But William Saroyan does almost just that. The real way to become a philosopher, he argues, is not to be found in profiting by the sum of human wisdom, but rather by intensifying personal attitudes. He even becomes quite practical in illustrating this point of view by suggesting a nice little poker game as the best place in which to become a philosopher. Sit down, deal when it's your turn, take an occasional swig of whiskey. *That* will teach you about our universe! Ten hours of this and you will know more about the world than any six scientists could ever know! Above all, you will learn enough about the universe to realize that but one gesture is necessary in explaining it — and "that gesture a comical one." [24]

Creating oneself endlessly. Clinging to Mr. Saroyan like a Nessus-shirt is another one of the Bergsonian ideas, already referred to : the idea that "to change is to mature, to mature is to go on creating oneself endlessly." Now when Mr. Dooley observed that the trouble with our knowledge is not that we haven't learned enough, but that we have learned so many things that "jest ain't so," he uttered a remark that applies nicely to the young William Saroyan gazing about the world in wild-eyed surmise and turning out stories — projections of intense personal impulses and attitudes — at the rate of almost one a day.

For to change is *not* necessarily to mature. Nor does it follow that we mature by an endless creation of ourselves. The artist matures by *transfiguring* experience — by deriving from it, to quote Saroyan's "big brother," Thomas Wolfe, "the palpable and living substance of his art."

But most of the Saroyan stories are *transcripts* of experience — usually of traumatic experience — rather than transfigurations of it. Indeed, it is to be noted that he has little skill in creating any character other than an *alter ego*: all of his characters speak and feel exactly alike. The "art" of his work is not the result of a richly endowed mind focusing a highly creative intelligence upon life and distilling from it some rarely concentrated beauty. It is the result of a mind caught in the flux of life, with little time to fuse experience with imagination, and forced to compensate itself by highly magnifying its own ego.

On his Bergsonian bark, and seeing only his own shadow upon the water, he tries feverishly to distract himself too often with the mere flotsam and jetsam carried along by the current.

"A thing of many fragments." William Saroyan tells us that a novel is "a thing of many fragments held together by the frequent perishing and frequent resurrection of a brave and stubborn man"; [25] and by way of giving point to this theory he generously concedes that Christ actually lived a novel that is "almost a first-rate" one. He has not himself as yet essayed the writing of a novel; but, significantly enough, his stories are just such "fragments"— fragments held together by their author's frequent perishing in disillusionment and his resurrection into an intensely passionate, but uncontrolled, exaltation. (Even his publishers, it is to be noted with interest, refer to his *"fever* of exaltation.")

Perhaps it is this effect of violent contrast in Saroyan's moods which makes many of his admirers think him powerful: as warmth may even be mistaken for heat by a man who has just come out of the cold. For, although in some of his stories he rises to a genuine feeling, he usually fails to sustain that feeling: vulgarisms, blasphemies, crude or annoyingly incompetent writing, characters that expectorate and curse on every page — these matters distract from the effect of real beauty and often leave its object just another piece of wreckage on the stream.

A fresh voice in our literary wilderness. It must be conceded that many of his techniques are effective. The method, for example, employed in "1,2,3,4,5,6,7,8" advances the narrative swiftly by alternating the speech in the first and third persons; the individualized technique in "The Daring Young Man on the Flying Trapeze" lends, I think, both urgency and freshness to the story; his handling of subjective moods is often not without verve and a sort of hard, cold brilliancy.

Too often, however — and we might as well admit it — he is *neither* original *nor* effective. He can ape Faulkner in such passages as the following: *"I am now almost seventeen and I have lived all these years upon the earth, thinking, no matter what happens, I shall be somewhere upon this earth forever, thinking, it is because of Maria, because I love her and am now walking to her, thinking, tomorrow all of us will turn away from the fields, our earth, and go to our houses, waiting for their wrath."* [26]

In "Secrets of Alexandria," and other tales, he uses headlines to get effects in a cinematographic manner which Dos Passos long ago proved would get at least one effect — that of an "art" surprisingly suggestive of the morning newspaper. And like the same author, he has hit upon routine descriptions of brothel scenes, etc., that have become a formula with him.

Many of his cynicisms were uttered long ago by Dreiser even before that confused writer began pouring out his tired soul into numerous autobiographies. Some of the shadows which he casts are merely those of Freud and Lawrence elongated into grotesque fancies. He omits punctuation; but so do a score of other published writers — and a million who are not yet published, though it is beginning to seem that they will be. In short, I think Saroyan's claims to originality have been egregiously exaggerated.

Also, I think unjustified his claim to being considered a "fresh" voice. He pretends to throw overboard all "rules" of writing. He does throw most of them overboard — with the exception of his own. We are told that he is free from that kind of literary self-consciousness which so often fails in producing anything truly creative. As a matter of fact, Mr. Saroyan is nothing if he is not self-conscious. He is self-conscious in the very way in which he is continually assuring us that he is not self-conscious. He is supposed to be creating a more intense art form, when he and his school are actually turning what was formerly a perfected form of art, into an intense projection of personal experience — making of it an immense proving ground for experimentation.

Emotional somersaults. Meanwhile, he threatens, unless his future work shows an advance over that so far published, to perish in the sea of his own egoism, endlessly trying to create himself, to keep himself afloat by depending upon fevered strokes of irony. His *Three Times Three* (1937) — the most recent Saroyan book at the moment of this writing — is a collection of nine "stories" as fevered and formless as those in his previous volumes.

Real irony, of the classic kind, might help him. But Mr. Saroyan's irony does not happen to be of the classic kind. It is rather what Jean Paul Richter described as "hot baths of sentiment alternating with cold douches of irony." Writing on another author than Saroyan, Alan Reynolds Thompson refers to such emotion as "a device of emotional somersaults . . . because it is the revulsion of the author's intelligence against his own romantic sentiments, and because it thus differs essentially from the classic irony which is based on the objective observation by a normal individual of extravagances in others." [27]

Perhaps that is it. Perhaps the author of *The Daring Young Man on the Flying Trapeze* has been merely performing emotional somersaults!

CHAPTER XI

A FOOTNOTE ON JAMES T. FARRELL

"The novelist of today chooses characters who will attract you from the opening sentence, men of audacious achievement, women of flamboyant picturesqueness, people whose lives would make effective scareheads in the yellow journal. They will not, they dare not, take time to make the reader understand the quiet beauty of unpretentious lives, outside the rush and turmoil of the world at large."— Frederic Tabor Cooper, in *The Bookman,* March, 1905.[1]

CHAPTER XI

A FOOTNOTE ON JAMES T. FARRELL

"WHAT in hell is art, anyway?"

Two decades ago that famous *jeune fille* whom Stuart Sherman had created as a symbol of the new spirit in our American literature, ran—"with somewhat more than a flash of her silken perfections"—down the steps of her home and onto the street where she met a prominent young critic who greeted her with a quotation from a rather famous book he happened to be reading: "*Où il n'y a point de délicatesse, il n'y a point de littérature.*" "That's a new one on me," said the young lady, as she hurried on her way.[2]

It was perhaps a decade later that a girl, in whom can be recognized the psychological lineaments of the same *jeune fille,* chanced to receive from an old friend a copy of verses by a poet even then still considered modern. She lighted a cigarette; displayed, I am sure, the same "flash of silken perfections"; and, sinking into the luxurious embrace of a sofa, prepared to read the book merely to oblige the friend who had given it to her. At first she was coldly indifferent to it; then she became slightly amused. Finally, she stopped smoking. And, at last, she sat up and exclaimed: "Why—hell! These are wonderful. I am going to write some religious things myself."[3]

With a knowledge of contemporary literature dating not much further back than Woodrow Wilson, either one of these young ladies mentioned as types of the "new" spirit in our letters during the second and third decades of our century—either of these young ladies, I say, might have uttered the undeniably direct interrogation with which I begin my chapter. Or, the *jeune fille* of our own decade—with perhaps even a greater flash of silken perfections—

might ask the same question, as she meets some young friend on the street, or as she perches beside him at a drug-store counter.

"What in hell is art, anyway?" Any charming young thing of today might ask this with the sip of a Walgreen soda, or a Bacardi at the Biltmore bar.

Let me add at once, however, that I take my opening sentence from the rouged lips of no light-headed *jeune fille,* conceived merely as a symbol of a new reader spirit in our literature. For by now this "new spirit" is an even newer spirit : — our *critics* are assuming the that's-a-new-one-on-me attitude when confronted by certain problems in aesthetics and certain distinctions between sociology and art. One of them has just been reading Mr. James T. Farrell's *Studs Lonigan* trilogy. He discovers that Mr. Farrell's books have "depth and pace." He confesses himself overwhelmed by their climaxes and "deep meanings."

He gets a "tremendous emotional wallop" from Mr. Farrell's rape scenes. Let people think this is sociology if they want to ! It is really enduring art ! For — "What in hell is art, anyway?" And anyone who insists that Mr. Farrell is not an enduring artist, is uttering, he says, not criticism, but merely "an incantation designed to exorcise the uncomfortable memory of Studs and his frightening palsy-walsies, with their broads, their movies, their pool, their alky, their poker and their craps." [4] In brief, we had better keep our eyes on James T. Farrell, for he "is going places." In this judgment, let me add, most of our other critics have concurred. Some of them have even gone so far as to rank Farrell "above all contemporary American novelists" and, in one critical circle at least, his trilogy has been rated the most significant American fiction since the War.

With his "palsy-walsies," "their broads," "alky," and "craps," James T. Farrell was first discovered in a serious way upon our literary horizons, when in 1932 he published his *Young Lonigan,* the first volume of the trilogy already referred to. Recorded with a merciless fidelity toward fact, this novel is a commentary on Chicago's South Side that constitutes a revealing textbook of the moral and social decay of our generation. The study introduces us to young Studs Lonigan as he is about to graduate from the elementary grades; and records this adolescent's life, in painfully repulsive detail, through the early years he is supposed to be spending in high school.

"He was a hard-boiled egg that they had left in the pot a couple of hours too long." [5] Studs is tough; and he is proud of it! He rebels against the simple piety of his Irish parents: against his father, a hard-working contractor who saves his money and continually resolves to take his wife back to the "old sod" on a second honeymoon; and against the mother, whose most fervent prayer is that Studs will enter the priesthood. Locked in the bathroom that he might enjoy a surreptitious smoke, Studs looks at himself in the mirror and decides that, after all, he has a "pretty good mug." "He twisted his lips in sneers, screwed up his puss, and imagined himself telling some big guy where to get off at." [6] Studs' young enemies dream of knifing him — so much do they hate him. In the meantime, he and his friends fight, curse, smoke, and engage in an early series of moral defections with a fourteen-year-old girl. By and large, Studs Lonigan is sufficiently matured by the end of the novel to be able to affirm that "the world was lousy and he was going to give it one Goddam run for its lousy money all right." [7]

This affirmation he puts to the test in *The Young Manhood of Studs Lonigan* (1934). The test is made somewhat difficult, it is true, by the fact that his young sister attempts to reform him with such an obnoxious persistence that our young hero reflects seriously on the pleasures that could be derived from kicking "her teeth in for her." The "old

lady" and the "old man" also interfere; but not quite sufficiently to keep their son from running the entire gamut of
sexual experiences, or to keep him from suffering certain
consequences to his health which sociologists and medical
men have long had an interest in, but which, until Hemingway and Dos Passos, had hardly constituted material for
literary reflection.

In the meantime, life is lively enough for young Lonigan.
It is pleasant to stand in front of the poolroom and watch
the girls go by, and with a slight effort of the imagination
quickly to see each disrobed in the sun. It is pleasant,
also, to torture the small negro boys in the neighborhood:
"They only caught a ten-year-old negro boy. They took
his clothes off, and burned them. They burned his tail
with lighted matches, urinated on him, and sent him running off naked with a couple of slaps in the face." [8]

Studs decides to go to war on adolescent principles that
are vaguely general; but he vows that he will never marry,
on principles sufficiently specific in their expression for me
to prefer not to quote them here. And, why marry, anyway, with such pleasurable experiences as the following, to
take part in?

Weary pumped his right into the ox's eyes. Two fellows
jumped Weary. Buddy Coen swung and brought his knee into
a groin. A fellow went down moaning. The ox swung at Studs.
Studs ducked. He hit the wall and winced. Studs swung. The
ox dropped, and Buddy kicked him in the head. He moaned,
and crawled towards the door. Studs jumped on the back of a
guy tackling Weary and got a stomach hold. . .[9]

Judgment Day (1935) carries the adventures of Studs
Lonigan through the remaining year or two of his life. He
falls in love, loses his savings in Imbray [Insull?] stocks,
continues a pre-marital relationship with Catherine, sees his
father ruined, suffers a complete physical collapse, and dies
of pneumonia before he has quite fulfilled his intention of

giving the "lousy world" a "run for its lousy money." On
the evening of his death, both his father and his brother
go out to become, in the words which Sinclair Lewis has
made famous, "gloriously drunk."

Just a word must be said about the technique employed
in these novels. Reminiscent of Dos Passos — with whom
Mr. Farrell has much in common — are such cinematic devices as those in which the younger novelist flashes news
reels upon a screen, or uses placards, carried by members
of a protest parade, to review sardonically certain phases of
contemporary life. Large slices of smurky satire are wedged
into the novels by means of devices which include long
sermons reproduced in full for the sole purpose of denigrat-
ing religion; the whole trilogy is sandwiched with inter-
chapters that effectively contrast the prayers and pieties of
certain characters with their entirely contradictory conduct;
and, finally, in *Judgment Day,* the stream-of-consciousness is
employed to suggest a weird and phantasmagoric procession
of friends which Studs sees as he lies dying.

"Lost, wholly lost, without an inward fire." The San-
tayana quotation which is prefixed to Mr. Farrell's collection
of short stories entitled *Guillotine Party* (1935) suggests this
volume's principal concern: with that "lost generation"
spoken of by Miss Stein, and written about by Mr. Hemingway in *The Sun Also Rises.* Compared, however, with Mr.
Hemingway's fresh, and often brilliant, picture of post-War
Europe, Mr. Farrell's indictment sounds like an account
received, even at best, only second hand. In the Hemingway portraits there is at least something akin to vitality and
real energy. The characters have something of that zest
which we look for in human beings — even when they are
lost human beings. They are enthusiastic and colorful in
their bull-fighting, fishing, damning, and drinking. It is
true that Mr. Hemingway's men and women sometimes sin
without much enthusiasm. But they at least fish, fight

bulls, and pound the typewriter like men who are awake. On the other hand, the bored sophisticates in *Guillotine Party* do everything with a yawn: "They talked on, and drank wine, and yawned." [10] As an indictment of Miss Stein's lost generation, *Guillotine Party* is exhausting because its themes have been exhausted — by fresher and more creative intelligences than that which Mr. Farrell possesses.

The Farrell stories have all the Hemingway hiccups without the Hemingway cold showers.

Furthermore, those tales that deal with material with which Farrell seems more honestly familiar sift out indiscriminately and rehash too much of the material from their author's previous trilogy. "The Open Road" merely reviews the travels of the Jew in the novels; "The Merry Clouters" is only a slight variation of one of young Lonigan's brawls; the incident of the young Greek who made his money at dance marathons had previously been run off the mill in one of the earlier novels; "Big Jeff" makes use of the interior monologue to re-introduce one of the Farrell perverts in a language which makes the reflections of Mrs. Bloom in *Ulysses* seem like a Chaucerian chuckle; "In Accents of Death" does no more than reflect one of Studs' school incidents; "The Little Blond Fellow" re-emphasizes another one of the sexual experiences of the same early group of boys; and at least four more of the sketches are only further smurky satires upon previous denigrations of women and religion.

The tale entitled "Studs" deserves, however, special comment; for it is the nucleus out of which grew the entire bulk of the Lonigan trilogy. In it a crowd of Studs' friends are depicted just after they have attended his wake. "If only they had not sent him to Heaven where there are no whores and poolrooms," [11] Mr. Farrell comments. And the boys reflect:

. . . the spiritual bouquet (further assurance that his soul would arrive safely in Heaven) was a dirty trick. So was the administration of the last sacraments. For Studs will be miserable in Heaven, more miserable than he was on those Sunday nights when he would hang around the old poolroom . . . waiting for something to happen. He will find the land of perpetual happiness and goodness dull and boresome, and he'll be resentful. There will be nothing to do in Heaven but to wait in timeless eternity. . . He will loaf up and down gold-paved streets where there is not even the suggestion of a poolroom, thinking of Paulie Haggerty, Sport Murphy, Arnold Sheehan and Hink Weber, who are possibly in hell together because there was no priest around to play a dirty trick on them.[12]

Studs "was a slob; but he died without having to live countless slobbish years."[13] These words from the concluding pages of *Guillotine Party* label their author's conception of fiction — as a sociological study, highly documental, *but not judgmental*. Both the characters and the environment are to be, in other words, purely functional material for sociology. Fiction is to be no more than a photograph of our "countless slobbish years."

A World I Never Made (1936), the most recent Farrell novel, covers only one year in the life of young Danny O'Neill; but it finds enough slobbishness in those twelve months at least to make our leading American newspaper refuse, according to its author's own recent admission at the New York Book Fair, even to accept any advertising for the book! The scene of this novel is again set on Chicago's South Side; the year which the book deals with is 1911 — when Danny is about six or seven years old. He might, in a sense, therefore be thought of perhaps as an autobiographical character, as Mr. Farrell was in 1911 himself a boy of seven living in Chicago.

Danny's mother, Lizz O'Neill, is a querulous woman with "her decayed teeth sticking out of her smile like sores, the dirty rag under her chin almost falling off." [14] His father is borne down under the burden of trying to support a large, and ever increasing, family upon the paltry sixteen dollars a week he earns driving an express truck, listening to Lizz's nagging, and attempting to reconcile himself to the squalid poverty and the dirt in his home. But the burden has grown too great for him, and so Danny has been sent to live with his Aunt Margaret, his Uncle Alf, and his grandmother, old Mrs. O'Flaherty. Margaret is a neurasthenic who has graduated by difficult stages from the life of a prostitute to that of mistress of a financier; Alf O'Flaherty is a shoe salesman who returns from his trips at least frequently enough to make young Danny continually look forward with dread to the cuffings his uncle gives him; and the grandmother is a vicious and gossipy old hag who is always offering some one a sum of money for bashing in the faces of her imagined enemies. "In the old country, if me father didn't like a man, he'd rip his guts out and bring them home to show to me mother." [15]

In such an environment what chance, Mr. Farrell implies, what chance has the boy? The world he lives in is a world *he* never made! (The title of the book, by the way, is derived from a line in Housman's *Last Poems*.) And so Danny passes this year of his childhood: from his older brother he learns of the "mysteries" of birth; his own curiosities about the world of sex are reported in long detail; and, what is probably worse, are focused against the most repulsive, abnormal, brawling, blasphemous, and sordid experiences of his elders. Nothing is spared the reader: Mr. Farrell's imagination — which, be it emphasized, is a *reproductive* and a *mechanical* one, rather than a *productive* and *creative* one — prompts him to fill in every detail. In the matter of language alone, in his use of four-letter words, this novelist would seem to have been actuated by a feverish desire to get as many vulgarisms on each page as possible.

The only punches that count are those below the belt!

Since the appearance of *A World I Never Made,* its author has brought out but one other volume of fiction — a book entitled *Can All This Grandeur Perish?* (1937). This is a collection of sixteen short stories and one short novelette called "Seventeen." The tales concern a number of subjects, for the most part set against the particular South Side of Chicago background which its author has dealt with in his previous books. There is a story about a wealthy Chicagoan who spends his time smoking expensive cigars and uttering platitudes about success; one about a young writer and his artist-wife in Paris; one which describes the activities of a Chicago precinct captain; another about a seventeen-thousand-dollars-a-year college professor thwarted in his ambition to write; another which tells of two young people, on relief, who hold a dog for ransom and are sentenced to prison; and several, of course, which go into detail about the sex life of adolescents.

Let me add, however, that in a very few of the stories Mr. Farrell has achieved the, for him, almost unique distinction of having found his inspiration in very normal impulses. Thus in "The Oratory Contest" — to give but one example — he tells of a proud father going off to watch his son win a school prize for oratory. Mrs. O'Dell is expecting another child; and before her husband leaves for the contest, she breaks down and tells him of a gnawing fear that she might not live.

She sobbed in his arms. Holding her, he felt as if paralyzed. He sensed in her the mystery of woman which enabled them to bring forth a man's child. He was filled with respect, awed into speechlessness. He kissed her, clasped her tightly, his feelings reverential. He thought of how they were going along now, and of how they were past knowing and feeling again what they had known and felt in those first burning days of their marriage. Now it was just having sympathy with each other, being used to one another, having their family, their duties, and the obligations which they had to meet together, the feeling of liking, more than loving, each other, and wanting to be proud of their kids. He kissed her again.[16]

And then, as father and son go down the street, Mr. O'Dell suddenly turns to Michael:

"Mickey, you always want to be good to your mother. Help her all you can while you've got her, because you'll never realize how much she means to you until she's gone," he said.

"Yes, Dad," the boy dutifully replied, the father's words merely giving him the feeling that the old man was just preaching a little in order to hear himself talk.

"You won't have her with you always, you know."[17]

In one of the tales, a student in a short-story class insists that a story have "the Misery, the Rawness, the Squalor, the Tragedy, the Beauty, the Glory of Life."[18] Of misery and rawness and squalor, Mr. Farrell has given us much. If only he would give us more often such approaches to tragedy, and beauty, and honest glory as characterize stories like "The Oratory Contest"! And if only he would learn something about writing—would learn how to end a story; how to describe characters without depending almost entirely on strings of adjectives; how to write dialogue without having about every line end with "said":

"Lizzie, June made me cry," Aggie said.
"I wasn't so good today," June said modestly.
"But, say, June, you've lost weight," Aggie said.
"I lost ten pounds on the Hollywood diet," June said smiling.
"Is it a good one?" asked Mrs. Brown.
"It's wonderful, Lizzie," June said.
"Lizzie, what happened to the diet you were on?" Aggie asked.
"I lost two or three pounds, but I had so much housework to do for the holidays, I forgot. I got hungry and ate," Lizzie said, and they laughed.

"Lizzie is like me. She likes her steaks thick and juicy," Myrtle, Fred Van Duym's wife, said.

"Yes, but, Myrtle, you can afford it. You're not an old tub like me," Mrs. Brown said.

"Well, none of us are spring chickens any more," Ella Markham said.

"You said it, Ella," Myrtle Van Duym said.

"We're too old to be worrying about the vanities of the flesh. The soul is what should interest us," Ella Markham said.

"Ella, here, is as religious as Tom," Mrs. Brown said.[19]

Mr. Farrell's *A Note on Literary Criticism* (1936) is interesting for its clear statement of its author's idea of art — that which I have already suggested. The artist is to be concerned primarily with the "use values" of experience: in place of the idealistic, imaginative, and judgmental values of literature, he is to substitute that sort of factual functionalism which, in philosophy, John Dewey has popularized. Elsewhere Farrell has abridged the thesis of *A Note On Literary Criticism* by drawing a sharp distinction between the aesthetic and functional aspects of human experience:

Literature is to be viewed both as a branch of the fine arts and as an instrument of social influence. As a consequence there arises a duality which produces unresolved problems in literary criticism. For purposes of understanding and convenience we may divide human experience into two general categories, the aesthetic and the functional. The aesthetic aspect of human experience is revealed in the pleasure or the elation which we derive from things, from qualities, and from intellectual, emotional, or physiological states for their own sake. Experience in its functional aspect is concerned with objects and actions in terms of their use values.[20]

It is, of course, nothing new to learn that literature may be thought of as both a branch of the fine arts and as a social instrument. But when writing concerns itself almost exclusively with the functional aspects of experience, it may become no longer a branch of the fine arts. When it reveals

only the "pleasure or the elation which we derive from
things . . . for their own sake" it may even continue to
give a hard-pressed reviewer "a tremendous emotional
wallop." When it reports chiefly the use values of experience, it may be good sociology. But in not one of these
cases will it necessarily reflect that *creative* intelligence which
we expect in the artist.

Intensely photographic realism may reflect cancerous
growths on civilization (and thus have certain sociological
"use values") without enlarging upon life. Writing may be
vivid and even technically skilful without advancing one
point the niceties and the discriminations we think of when
we view literature as "a branch of the fine arts." *"Où il n'y
a point de délicatesse, il n'y a point de littérature."* Furthermore, I doubt very much if Mr. Farrell's work has even the
"use values" which have been attributed to it. I think it
an X-ray which reveals cancerous growths without having
any great therapeutic value — that it is rather intended to
attract by its morbid detail.

But — "That's a new one on me," our critic can be heard
to say. One young critic[21] asks: Doesn't James T. Farrell
have "depth and pace"? And doesn't his work continually
"flash with new meanings"?

Perhaps. From the time that Studs Lonigan "screwed up
his puss" in front of the mirror, to the time when death ends
all his "slobbish years," perhaps the trilogy *does* flash with
new meanings. But only of a certain kind: we watch a
long chapter given over to the physical details of a rape in
a cheap hotel room; we follow the progress of a boy's perversions; we have pictured for us a young fourteen-year-old
girl giving herself to several boys within an hour; we read
another long chapter telling of a young housewife who
gambles her weekly allowance away and gets it back again
by bringing three strange men home with her. New meanings?

But — the work of James T. Farrell "coordinates one's own scattered and spasmodic experiences and reflections," the same critic claims.

I think not. I prefer to think that, with few exceptions, neither the novels nor the tales coordinate many human experiences that are *worth* coordinating. Studs Lonigan "was a slob; but he died without having to live countless slobbish years." "Life was evil . . ." [22] to one of the other Farrell characters. Another "had permitted himself to be pushed and shoved into" [life], "and these last years he had gone on in his rut. He was a pawn." [23] Another sums up all *his* "scattered and spasmodic experiences and reflections" by concluding: ". . . as you Americans say, what the hell!" [24] Another offers his reflections in an interesting Nietzscheism: "Men are fools, except for . . . artists and noblemen. They are pigs. Your common people! Pigs. Beasts!" [25] Another finally becomes a pimp, gets syphilis, dies. Another gives forceful affirmation to this philosophy: "Women are bitches. . . They're bitches, I tell you." [26] And — to cut this list of "scattered and spasmodic" reflections short — we are told of Studs, just before his death:

He thought of how when you went out and listened to what people said, you heard all kinds of things; people washing their dirty linen in public, talking about friends and business . . . and it made him think how the world must be, at every minute, so full of people fighting . . . and dying, and working, and losing jobs, and it was a funny world, all right, full of funny people, millions of them.[27]

". . . one's own scattered and spasmodic experiences and reflections"?

But — the Farrell books mount "to climaxes that suddenly reveal by artistic mutation what has been imperceptible and latent in a character." [28]

Do they? When Studs was a boy the world was "lousy" to him. When he came to die it was merely full of "funny people." When he was a boy his defections were with a very young girl; later on, he arrives at the brothel stage. When young, he had "screwed up his puss" and decided to give the world "one Goddam run for its lousy money." As he grows older, he acquires even further proficiencies in cursing which need not be recorded here. His characteristics are "latent" enough, but hardly "imperceptible"! And where is the "artistic mutation"? In the violence? In the tedious minutiae?

But — "*Studs Lonigan demands* the minutiae, the stretches of comparative tedium about humdrum life, if only to point up the sudden wild flaring into brutality of some of his characters."

I think that what the critics really should say is this: *Studs Lonigan* is very badly in need of those wild flarings into brutality to point up its dreadful and painful tedium. In this matter, Farrell is extremely proficient: his books are seasoned, at almost mathematically calculated intervals, with sex, violence, and brutality. It is these scenes chiefly which carry the reader through the humdrum pages, through the medical reports, psychopathic studies, and sociological investigations.

That brings us, of course, to even further distinctions between sociology and art. Into these we need not inquire. It would perhaps be futile. For some critic can always counter by asking:

"What the hell is art, anyway?"

CHAPTER XII

TOWARD THE CENTRE OF THE STREAM

". . . literature is greater than social history: it aspires to embody the meaning of life in terms at once timeless and universal and beautiful . . . let us develop a new respect for personality —for personality richly varied and healthily individual."— "Pandora's Box in American Fiction," by Harry Hayden Clark. In *Humanism and America*, edited by Norman Foerster. Pages 202-203.[1]

CHAPTER XII

TOWARD THE CENTRE OF THE STREAM

THE significant body of Theodore Dreiser's work, compelling for its color and cumulative detail, rich in what is humanitarian but poor in what is human: some of the clumsiest writing ever done by an American and, occasionally — some of the most warm, tender, moving. . . The brilliantly urbane style of Branch Cabell continually pointing itself on the sharp-edged instruments of cynicism and indiscriminate mockery. . . Our Freudians and stream-of-consciousness writers, who have some genuine veins of ore to mine, but who often bring up tons of muck to prove they have real ore — who put the cellar where the attic should be, and make the abnormal a key to the normal. . . Sherwood Anderson, who has written some stories that must last as long as boys wish to "die gloriously" or race horses are "full of spunk"; who has written others that only prove that Truth cannot be found under the bed. . . Ernest Hemingway, original, virile, with many fine answers to the hiccuping queries of a lost generation, but unable, quite, to say the last word.

John Dos Passos, who has proved the value of experiment and the ineffectiveness of mere experiment; who has an alert awareness of the problems of our social order, and yet finds an answer for those problems only in a further breakdown of that order. . . William Faulkner, and the cruelty cult, thrown, at last, against the dilemma of being either only horrible or only ridiculous. . . Thomas Wolfe, who writes prose as surging as his rivers — certainly the most promising of the younger men now writing in America, if he can only "corset" his art a bit. . . William Saroyan, paddling the bark of his own individual (but not necessarily original) personality on the Bergsonian stream. . . And James T.

Farrell, whose sincerity, perhaps, cannot be questioned; but whose failure to distinguish between sociological and judgmental values has resulted in some of the most vulgar and orgiastic writing of our day.

1

In the studies that I have made, I have not, of course, given a complete picture of American literature during the last three decades. There is much of which I have said nothing: the penetrating and, as a rule, infallibly accurate analyses which Sinclair Lewis has made of our social scene; the trenchant satire in the earlier work of Edith Wharton; the richly textured and superbly ironic style which should, before this, have brought Ellen Glasgow the Nobel Prize; the artistic undertones, the impeccable writing, and the poignant beauty to be found in Willa Cather's novels; the fine restraint, understanding, and sensitivity which characterize most of Mrs. Fisher's books; the accomplishments, as a matter of fact, of a dozen other novelists whom I found outside the province of my investigations.

On the whole, however, it is exactly those attractive literary currents which I have traced that have tended to make us somewhat blind to our more solid literary achievements. While watching the eddies, we are inclined to forget the real and stronger current in the centre of the stream: that writing which has a sound regard for the traditional and unceasing flow of human values, instinctive and enduring, that literature cannot long ignore if it is to be thought of as an affair of the spirit or a concern of the heart. I have written this book because I believe re-evaluations (which distinguish between these eddies and this stream) are especially in order today. I have written this book because I think that a large number of our readers likewise believe such re-evaluations to be in order.

For, certain signs already point to a veering away from the unrelieved "realism" of present-day literature. The immense popular success, in recent years, of such books as Hervey Allen's *Anthony Adverse* (1933) and Margaret Mitchell's *Gone With the Wind* (1936); the appeal which the work of two "incurably" romantic British novelists, James Hilton and J. B. Priestley, has had in this country; the avidity with which we have devoured the romantic tushery of Lloyd C. Douglas; the keen interest reflected in biography and "personal" history, where we are at least permitted to enjoy a character who is not a puppet, one who dominates his environment; the crest of a wave of historical fiction on which we now seem to be riding — do not such tendencies indicate significant literary hungers which our fiction is attempting to satisfy?

2

Margaret Mitchell's *Gone With the Wind* is a case in point. Miss Mitchell's father, a prominent Atlanta lawyer, had a deep interest in the history of Georgia; the daughter, even as a child, inherited this interest, and devoured volume after volume about the South. She planned on studying medicine; but an accident forced her to use crutches for three years and destroyed that ambition. Instead, she became a feature writer for the Atlanta *Journal;* and as early as 1926 began work on her monumental novel, scribbling it on copy paper and even laundry slips, storing the massive bundles in the closet, as the book took gradual shape.

And then Mr. H. S. Latham, of the Macmillan Company, came to Atlanta, one day, in search of new authors. At lunch with Miss Mitchell (she is Mrs. John R. Marsh in private life) and one of her friends, he learned of the former's manuscript; found it so large that he had to go out and buy a new suitcase to bring it back with him; and, as we all know by now, made a rather handsome investment by getting that suitcase. By April, 1937, Miss Mitchell's book had sold 1,350,000 copies; in the first part of the following month it was announced as a Pulitzer Award winner; and it is now reported that it is very soon to be published in Germany and in Sweden.

Most of us know the story of *Gone With the Wind*. Scarlett O'Hara, the daughter of an Irish plantation owner in Georgia at the time of the Civil War, has had many beaus; but when she learns that Ashley Wilkes is to announce his engagement, to Melanie Hamilton, at a great barbecue the following day, she suddenly decides that it is he whom she loves. She will confess her love to him boldly; they will elope together. And so she prepares to attend the affair — under Mammy's eyes, carefully eating a great quantity of food before she leaves home, in order that she might, at the barbecue, have the delicate appetite expected of a Southern "lady." But her "confession" does not have its intended effect. Ashley insists upon keeping his pledge to Melanie; and she is further embarrassed by learning that her avowals had been overheard by one Rhett Butler, a strange guest at the barbecue. As the party ends, news is brought of the outbreak of the War.

Ashley marries Melanie; to spite him, Scarlett marries Melanie's brother who is soon killed in battle, leaving her with an unborn child. Later she goes to Atlanta where, while trying to live the decorous life of a widow, she again meets Butler, who is now, for purely mercenary reasons, a blockade runner for the South. During the siege of the city she bravely keeps a promise she has made to Ashley that she would always take care of Melanie; and with a great deal of resourcefulness and personal heroism stays with Melanie until the latter's child is born. Then they make their way back through the Yankee lines, to Tara, the family plantation, where Scarlett finds that two of her sisters are ill with typhoid, her mother has died, and her father has lost his mind.

The following weeks are filled with terror for them all. To pay a prohibitive tax which the Scalawags and Republicans have levied on Tara, Scarlett offers herself to Rhett Butler. But he refuses to give her the money she needs; and so, by lying, she manages to win, instead, Frank Kennedy, who had been engaged to her own younger sister. With her new husband's business, and certain other ventures, she prospers; and, when Frank is killed in a Klan foray, she marries Butler without delay. Later, she comes to realize that it was really he whom she had loved all the while! But, too late! At this point, Butler leaves her; and she goes back to Tara to recover her determination to win him back, for she had yet to see the "man she couldn't get" once she had determined to get him!

Gone With the Wind has many scenes that are richly humorous: the scene in which old Uncle Henry Hamilton rides to war, with his negro valet walking beside him with a raised umbrella; that in which Gerald comes to town to rebuke his daughter, gets drunk, and finds Scarlett holding the whip hand with a threat to tell Mrs. O'Hara of his own disgraceful conduct; that in which Grandpa Merriweather recalls the time his wife had given him a surprise party and had herself been the most surprised one at the party, for she had neglected to apprize him of the coming affair and he had done much drinking during the day; and many others that readers will long remember. It is also a novel which, though undoubtedly over-long and crowded, is still surprisingly rewarding in detail, in charming descriptions of Southern life, in sharply individualized characters, in skilful suspenses, in its handling of emotions that are elemental in the best sense, and in its complete absorption with an idea:

that some things may be gone with the wind, but that others endure forever.

I am not interested in all of this. I am interested in *Gone With the Wind* not as a literary triumph of our day, but as a challenge to our day. At a time when extreme and literal realism would seem to be the fashion, Margaret Mitchell has proved again what can be done by the novelist who writes with a realization that the values of art should be transcending values. Let me suggest but one example. Recall that long description of the birth of Melanie's child — a terrifyingly vivid description, to be sure, but not an orgiastic or purposeless one as is, let us say, the birth scene in Sherwood Anderson's *Tar*. Rather is it imaginative and redemptive, filled with highly significant overtones, as such a scene should be — as is the similar scene in *Kristin Lavransdatter*.

Also, Margaret Mitchell has shown us what can be done by a novelist who thinks of men and women as *human* beings. Scarlett O'Hara has an extremely volatile temperament; but she is no bottle of "fluid dynamite." She lives powerfully in our memories, not because she is a "moth" or a "little mannikin," but because she is a woman. Rhett Butler is the very incarnation of evil; he is one of the most gigantic devils ever created for our fiction. But he is an arresting devil, even a fascinating one; and Miss Mitchell has been able to create him as such because she has created him, also, as a man. The same is true of the other people in the novel. Their emotions are not "agglutinated" hysterias, but genuine passions. They are not merely "caught up" in the "flux" of life. In short, they are men rather than mechanisms, women rather than mere chemical compounds.

And have we not proved that we like them as such?

3

Josephine Johnson, who received the Pulitzer Award in 1935, offers another illustration of a writer with satisfyingly human attitudes. "Now in November I can see our years as a whole. This autumn is like both an end and a beginning to our lives, and those days which seemed confused with the blur of all things too near and too familiar are clear and strange now." [2] From the very opening sentences of her *Now In November* (1935) there was the promise of a book that would contain some of the most distinguished writing yet done by any living American novelist. That promise was not unfulfilled.

Now In November is concerned chiefly with a final spring and a desolate summer in the lives of Mr. and Mrs. Haldmarne and their three children (Marget, Merle, and Kerrin) some time after they have settled down upon a Midwestern farm. By making use of a skilful series of "throw-backs," however, the novel actually covers the entire period of their life on this farm, with the final spring and summer emphasized only as the culmination of their miseries.

Mr. Haldmarne loves the land and hopes to find in it a source of security for his children, a means of saving them from that "fierce crawling" against debt which he himself had always known. But he can make no headway against the crushing mortgage which the farm carries: "There was a bitterness in sowing and reaping . . . when all that it meant was the privilege of doing this over again and nothing to show but a little mark on paper." [3] One tragedy after another besets the cruelly pressed family. Kerrin gradually loses her sanity after an unrewarded love affair, and finally kills herself. The mother dies from burns which she receives in fighting a fire which threatens to destroy their buildings. To add to it all, a merciless drought and scorching heat crisp everything that is green on the face of their small part of mortgaged earth.

A sombre tale? And "bleak, and bitter, and tragic"? Yes. But not a tale of frustration or despair. It is intense, but even its "bitterness" has a kind of resonance; and the novel is filled with snatches of such beauty as that suggested by Marget:

> But sometimes, even in this year, the beauty of certain hours and places was so intolerable that it contracted the heart and left me without words. There was an unearthly smell in evenings, a strange mingling of wild grape and catalpa sweetness with honeysuckle come to flower and unknown blossoming things, and I woke up at night to blinding moonlight and the complaining of a catbird in the firebushes. The black marsh-fields swarmed with fireflies that seemed to stand still in the air for seconds at a time. The earth was overwhelmed with beauty and indifferent to it, and I went with a heart ready to crack for its unbearable loveliness.[4]

Beauty that contracts the heart! And hope that all men and women know who live close to the earth! Under the pressure of almost unendurable suffering, these people may, at times, think of themselves as "crawling along the ruts and shoving . . . debts ahead like the ball of dung-beetles." But always they rise "to face the mornings":

> Love and the old faith are gone. Faith gone with Mother. Grant gone. But there is the need and the desire left, and out of these hills they may come again. I cannot believe this is the end. Nor can I believe that death is more than the blindness of those living. And if this is only the consolation of a heart in its necessity, or that easy faith born of despair, it does not matter, since it gives us courage somehow to face the mornings. Which is as much as the heart can ask at times.[5]

The reputation which Miss Johnson achieved with this book, she more than sustained in her *Winter Orchard* (1935), a collection of stories that will be remembered for its many warm character portraits and limpidly beautiful writing. *Jordanstown* (1937), her most recent novel, adds to these qualities a passionate sympathy and a new power born of an awareness of suffering in a small town. Jordanstown, the scene of the book, is described as "a cluster of parallel, isolated lives. . . A town poised on the borderland between North and South, sourced by French and Swedish and German and plain English stock. It had none of the beauty or fierce brutality of the South, but a starched and simple savagery of its own." [6] Part of the town (the Bluff) is inhabited by the successful; below lies Fox Basin, inhabited by the poor; but over both sections blow the "four great winds of life":

> . . . *the fierce west wind of passion, of hate and anger, that drives men howling in mobs together; the foul east wind of the desire for power; the bitter and arctic wind of necessity, driving each life before it; the strong south wind of love.*[7]

When his father dies, Allen Craig manages to buy the town's small newspaper from its dying owner; and, together with his friend, Dave Woolf, he sets about the business of rousing the exploited laborers in Fox Basin. He wants to give them pride in themselves, to make them more articulate in their need. For it does not seem right to Allen that Fox Basin should know always the bitterly cold "north wind of necessity," while the Bluff lives in abundance:

> Above, on the surface of the town, lay the pattern of good things, normal things: the sewing circles, the light on supper tables, the clubs, the plays, the literary societies, the sudden comprehensions of beauty, the church socials, the gingerbread and prayers; men standing in sun on street corners, talking; the heavy grocery sacks, the picture shows; children laughing, shouting, licking their ice-cream cones; the school pageant, weddings, the car tied with white ribbons, the church full of lilies and asparagus fern. Law and order going on, life moving on the surface. . .[8]

Under Craig's leadership the workers build a crude hall which they intend to use as a meeting place and a kind of cooperative market. But when they finally try to take possession of their building, they are driven from its steps by a posse of deputies and thugs hired by the "organized" wealth of the Bluff. Dave is shot and dies; Allen and a number of the other laborers are jailed. For a time, after he is released, Allen despairs. But not for long. Remembering Dave's death, he comes to see that in its very "chill and terrible finality" there was something demanding that he carry on. *"He had felt the south wind, the wind without salt, at last."*

I have said nothing about some of the splendid portraits in this novel: such as that of the big negress, Anna, who leads the workers on with her improvised songs; or the desperate Avery, who has been without a job for years but who manages to keep himself and his cancer-ridden wife alive by driving a bakery wagon in exchange for left-over buns; or the golden-hearted little baker, Stefan, whose business is almost ruined because he cannot resist the proud, tear-stained, hungry faces that press against his windows. The social order in which *these* people live is just as trying as that, for example, in which John Dos Passos' characters exist. But, whereas John Dos Passos and his school give us puppets who, figuratively speaking, allow themselves to be beaten to the railroad crossing, Josephine Johnson gives us characters who, if necessary, will manage, like men, to keep alive by driving a bakery wagon in exchange for a few buns.

4

Earlier in this chapter I suggested that our recent avid interest in biography, historical fiction and "personal" history might, from one point of view, be interpreted as a sign of our growing dissatisfaction with that extreme realism which is the reflection of the realistic temper of our day. Does this not seem plausible?

That we are devouring biographies because — among other reasons, of course — our instinctive admiration for characters who are not dwarfed by their environment, is beginning to reassert itself?   That we are boosting the sales of historical novels — interesting ourselves for a while in the past — because we are beginning to find the ultra-realism of the present a bit uninteresting? [Such novels as Hervey Allen's *Anthony Adverse* (1933), Stark Young's *So Red The Rose* (1934), Walter D. Edmonds' *Drums Along the Mohawk* (1936), Vincent Sheean's *Sanfelice* (1936), Caroline Gordon's *None Shall Look Back* (1937), Kenneth Roberts' *Northwest Passage* (1937), and Royce Brier's *Boy in Blue* (1937) would seem to support my argument.]   That we are making best sellers out of such "personal" histories as Marie Sandoz's *Old Jules* (1935), Vincent Sheean's *Personal History* (1935), Negley Farson's *The Way of a Transgressor* (1936), and Victor G. Heiser's *An American Doctor's Odyssey* (1936), because we really do believe that man can, and does, add a cubit to his stature?

Still other signs are not, perhaps, insignificant.   Not long ago we saw the way in which readers welcomed Donald Culross Peattie's *Green Laurels* (1936), that faultlessly written study of naturalists that never once subscribes to Naturalism, because its "real hero . . . is *man's* mind."   Here is a book which owed, I think, no small measure of its popular appeal to the way in which it satisfied a kind of universal and inextinguishable interest which we have in people who survive when pitted against the problems, and even the hostilities, of our physical world.   We read, let us say, that chapter in it telling of the heroic Wallace rising from his fevered Ternate bed to take notes; and we received a pleasing confirmation of our instinctive faith in the invincibility of the human spirit.   We read of Buffon humbly getting out of his fine carriage to watch an ant, or Linnæus, when he saw the gorse in flower, falling on his knees to pray. And we were glad to be told again of the divine, aspiring nature of that same spirit. In somewhat the same way Dr. Alexis Carrel's *Man The Unknown* (1935), that searching inquiry by a scientist of indisputable reputation, found a welcome among a good many thousands no longer quite satisfied with the older "scientific" monism.

Following in the footsteps of Nordhoff and Hall (whose rousing "Bounty" trilogy was succeeded by their *The Hurricane,* 1937, a Conrad-like story of Polynesia) a small, but not negligible, number of our writers have also begun to turn to the sea again for inspiration. I think we may safely predict a growing interest in such imaginative and romantic material; and this, too, indicates a veering, however slight, away from extreme "realism," defeatism, and morbid pathology. Somehow, psychoanalysts do not especially flourish on salt water; on a full-rigged ship there is little time for despair; and men who climb masts in ice and sleet do not think of themselves as "bulbous, spewing, puling" creatures.

Also, we might note with interest a few of the books which now actually suggest that family relationships can be normal — and that normal relationships can be extremely interesting. To those of us who have come to believe that every son is suffering from an Œdipus complex and every daughter from an Electra complex, that every mother has a "chemical affinity" for her neighbor's husband and every husband a "biological compulsion" toward his neighbor's wife — to such of us, books like Ruth Suckow's *Country People* (1924), *The Bonney Family* (1928), and *The Folks* (1934), Clarence Day's *Life With Father* (1935), Nancy Pope's *We Three* (1936), and John P. Marquand's *The Late George Apley* (1937) came as agreeable surprises.

Mr. Marquand's book is particularly rewarding for its presentation of what we might call "old-fashioned" relationships, for its sly humor, and for its effective irony. His central figure, George Apley, (whose life is presented to us chiefly through the letters he had written his son) is one of the past year's memorable character portraits. Writing to John, who was in the Army at the Mexican border, old George complains that John's mother is about to have some rose-bushes removed from the premises — rose-bushes cherished because they had come from his own grandfather's garden in Salem. He begs his son to send a telegram — if necessary, getting his Colonel's special permission to go to the telegraph office! — urging the mother to let the bushes stand.

When John's aged great uncle scandalizes all of them by marrying his trained nurse, George nevertheless insists that "the family must stand together"; and spends a whole day calling on people to assure them how "completely delighted" the family really is! Again, when the son secretly marries a woman from Long Island, the father is shocked — until he learns that his daughter-in-law is actually "one of the Hogarths of Connecticut." *That* makes all the difference in the world! And when he finds his daughter reading Freud, old George again writes his son. I find a double pleasure in quoting from this letter: in itself it is irresistible for its humor and irony; and my using it, may, I hope, let my readers know that, despite my strictures on Fraudism, I am not unaware of that genuine influence of Freudism which Mr. Marquand so slyly emphasizes.

Dear John : —
   At a small dinner last night, which your mother and I gave for Eleanor, your sister suddenly began discussing psychology. To my amazement, she seems to have been spending a great deal of time in the Athenæum lately reading the works of a certain doctor named Sigmund Freud. Have you ever heard of this man? I believe I recall overhearing some of your friends mention his name in New York. I am writing by this same mail to the Trustees of the Athenæum asking that all works

by Freud be put into the Locked Room. They are certainly too strong for public consumption. . .

. . . Now you have more influence with Eleanor than we have, John. I wish when you get this letter you would ask her down to New York, or better come up here and speak to her sensibly. This letter is, of course, completely confidential as man to man and it might be just as well if you would burn it.

This disposition to throw all reticence to the wind, to speak frankly of things which had better not be mentioned, may be all right in a way. Certainly it seems hard these days to find a good clean novel, so hard that I have given up reading any but the works of Conrad and Archibald Marshall. At any rate this sort of thing is distinctly not good for women. Yesterday, I found that your mother had actually taken this Freud book out of the Athenæum. She was embarrassed when I found her reading it in the small music-room, and gave as her reason that she wished to know what Eleanor was doing. I am now reading the book myself for the same reason. . .[9]

But of all the literary portents somewhat indicative of a new tendency in our fiction, I believe the most promising to be found in the work of that small group of our novelists who are beginning more and more to turn to regional material — especially that regional material to be found in older ways of life, or in life closer to the soil. They are re-emphasizing values which greatly need to be re-emphasized; and they are doing much to strengthen again our perishing faith in the simple, the abiding, and the fundamental. The work of even some of our more established writers would now seem, indeed, often to be most enduring in those of their books which are based upon the unfailing, elemental virtues discovered by people who live near to the earth.

One has only to compare, by way of illustration, some of Joseph Hergesheimer's earlier novels (and their sickeningly rococo descriptions of jade, tassels, moonstones, satins, flower petals, and lotus buds) with his *The Limestone Tree* (1931), a sturdily textured novel about Kentucky pioneers ("passionate and courageous men") — one has only to make this comparison, I say, to be convinced of the power and literary worth of simple emotions that really do satisfy the human heart. Or, one has only to compare Louis Bromfield's *Twenty-four Hours* (1930) with his *The Farm* (1933), which tells, in its author's words, of a manner of living "largely gone out of fashion," but still "a good way."   For, as Rose Wilder Lane says in her *Let the Hurricane Roar* (1933), it is a way rich in its lessons about the invincibility of the human spirit. Life batters Mrs. Lane's Caroline, but it does not crush her :

. . . she knew the infinite smallness, weakness, of life in the lifeless universe. She felt the vast, insensate forces against which life itself is a rebellion. Infinitely small and weak was the spark of warmth in a living heart. Yet valiantly the tiny heart continued to beat. Tired, weak, burdened by its own fears and sorrows, still it persisted, indomitably it continued to exist, and in bare existence itself, without assurance of victory, even without hope, in its indomitable existence among vast, incalculable, lifeless forces, it was invincible.[10]

Readers interested in lists of earlier regional books can be referred to such an excellent volume as Harry Hartwick's *The Foreground of American Fiction* (1934).   But let me mention just a few books of this type which have appeared since Mr. Hartwick's study : Bess Streeter Aldrich's *Spring Came On Forever* (1935), a story about the descendants of Nebraska pioneers; Phil Stong's *Career* (1936) and *Buckskin Breeches* (1937); Hubert Skidmore's *I Will Lift Up Mine Eyes* (1936), a simple and compelling chronicle of a family in the Blue Ridge Mountains; Claude Morrow Wilson's *Rabble Rouser* (1936), an account of Arkansas pre-War politics; Jesse Stuart's *Head O'W-Hollow* (1936), a collection of highly flavored stories; Owen P. White's *My Texas 'Tis of Thee* (1936), a group of virile, legendary "tall tales" about the Lone Star State; Virginia Watson's *The Featherlys* (1936), a study in the "beauty, courtesy and grace of living" of the early Virginia aristocracy; Thad St. Martin's *Madame Toussaint's Wedding Day* (1936), a colorful novel of the Louisiana bayous; Theodore Pratt's *Big Blow* (1936), a narrative about a courageous young farmer in Southern Florida; Warren Howard's *The Littlest House* (1936), a romantic novel with a Maryland setting; Paul Horgan's *The Return of the Weed* (1936), a group of stories about New Mexico; Robert P. Tristram Coffin's *John Dawn* (1936), a tale of hardy Maine seafarers; Margaret Cabell Self's *Red Clay Country* (1936), a colorful romance of Virginia country life; and Sophus Keith Winther's *Take All To Nebraska* (1936), a story of Midwestern pioneering and farm life.

Other titles could be named: Elma Godchaux's *Stubborn Roots* (1936), a novel about a Louisiana sugar plantation; William McNally's *The Roofs of Elm Street* (1936), a book with a setting in a small Minnesota town; Alvin Johnson's *Spring Storm* (1936), a tale of hardy Nebraska life; Elizabeth Corbett's *Mount Royal* (1936), four short novelettes about a small Illinois town; Stuart David Engstrand's *The Invaders* (1937), a narrative of the Southwest; Roark Bradford's *Three-Headed Angel* (1937), a novel with a Tennessee background; Conrad Richter's *The Sea of Grass* (1937), an artistic story of the Southwest cattle country, which has been compared with *My Ántonia;* Wellington Roe's *The Tree Falls South* (1937), a grim depiction of the Dust Bowl; Esther Forbes' *Paradise* (1937), and Frances Winwar's *Gallows Hill* (1937), both of which are chronicles of the Massachusetts Bay Colony.

I do not say that all of these books meet with my unqualified recommendation. But each, in some way or another, suggests something of the hard courage and the fullness which the novelist can find by looking deeply into American life, and searching for characters who, in the words Miss Cather uses to describe Ántonia, lend themselves "to immemorial human attitudes which we recognize by instinct as universal and true."

5

It may be objected, of course, that I seemingly want our writers to flee from their own times, to seek an evasion of present-day problems by working out patterns of life that belong to the past. It may further be objected that our age — in itself sordid, Naturalistic, and abnormal — must, for the writer who does *not* want to "flee" from it, lend itself of necessity to representations of the sordid, Naturalistic, and abnormal. And it may be argued that in either case — whether he avoid the present entirely, or fail in representing it as it is — the writer is falsifying his intuitions.

And yet, is this true? May a writer not be true to the material of his age, the incidents of his day, and still possess that greatness of vision which enables him to fuse, through the alembic of a powerful imagination, both that material and those incidents, into a transcending art? For realism — if that is what our writers are after — is not truth to a writer's *day*: it is truth to *life* — to *all* life. It does not necessarily inhere in any material, or in any incident. As Hugh Walpole has pointed out, there may be just as much realism in the tap of blind Pew's cane as in "any number of adulteries." [11]

Consequently, much would seem to depend — almost everything would seem to depend — on the vision of the author himself : he is today often imposing falsifications upon his art by mistaking "realism" for realism, no less than if he were substituting maudlin sentiment for genuine romanticism. The important thing, as I see it, is that he not confuse the eddies with the strong central current of human values.

Let him write of his day if he wants to ; but let him do so without forgetting that his day is but one in the years.

14937

ACKNOWLEDGMENTS AND REFERENCES

I. *On Falling Off the Floor*

[1] Reprinted with the kind permission of the New York *Evening Post.*

[2] *The Critique of Humanism* (1930), p. 333.

[3] Introduction to *On Contemporary Literature*, 1917.

[4] P. 267. By permission of Harcourt, Brace and Company, Inc.

[5] Young's *Night Thoughts,* ll. 67-68.

[6] *Beyond Life,* p. 42.

[7] These comments by Messrs. Hazlitt, Chamberlain, and Grattan are to be found in *The Critique of Humanism,* edited by C. Hartley Grattan. Brewer and Warren, Inc., 1930.

[8] *The Modern Temper* (1929), by Joseph Wood Krutch. P. 20. My quotations from this volume are all reprinted with the most gracious permission of Harcourt, Brace and Company, Inc.

[9] *Man and Technics* (1932), by Oswald Spengler. P. 22. By permission of Alfred A. Knopf, Inc., the authorized publishers.

[10] *Ibid.,* p. 28.

[11] From *No Villain Need Be,* by Vardis Fisher. Copyright, 1936. P. 304. Reprinted by permission from Doubleday, Doran and Company, Inc.

[12] From *This Body the Earth* (1935), by Paul Green. P. 388. By permission of Harper & Brothers, publishers.

[13] From *Thus Spake Zarathustra,* by Friedrich Nietzsche. P. 11. By permission of The Macmillan Company, publishers.

[14] Quoted in René Lalou's *Contemporary French Literature* (1924), p. 36.

[15] *The Modern Temper,* by Joseph Wood Krutch. P. 66.

[16] From *God's Little Acre,* by Erskine Caldwell. P. 298. Copyright, 1933. Published by The Viking Press, Inc., New York.

[17] *The New Statesman,* Dec. 7, 1929. By courtesy of the Editor of *The New Statesman and Nation.*

II. *Theodore Dreiser and the Rise of American Naturalism*

[1] By courtesy of Mrs. Woodrow Wilson.

[2] Certain ideas which I advance in this book, I have previously made the subjects of papers published in *The Catholic World*. To the Editor of that magazine I am deeply grateful for permission to make this new use of that material.

[3] *The Ordeal of Richard Feverel*. By courtesy of Charles Scribner's Sons.

[4] My brief quotations from Stephen Crane's *Maggie* are used by permission of Alfred A. Knopf, Inc., authorized publishers of the novel.

[5] The brief quotations from Stephen Crane's *The Red Badge of Courage* are used by permission of the D. Appleton-Century Company, publishers.

[6] I quote from Stephen Crane's "The Blue Hotel" with the permission of Alfred A. Knopf, Inc., the authorized publishers.

[7] The few phrases from Stephen Crane's "The Open Boat" are used with the permission of Alfred A. Knopf, Inc., the authorized publishers.

[8] From *Vandover and the Brute*, by Frank Norris. Copyright, 1924, by Doubleday, Doran and Company, Inc.

[9] From *McTeague*, by Frank Norris. Copyright, 1899, 1927, by Doubleday, Doran and Company, Inc.

[10] *Ibid.*, p. 32. Quoted in Vernon Louis Parrington's *Main Currents in American Thought*, vol. III, p. 331.

[11] From *The Octopus*, by Frank Norris. Copyright, 1901, by Doubleday, Doran and Company, Inc.

[12] From *The Pit*, by Frank Norris. Copyright, 1903, by Doubleday, Doran and Company, Inc. See the whole passage, pp. 419-420.

[13] The brief quotations from Jack London's *The Sea-Wolf* are used with the kind permission of Eliza London Shepard.

[14] From *Thus Spake Zarathustra*, by Friedrich Nietzsche. By permission of The Macmillan Company, publishers.

[15] *Newspaper Days*, p. 396. The quotations in this volume from Theodore Dreiser's books are used by courtesy of the author. I am very grateful to Mr. Dreiser, and also to his publishers, Simon and Schuster, Inc.

[16] Quoted in *Living Authors,* by Dilly Tante. P. 109. The H. W. Wilson Company, 1931.

[17] *Newspaper Days.* Copyright, 1922. P. 59.

[18] *Ibid.,* p. 380.

[19] *The Bookman.* January, 1930, p. 536. Throughout this volume I quote from *The Bookman* with the gracious permission of Mr. Seward Collins.

[20] From "Theodore Dreiser," by Isidor Schneider. *The Saturday Review of Literature,* March 10, 1934. For all of my quotations from this magazine I am grateful to Miss Amy Loveman, the Associate Editor.

[21] By courtesy of the New York *Herald-Tribune.* Quoted in Charles C. Baldwin's *The Men Who Make Our Novels,* p. 143.

[22] From *Horses and Men,* by Sherwood Anderson. Copyright, 1923. Published by The Viking Press, Inc., New York.

[23] From *Dawn.* Copyright, 1931. P. 63.

[24] *Newspaper Days,* p. 107.

[25] *Ibid.,* p. 67.

[26] "What I Believe," by Theodore Dreiser. *The Forum,* November, 1929. Quoted with the permission of the Editor.

[27] *Hey Rub-A-Dub-Dub.* Copyright, 1920. P. 7.

[28] *The Bookman.* September, 1928, p. 25.

[29] *Hey Rub-A-Dub-Dub,* p. 117.

[30] *Ibid.,* p. 120.

[31] *Ibid.,* pp. 242-243.

[32] *Newspaper Days,* p. 106.

[33] *Hey Rub-A-Dub-Dub,* p. 88.

[34] *A Hoosier Holiday.* Copyright, 1916. P. 253.

[35] *Hey Rub-A-Dub-Dub,* p. 17.

[36] *Newspaper Days,* pp. 196-197.

[37] See *Hey Rub-A-Dub-Dub,* pp. 12-16.

[38] *The Financier.* Revised edition. Copyright, 1927. Pages 3-4.

[39] *Ibid.,* p. 503.

[40] An especially good illustration of the way in which Mr. Dreiser sometimes parodies himself, is that passage in *Jennie Gerhardt* beginning on p. 129 and continuing to the end of the chapter.

[41] *In the Worst Possible Taste,* by Corey Ford. Pages 24-25. Quoted by courtesy of Charles Scribner's Sons.

42 *The Financier,* p. 141.
43 *Ibid.,* pp. 146-147.
44 *The Titan.* Copyright, 1914. P. 188.
45 *Humanism and America,* edited by Norman Foerster. P. 163. By permission of the publishers, Farrar and Rinehart, Inc.
46 *Ibid.,* pp. 164-165.
47 Pages 85-86. Quoted with the kind permission of Calmann-Lévy, the publishers.
48 Brother Leo, in *Columbia,* March, 1930. By courtesy of the Editor.
49 *Newspaper Days,* p. 499.

III. *Something More about Cabell*

1 I have been permitted to quote from the Cabell books through the courtesy of the publishers, Robert M. McBride & Company.
2 Printed by the Colophon Club of Cleveland.
3 *Smirt, Smith,* and *Smire* constitute a series. Mr. Cabell has carefully explained the genesis of these novels in a little pamphlet entitled "The Nightmare Has Triplets." Doubleday, Doran and Company, 1937.
4 From *The Men Who Make Our Novels,* by Charles C. Baldwin. P. 75. Copyright, 1924, by Dodd, Mead & Company, Inc.
5 *Beyond Life,* p. 43.
6 *Ibid.,* p. 42. Quoted with the permission of the publishers, Robert M. McBride & Company.
7 *Straws and Prayer-Books,* p. 176.
8 From *The Men Who Make Our Novels,* by Charles C. Baldwin. P. 76.
9 *Beyond Life,* p. 59.
10 P. 195. Quoted through the courtesy of Charles Scribner's Sons.

IV. *Freudism and the Stream-of-Consciousness*

1 By permission of the publishers, the D. Appleton-Century Company.
2 Quoted in *Living Authors,* by Dilly Tante. P. 202. The H. W. Wilson Co.

[3] *Ibid.*

[4] *Ulysses,* p. 14. Reprinted by courtesy of Random House, Inc., New York.

[5] Paul Jordan Smith, in his *A Key to the Ulysses of James Joyce.* Copyright, 1927, by Pascal Covici. Reissued, 1934, by Covici, Friede, Inc. By permission.

[6] Quoted in *Modern Fiction,* by Dorothy Brewster and Angus Burrell. P. 156. Columbia University Press, 1934.

[7] *Ibid.,* pp. 156-157.

[8] From Katherine F. Gerould's "Stream of Consciousness." *The Saturday Review of Literature,* October 22, 1927.

[9] Serviceable summaries may be found in *A Key to the Ulysses of James Joyce* or *Modern Fiction,* both mentioned above.

[10] Quoted in *Living Authors,* p. 204.

[11] P. 11. Reprinted by courtesy of Random House, Inc., New York.

[12] *The Twentieth Century Novel,* by Joseph Warren Beach. P. 517. By permission of D. Appleton-Century Co., publishers.

[13] P. 51. Reprinted by courtesy of Random House, Inc., New York.

[14] P. 666. Reprinted by courtesy of Random House, Inc., New York.

[15] P. 676. Reprinted by courtesy of Random House, Inc., New York.

[16] P. 722. Reprinted by courtesy of Random House, Inc., New York.

[17] From *1919,* p. 102. Published by Harcourt, Brace and Company, Inc. Copyright, 1932, by John Dos Passos.

[18] *Sword Blades and Poppy Seed,* by Amy Lowell. By permission of Houghton Mifflin Company, the publishers.

[19] *A Farewell to Arms,* p. 6. By permission of Charles Scribner's Sons.

[20] *Ulysses,* p. 172. Reprinted by courtesy of Random House, Inc., New York.

[21] P. 19. Reprinted by courtesy of Random House, Inc., New York.

[22] *Plagued by the Nightingale* (1931), p. 176. Reprinted by courtesy of Random House, Inc., New York.

[23] *Year Before Last,* p. 12. Reprinted by courtesy of Random House, Inc., New York.

[24] P. 233. Quoted by permission of Charles Scribner's Sons.

[25] *City Block*, by Waldo Frank. Pages 127-128. Copyright, 1922. Quoted by permission of Charles Scribner's Sons.

[26] P. 227. By courtesy of Henry Holt and Company.

[27] *Appointment in Samarra*, by John O'Hara. Pages 221-222. Copyright, 1934, by Harcourt, Brace and Company, Inc. Quoted with the permission of the publishers.

[28] *Ulysses*, p. 363. Reprinted by courtesy of Random House, Inc., New York.

[29] *Expression in America*, by Ludwig Lewisohn. Pages 405-406. Copyright, 1932, by Harper & Brothers. Quoted through the courtesy of the publishers.

[30] Lines 85-92.

[31] From Matthew Arnold's "Resignation," ll. 146-147. By permission of The Macmillan Company, publishers.

[32] From *1919*, p. 175. Published by Harcourt, Brace and Company, Inc. Copyright, 1932, by John Dos Passos.

[33] *Look Homeward, Angel*, by Thomas Wolfe. P. 342. By courtesy of Charles Scribner's Sons.

[34] *Year Before Last*, p. 49. Reprinted by courtesy of Random House, Inc., New York.

[35] *Ibid.*, p. 369. Reprinted by courtesy of Random House, Inc., New York.

[36] From *City Block*, by Waldo Frank. Copyright, 1922, by Waldo Frank. Quoted with the kind permission of the publishers, Charles Scribner's Sons.

[37] *Of Time and the River*, by Thomas Wolfe. P. 867. By courtesy of Charles Scribner's Sons.

[38] "What Has 1932 Done for Literature?", by Lewis Mumford. *The Atlantic Monthly*, December, 1932. My quotations from this magazine are used with the kind consent of the Editor.

[39] Each year sees the publication of at least a score of such volumes as Dorothy R. Blitzsten's *Psychoanalysis Explained* (1936), Sigmund Freud's *The Problem of Anxiety* (1936), Dr. William Malmud's *Outlines of General Psychopathology* (1936), etc.

[40] From *False Prophets*, by James M. Gillis, C.S.P. By permission of The Macmillan Company, publishers.

[41] *The Interpretation of Dreams*, by Sigmund Freud. Pages 109 ff. Authorized translation by A. A. Brill. London:

George Allen & Unwin, Ltd., 1932. My quotations from this volume are used with the kind permission of Dr. Brill.

[42] From *Freud's Theories of the Neuroses.* Hitschmann, trans. by Payne, 1921. P. 195. By courtesy of Dodd, Mead and Company, the publishers.

[43] *The Interpretation of Dreams,* p. 165.

[44] I take examples from Freud's *The Interpretation of Dreams.*

[45] From Maxwell Bodenheim's "Psychoanalysis and American Fiction." *The Nation,* June 7, 1922. By courtesy of the Editor. This passage is also quoted in Harry Hartwick's *The Foreground of American Fiction,* pp. 133-134.

[46] From *No Villain Need Be,* by Vardis Fisher. P. 320. Copyright, 1936. Reprinted by permission from Doubleday, Doran and Company, Inc.

[47] *Ibid.,* p. 165.

[48] *Moon-Calf,* p. 295. I quote from this book with the courteous permission of Mr. Dell.

[49] *Ibid.,* p. 120.

[50] Pages 90-91. By courtesy of Charles Scribner's Sons.

[51] *Ibid.,* p. 57.

[52] *A Jew in Love,* by Ben Hecht. P. 245. Published by Covici, Friede, Inc. Quoted by permission.

[53] From *Manhattan Transfer,* p. 234. Published by Harper and Brothers. Copyright, 1925, by John Dos Passos.

[54] *Ibid.,* p. 235.

[55] *A History of the American Drama,* by Arthur Hobson Quinn. Vol. II, p. 199. By permission of the publishers, Harper and Brothers.

[56] My brief quotations from the O'Neill plays are reprinted by courtesy of Random House, Inc., New York.

[57] See John Corbin's "O'Neill and Æschylus." *The Saturday Review of Literature,* April 30, 1932.

[58] From *No Villain Need Be,* by Vardis Fisher. P. 239. Copyright, 1936. Reprinted by permission from Doubleday, Doran and Company, Inc.

[59] *Ibid.,* p. 241.

[60] *Ibid.,* p. 126.

[61] *King Coffin,* by Conrad Aiken. P. 100. Copyright, 1935, by Conrad Aiken. By permission of the publishers, Charles Scribner's Sons.

[62] *Among the Lost People,* by Conrad Aiken. P. 43. Copyright, 1934, by Conrad Aiken. By permission of the publishers, Charles Scribner's Sons.

[63] *Meat,* by Wilbur Daniel Steele. Pages 142-143. Copyright, 1928, by Wilbur Daniel Steele. By permission of the publishers, Charles Scribner's Sons.

V. *Sherwood Anderson: Congenital Freudian*

[1] By courtesy of Dr. A. A. Brill, the authorized translator.

[2] Quoted in Cleveland B. Chase's *Sherwood Anderson,* p. 7.

[3] From *A Story Teller's Story,* by Sherwood Anderson. Pages 312-313. Copyright, 1922. Published by The Viking Press, Inc., New York.

[4] From *Mid-American Chants,* by Sherwood Anderson. P. 27. Copyright, 1918. Published by The Viking Press, Inc., New York.

[5] From *A Story Teller's Story,* by Sherwood Anderson. P. 293. Copyright, 1922. Published by The Viking Press, Inc., New York.

[6] From *Windy McPherson's Son,* by Sherwood Anderson. P. 75. Copyright, 1920. Published by The Viking Press, Inc., New York.

[7] *Ibid.,* final paragraph.

[8] From *Marching Men,* by Sherwood Anderson. Copyright, 1917. Published by The Viking Press, Inc., New York. The reader should refer to the whole passage beginning on p. 148.

[9] From *Marching Men,* by Sherwood Anderson. Copyright, 1917. Published by The Viking Press, Inc., New York. Passage quoted in Chase's *Sherwood Anderson,* p. 30.

[10] P. 63. Quoted with the kind permission of Charles Scribner's Sons.

[11] From *Winesburg, Ohio,* by Sherwood Anderson. Copyright, 1919. Published by The Viking Press, Inc., New York.

[12] From *The Triumph of the Egg,* by Sherwood Anderson. Copyright, 1921. Published by The Viking Press, Inc., New York.

[13] From *Poor White,* by Sherwood Anderson. Copyright, 1921. Published by The Viking Press, Inc., New York. I quote the opening lines of the novel.

[14] From Cleveland B. Chase's *Sherwood Anderson,* p. 54. By courtesy of the publishers, Robert M. McBride & Company.

[15] "A Small-town Editor Airs His Mind," by Mildred Adams. The New York *Times,* September 22, 1929. By courtesy of Miss Adams and the New York *Times.*

[16] P. 221. By courtesy of Charles Scribner's Sons, the publishers.

[17] Quoted in Harry Hartwick's *The Foreground of American Fiction,* p. 112. American Book Company, 1934. I have found Mr. Hartwick's scholarly volume very helpful in preparing my own — especially in doing this chapter on Anderson.

[18] See *Tar,* p. xii.

[19] From *The Men Who Make Our Novels,* by Charles C. Baldwin. P. 26. Copyright, 1924, by Dodd, Mead & Company, Inc.

[20] *Winesburg, Ohio.*

[21] *The Interpretation of Dreams,* p. 165.

[22] *Winesburg, Ohio.*

[23] *Kit Brandon,* p. 9. By courtesy of Charles Scribner's Sons.

[24] *Taking the Literary Pulse,* p. 33. Quoted with the kind permission of Dr. Collins.

[25] From *Many Marriages,* by Sherwood Anderson. Pages 190-191. Copyright, 1923. Published by The Viking Press, Inc., New York.

[26] Both of these poems are in Sherwood Anderson's *Mid-American Chants.* Copyright, 1918. Published by The Viking Press, Inc., New York.

[27] From *The Modern Novel,* by Elizabeth A. Drew. Pages 119-120. Quoted with the kind permission of the publishers, Harcourt, Brace and Company, Inc.

[28] The poem is in *Mid-American Chants.*

[29] See p. 119 of Mr. Sinclair's *Money Writes.* Quoted in Hartwick's *The Foreground of American Fiction,* p. 115.

VI. *Ernest Hemingway: Spokesman for His Generation*

[1] Reprinted with the kind permission of the publishers, Charles Scribner's Sons.

[2] Pages 260-261. Reprinted by courtesy of Random House, Inc., New York.

[3] P. 265. Reprinted by courtesy of Random House, Inc., New York.

[4] The *Autobiography of Alice B. Toklas,* p. 262. Reprinted by courtesy of Random House, Inc., New York.

[5] *Ibid.* Reprinted by courtesy of Random House, Inc., New York.

[6] See "Ernest Hemingway: A Note," by Harry Sylvester. *The Commonweal,* October 30, 1936.

[7] From *In Our Time,* by Ernest Hemingway. Pages 184-185. I am grateful to the publishers, Charles Scribner's Sons, for permission to make certain quotations from this volume.

[8] *Ibid.,* p. 235.

[9] From *The Sun Also Rises,* by Ernest Hemingway. P. 255. Copyright, 1926, by Charles Scribner's Sons. I quote from this volume by courtesy of the publishers.

[10] *Ibid.* Pages 39-40.

[11] *Men Without Women,* by Ernest Hemingway. P. 58. Copyright, 1927, by Charles Scribner's Sons. My quotations from this volume are used with the most gracious permission of Charles Scribner's Sons.

[12] In the tale, "Hills Like White Elephants."

[13] *A Farewell to Arms,* by Ernest Hemingway. P. 355. Copyright, 1929, by Charles Scribner's Sons, who have most kindly permitted me to quote from this novel.

[14] *The Sun Also Rises,* p. 135.

[15] *The Autobiography of Alice B. Toklas,* p. 271. Reprinted by courtesy of Random House, Inc., New York.

[16] See William Troy's review of *Winner Take Nothing* in *The Nation* for November 15, 1933. Quotations from this magazine by permission of the Editor.

[17] From *No Villain Need Be,* by Vardis Fisher. P. 276. Copyright, 1936. Reprinted by permission from Doubleday, Doran and Company, Inc.

[18] *The Autobiography of Alice B. Toklas,* p. 261. Reprinted by courtesy of Random House, Inc., New York.

[19] From Vernon Louis Parrington's *Main Currents in American Thought,* vol. III, p. 386. By permission of Harcourt, Brace and Company, Inc.

[20] *Three Worlds,* by Carl Van Doren. P. 176. By permission of the publishers, Harper & Brothers.

[21] *A Farewell to Arms,* p. 123.

[22] *The Sun Also Rises,* p. 216.

[23] *A Farewell to Arms,* p. 143.

[24] *Ibid.*, p. 181.

[25] *Ibid.*, p. 273.

[26] *Ibid.*, p. 249.   A few of these short quotations are quoted also in Harry Hartwick's *The Foreground of American Fiction.*

[27] Quoted in William Troy's review of *Winner Take Nothing. The Nation,* November 15, 1933.   By permission of Charles Scribner's Sons.

[28] *Men Without Women,* p. 196.

[29] *A Farewell to Arms,* p. 350.

[30] *Ibid.*, p. 148.

[31] *Ibid.*, p. 196.

[32] *Ibid.*, p. 350.

[33] *The Sun Also Rises,* p. 153.

[34] *Death in the Afternoon,* by Ernest Hemingway.   P. 4.   I quote from this volume with the kind permission of Charles Scribner's Sons.

[35] *The Sun Also Rises,* p. 153.

[36] *A Farewell to Arms,* p. 164.

[37] *Ibid.*, p. 32.

[38] *Ibid.*

[39] From "Chronicle and Comment."   *The Bookman,* February, 1930.

[40] *A Farewell to Arms,* p. 196.

[41] *The Modern Temper,* by Joseph Wood Krutch.   Pages 97-98. With the kind permission of Harcourt, Brace & Company, Inc.

[42] *A Farewell to Arms,* p. 146.

[43] *The Sun Also Rises,* p. 123.

[44] See *The Bookman,* February, 1930.

[45] *Lectures in America,* by Gertrude Stein.   P. 170.   Reprinted by courtesy of Random House, Inc., New York.

VII. *John Dos Passos and the Modern Distemper*

[1] Reprinted by permission of the publisher, The University of Chicago Press.

[2] See the 1904 edition of his *Letters.* Pages 52 ff.

[3] From *No Villain Need Be,* by Vardis Fisher.   P. 16.   Copyright, 1936.   Reprinted by permission from Doubleday, Doran and Company, Inc.

[4] *Ibid.*, p. 25.

[5] *Ibid.*, p. 276.

[6] "My Picture in the Paper"—in the volume, *Inhale & Exhale.*

[7] Reprinted by courtesy of Random House, Inc., New York.

[8] *As I Lay Dying*, p. 160. Reprinted by courtesy of Random House, Inc., New York.

[9] By courtesy of Charles Scribner's Sons.

[10] Reprinted by courtesy of Random House, Inc., New York.

[11] P. 199. By permission of The Vanguard Press.

[12] *Studs Lonigan*, p. 119.

[13] From *Three Soldiers*, by John Dos Passos. P. 250. Copyright, 1921, by Doubleday, Doran and Company, Inc.

[14] From *The Three Black Pennys*, by Joseph Hergesheimer. P. 167. By permission of Alfred A. Knopf, Inc., authorized publishers.

[15] *King Coffin*, p. 85.

[16] P. 73. Reprinted by courtesy of Random House, Inc., New York.

[17] From *Winesburg, Ohio*, by Sherwood Anderson. Copyright, 1919. Published by The Viking Press, Inc., New York.

[18] By permission of Frederick A. Stokes Company.

[19] P. 315. By permission of Coward-McCann, Inc.

[20] P. 3.

[21] From *Three Soldiers*, by John Dos Passos. P. 42. Copyright, 1921, by Doubleday, Doran and Company, Inc.

[22] *Ibid.*, p. 72.

[23] *Ibid.*, pp. 118-119.

[24] *Ibid.* See the whole passage beginning on p. 27.

[25] *Ibid.*, p. 231.

[26] *Ibid.*, p. 44.

[27] From *Manhattan Transfer*, p. 120. Published by Harper & Brothers. Copyright, 1925, by John Dos Passos. I wish to thank Messrs. Brandt & Brandt for their kind permission to quote from *Manhattan Transfer, The 42nd Parallel, 1919,* and *The Big Money.*

[28] *Manhattan Transfer*, p. 154.

[29] *Ibid.*, p. 3.

[30] *Ibid.*, p. 94.

[31] *Ibid.*, p. 113.

[32] *Ibid.*, p. 230.

[33] *Ibid.*, p. 295.

[34] *Ibid.*, p. 289.

[35] *Ibid.,* p. 12.

[36] *Ibid.,* p. 392.

[37] *Ibid.,* p. 371.

[38] Mr. Dos Passos says he quotes from *American Climatology,* by W. W. Hodgins. Chicago, 1865.

[39] From *The 42nd Parallel,* p. 5. Published by Harper and Brothers. Copyright, 1930, by John Dos Passos.

[40] From *The Big Money,* p. 556. Published by Harcourt, Brace & Company, Inc. Copyright, 1936, by John Dos Passos.

[41] See "John Dos Passos," by Granville Hicks. *The Bookman,* April, 1932.

[42] *The Big Money,* p. 434.

[43] *Ibid.,* p. 149.

[44] P. 220.

[45] *Manhattan Transfer,* p. 210.

[46] From *1919,* p. 190. Published by Harcourt, Brace & Company, Inc. Copyright, 1932, by John Dos Passos.

[47] See Robert Van Gelder's review of *The Big Money* in the New York *Times,* August 6, 1936.

[48] See p. 105 of *Living Authors,* by Dilly Tante.

[49] From *Three Soldiers,* by John Dos Passos. P. 237. Copyright, 1921, by Doubleday, Doran and Company, Inc.

[50] *Ibid.,* p. 225.

[51] *Manhattan Transfer,* p. 90.

[52] *Ibid.,* p. 168.

[53] *Ibid.,* p. 345.

[54] *Ibid.,* p. 194.

[55] *Ibid.,* p. 169.

[56] From *Three Soldiers,* by John Dos Passos. P. 27. Copyright, 1921, by Doubleday, Doran and Company, Inc.

[57] From *One Man's Initiation — 1917,* by John Dos Passos. P. 120. Copyright, 1917, 1922, by Doubleday, Doran and Company, Inc.

[58] *Manhattan Transfer,* p. 37.

[59] *New York Is Not America* (1927).

[60] *My Ántonia,* p. 398. By permission of Houghton Mifflin Company.

[61] *Giants in the Earth,* p. 424. By permission of the publishers, Harper and Brothers.

[62] *The Bonney Family,* by Ruth Suckow. P. 296. By permission of Farrar and Rinehart, Inc.

[63] *Mister Pitt,* by Zona Gale. P. 163. By permission of the D. Appleton-Century Company.
[64] *So Big,* p. 27. By courtesy of Miss Ferber.

VIII. *William Faulkner : Cretins, Coffin-worms, and Cruelty*

[1] Quoted with the kind permission of Mr. Seward Collins.
[2] From the Introduction to Stuart Sherman's *On Contemporary Literature.* By courtesy of Henry Holt and Company.
[3] From Henri Barbusse's *Under Fire.* Reprinted by courtesy of the publisher, E. P. Dutton & Co., Inc., New York, and J. M. Dent & Sons, (Canada) Ltd.
[4] Quoted by Alan Reynolds Thompson in "The Cult of Cruelty." *The Bookman,* January-February issue, 1932.
[5] See his Introduction to the Modern Library edition of *Sanctuary.*
[6] *Ibid.* Reprinted by courtesy of Random House, Inc., New York.
[7] See the review by Harold Strauss. The New York *Times Book Review* for November 1, 1936. I quote from the New York *Times* with the permission of Mr. J. Donald Adams, Editor of the *Book Review.*
[8] I italicize the word.
[9] P. 146. Reprinted by courtesy of Random House, Inc., New York.
[10] *Ibid.* Reprinted by courtesy of Random House, Inc., New York.
[11] P. 186. Reprinted by courtesy of Random House, Inc., New York.
[12] P. 96. Reprinted by courtesy of Random House, Inc., New York.
[13] *As I Lay Dying,* p. 174. Reprinted by courtesy of Random House, Inc., New York.
[14] *Sanctuary,* Modern Library edition, p. 379.
[15] P. 110. Reprinted by courtesy of Random House, Inc., New York.
[16] P. 111. Reprinted by courtesy of Random House, Inc., New York.
[17] P. 207. Reprinted by courtesy of Random House, Inc., New York.
[18] P. 315. Reprinted by courtesy of Random House, Inc., New York.

[19] *Light In August,* p. 217.   Reprinted by courtesy of Random House, Inc., New York.

[20] "Faulkner of Mississippi," by Marshall J. Smith.   *The Bookman,* December, 1931.

[21] *A Green Bough,* p. 26.

[22] Pages 97 ff.   Reprinted with the most gracious permission of Harcourt, Brace and Company, Inc.

[23] P. 152.   By courtesy of Harcourt, Brace and Company, Inc.

[24] *Sartoris,* p. 41.   By courtesy of Harcourt, Brace and Company, Inc.

[25] Alan Reynolds Thompson's review of *Sanctuary.*   *The Bookman,* April, 1931.

[26] *Sanctuary,* Modern Library edition, p. 2.   Reprinted by courtesy of Random House, Inc., New York.

[27] *In the Worst Possible Taste,* by Corey Ford.   P. 85.   Quoted with the permission of the publishers, Charles Scribner's Sons.

[28] Pages 151-152 of the Modern Library edition.   Reprinted by courtesy of Random House, Inc., New York.

[29] By Benjamin de Casseres.   Quoted on the jacket of *Cawdor.*

[30] P. 251.   Edition published by Duckworth, Henrietta St., London.

[31] Robert Van Gelder, in the New York *Times.*   October 8, 1936.

[32] P. 174.   Reprinted by courtesy of Random House, Inc., New York.

[33] P. 298.

[34] Reprinted from Paul Green's *This Body the Earth,* with the permission of the publishers, Harper & Brothers.   The flogging scene is on pp. 374-375.

[35] To the author, at the Bread Loaf School of English.

IX. *Thomas Wolfe Embraces Life*

[1] I wish to acknowledge the courtesy of Charles Scribner's Sons for permission to quote throughout this book from Thomas Wolfe's *The Story of a Novel* (Copyright, 1936), *From Death to Morning* (Copyright, 1935), *Of Time and the River* (Copyright, 1935), and *Look Homeward, Angel* (Copyright, 1929).

[2] For certain of these details I am indebted to Hamilton Basso's "Thomas Wolfe: A Portrait." *The New Republic*, June 24, 1936.

[3] *Ibid.*

[4] Much of this information I get from Mr. Wolfe's *The Story of a Novel*. This brief "autobiography" is revealing, sensible, and of great importance as the record of a very promising creative mind. With some slight modifications it first appeared as a series of three articles in *The Saturday Review of Literature* during December, 1935.

[5] *The Story of a Novel*, p. 39.

[6] Eugene Gant. See *Of Time and the River*, p. 150, for a long passage enumerating Eugene's ambitions. See also p. 91 for an account of his reading.

[7] *Of Time and the River*, p. 550.

[8] *Ibid.*, p. 661.

[9] *From Death to Morning*, p. 5.

[10] *Of Time and the River*, p. 90.

[11] *Ibid.*, p. 869.

[12] *Ibid.*, p. 230.

[13] *Ibid.*, p. 68.

[14] *Look Homeward, Angel*, p. 605. My page references to this novel are to the Giant Modern Library edition.

[15] *Ibid.* See the passage beginning on p. 59.

[16] *Ibid.*, p. 532.

[17] *Ibid.*, p. 353.

[18] *Ibid.*, p. 65.

[19] *Ibid.*, p. 150.

[20] *Of Time and the River*, p. 670.

[21] *Ibid.*, p. 792.

[22] *Look Homeward, Angel*, p. 505.

[23] *Ibid.*, p. 564.

[24] *Of Time and the River*, p. 270.

[25] *Look Homeward, Angel*, p. 200.

[26] *Of Time and the River*, p. 70.

[27] P. 113.

[28] *From Death to Morning*, p. 195.

[29] *Look Homeward, Angel*, p. 192.

[30] *Ibid.*, pp. 251-252.

[31] *Of Time and the River*, p. 4.

[32] *Look Homeward, Angel*, p. 243.

[33] *Ibid.*, pp. 571-572.
[34] *Of Time and the River*, p. 237.
[35] *Ibid.*, p. 89.
[36] *Ibid.*, p. 673.
[37] *Ibid.*, p. 419.
[38] *Ibid.*, p. 156.
[39] Henri Bergson's *Creative Evolution*, p. 4. By permission of Henry Holt and Company.
[40] *Ibid.*, p. 5.
[41] Pages 47 ff.
[42] *Of Time and the River*. See pages 169 ff.
[43] See the three numbers of *The New Republic* beginning with the issue of March 10, 1937.
[44] *The New Republic*, March 24, 1937. P. 207.
[45] See Bernard De Voto's penetrating "Genius Is Not Enough." *The Saturday Review of Literature*, April 25, 1936.

X. *That Daring Young Man, Mr. Saroyan*

[1] Reprinted by courtesy of Random House, Inc., New York.
[2] See the preface to *The Daring Young Man on the Flying Trapeze.*
[3] *The Daring Young Man on the Flying Trapeze*, pp. 57-58. Reprinted by courtesy of Random House, Inc., New York.
[4] See the jacket on *The Daring Young Man on the Flying Trapeze.*
[5] *The Daring Young Man on the Flying Trapeze*, p. 25. Reprinted by courtesy of Random House, Inc., New York.
[6] *Ibid.*, p. 242.
[7] *Ibid.*, p. 138.
[8] *Inhale & Exhale*, p. 3. Reprinted by courtesy of Random House, Inc., New York.
[9] *Ibid.*, pp. 56-57. Reprinted by courtesy of Random House, Inc., New York.
[10] *Ibid.*, p. 66.
[11] Henri Bergson's *Creative Evolution*, p. 27. By courtesy of Henry Holt and Company.
[12] *Ibid.*, p. 3.
[13] From the jacket on *The Daring Young Man on the Flying Trapeze.*
[14] Henri Bergson's *Creative Evolution*, p. 165.

[15] *Inhale & Exhale,* p. 12. Reprinted by courtesy of Random House, Inc., New York.

[16] *Ibid.,* p. 32.

[17] *Ibid.,* p. 25.

[18] *Inhale & Exhale,* pp. 57-58. Reprinted by courtesy of Random House, Inc., New York.

[19] *Ibid.* Pages 115 ff. Reprinted by courtesy of Random House, Inc., New York.

[20] *Ibid.,* pp. 193-194. Reprinted by courtesy of Random House, Inc., New York.

[21] *The Daring Young Man on the Flying Trapeze,* pp. 128-129.

[22] P. 7.

[23] *Inhale & Exhale,* p. 58. Reprinted by courtesy of Random House, Inc., New York.

[24] *Ibid.*

[25] *Ibid.,* p. 289. Reprinted by courtesy of Random House, Inc., New York.

[26] *Ibid.,* p. 212. Reprinted by courtesy of Random House, Inc., New York.

[27] "Farewell to Achilles." *The Bookman,* January, 1930.

XI. *A Footnote on James T. Farrell*

[1] From "The Touch of Nature and Some Recent Books." Quoted with the kind permission of Mr. Seward Collins.

[2] See "Mr. Mencken, the Jeune Fille, and the New Spirit in Letters," in Stuart Sherman's *Americans.* Copyright, 1922, by Charles Scribner's Sons.

[3] See "A Sublimated Puritan," by Rollo Walter Brown. *The Saturday Review of Literature,* October 6, 1928.

[4] See John Chamberlain's Introduction to the *Studs Lonigan* trilogy. I quote from this Introduction and from Mr. Farrell's books with the gracious permission of The Vanguard Press.

[5] *Studs Lonigan,* p. 8.

[6] *Ibid.,* p. 68.

[7] *Ibid.,* p. 119.

[8] *The Young Manhood of Studs Lonigan,* p. 74.

[9] *Ibid.,* pp. 269-270.

[10] *Guillotine Party,* p. 44.

[11] *Ibid.,* p. 305.

[12] *Ibid.*, p. 296.
[13] *Ibid.*, p. 305.
[14] *A World I Never Made*, p. 237.
[15] *Ibid.*, p. 318.
[16] *Can All This Grandeur Perish?*, pp. 161-162.
[17] *Ibid.*, pp. 163-164.
[18] *Ibid.*, p. 71.
[19] *Ibid.*, pp. 11-12.
[20] "A Note On Literary Criticism," by James T. Farrell. *The Nation*, March 4, 1936. By permission of the Editor.
[21] John Chamberlain, in his Introduction to the *Studs Lonigan* trilogy.
[22] *Guillotine Party*, p. 79.
[23] *Ibid.*, p. 77.
[24] *Ibid.*, p. 35.
[25] *Ibid.*, p. 37.
[26] *Ibid.*, p. 252.
[27] *Judgment Day*, p. 194.
[28] My critic's defenses of Mr. Farrell are those of Mr. Chamberlain.

XII. *Toward the Centre of the Stream*

[1] By permission of the publishers, Farrar and Rinehart, Inc.
[2] *Now In November*, by Josephine Johnson. P. 3. I quote from Miss Johnson's books with the kind permission of her publishers, Simon and Schuster, Inc.
[3] *Now In November*, p. 76.
[4] *Ibid.*, pp. 113-114.
[5] *Ibid.*, p. 231.
[6] *Jordanstown*, p. 6.
[7] *Ibid.*, p. 3.
[8] *Ibid.*, pp. 78-79.
[9] From *The Late George Apley*, by John P. Marquand. Pages 292-294. By permission of the publishers, Little, Brown & Company.
[10] From *Let the Hurricane Roar*, by Rose Wilder Lane. Pages 128-129. Copyright, 1933, by Rose Wilder Lane. Quoted with the kind permission of the publishers, Longmans, Green and Company.
[11] *The Cathedral*, p. 159.

INDEX